BREAKING OPEN
the LECTIONARY

CYCLE C

BREAKING OPEN
the LECTIONARY

CYCLE C

Lectionary Readings in their Biblical Context
for RCIA, Faith Sharing Groups, and Lectors

MARGARET NUTTING RALPH

PAULIST PRESS
New York • Mahwah, NJ

Cover design by Cynthia Dunne
Book design by John Eagleson

Library of Congress Cataloging-in-Publication Data

Ralph, Margaret Nutting.
    Breaking open the lectionary : lectionary readings in their biblical context for RCIA, faith sharing groups, and lectors, cycle C / Margaret Nutting Ralph.
       p. cm.
    Includes bibliographical references.
    ISBN 0-8091-4406-9 (alk. paper)
    1. Church year meditations. 2. Bible – Meditations. 3. Catechumens. I. Title.
BV30.R34 2006
264′.34 – dc22

2006008257

Published by Paulist Press
997 Macarthur Boulevard
Mahwah, New Jersey 07430

www.paulistpress.com

Printed and bound in the
United States of America

With heartfelt personal gratitude this series of books
Breaking Open the Lectionary Cycle A
Breaking Open the Lectionary Cycle B
Breaking Open the Lectionary Cycle C
is dedicated to
Father Raymond Brown,
who made Catholic biblical scholarship
available to the person in the pew,
and to
The North American Forum on the Catechumenate,
who taught parish RCIA teams
how to *break open the word.*

ACKNOWLEDGMENTS

This series of books, *Breaking Open the Lectionary, Cycles A, B, C,* is the end result of years of working with RCIA groups and other faith sharing groups, teaching scripture, and writing catechetical materials.

Thanks to the many parish leaders in the diocese of Lexington, Kentucky, who have invited me into their parishes to *break open the word* and to teach the contextualist approach to scripture. Conversations with catechumens and candidates taught me what questions the Lectionary texts raise in inquiring minds. I have tried to respond to those questions in these commentaries.

Thanks to Father Hilarion Kistner, O.F.M., of St. Anthony Messenger Press for inviting me to write the Gospel portion of Homily Helps for three years, and to Sister Susan Wolf, S.N.D., of Paulist National Catholic Evangelization Association (PNCEA) for inviting me to write the *Sunday Reflections* for *Share the Word* for three years as well as the Lectionary-based materials for small groups for *Disciples in Mission.* Six years of research for those projects gave me the necessary background to tackle *Breaking Open the Lectionary.*

Thanks to Father Lawrence Boadt, Paul McMahon, and Dr. Nancy de Flon of Paulist Press for accepting this project for publication, offering invaluable advice, and seeing it through to completion.

Finally, thanks to my husband, Don, who encourages me in every way possible and who doesn't mind at all that my idea of a good way to spend the weekend is to study and write.

To each of you I say, "I thank my God every time I remember you, constantly praying with joy in every one of my prayers for all of you, because of your sharing the gospel from the first day until now" (Phil 1:3–5, NRSV).

Contents

ORDINARY TIME: SUNDAYS 1–9

LENT

THE EASTER SEASON

INTRODUCTION

For those of us involved in the Rite of Christian Initiation of Adults (RCIA), the phrase *breaking open the word* is very familiar. This book is entitled *Breaking Open the Lectionary*. These are obviously two different things. So let us begin by defining what we mean by *breaking open the word* in the context of the Rite of Christian Initiation of Adults. Next we will explain why *Breaking Open the Lectionary* is an essential prerequisite to *breaking open the word* for RCIA groups, for faith sharing groups, and for lectors who proclaim the word to the assembly.

During the catechumenate stage of the Rite of Christian Initiation, the stage that begins after the period of evangelization and precatechumenate and continues until the period of purification and enlightenment, catechumens (those who are not baptized) are invited to attend the Liturgy of the Word with the gathered Sunday assembly. Before the Liturgy of the Eucharist the catechumens are formally dismissed to *break open the word,* that is, to gather in small groups in order to listen once more to the Lectionary readings for that Sunday and to share thoughts and insights that are triggered by the readings. The purpose of *breaking open the word* is to hear the living word, as it is proclaimed each Sunday in the Lectionary, in conversation with the lives of those gathered, both individually and communally.

This book is entitled *Breaking Open the Lectionary*. It is written to help those who *break open the word*—whether in a Rite of Christian Initiation setting, in a small faith group setting, or as part of lector or homily preparation—to avoid misinterpreting scripture while *breaking open the word*. In other words, it is written to help those who *break open the word* and those who proclaim the word to avoid inadvertently becoming biblical fundamentalists.

Those who are experienced in *breaking open the word* might well want to register an objection at this point. They might say, "People who *break open the word* are not misinterpreting scripture. They are simply sharing what they personally hear the words saying in the context of their own lives. The session is not about scripture study, but about hearing the word as a living word that cuts to the marrow of the bone."

It is true that the purpose of *breaking open the word* is to hear the living word in conversation with one's own life. However, it is also true that such a method, if carried on by people who have little knowledge of the Bible, can lead to misinterpretation and serious error.

We are certainly not suggesting that to *break open the word,* to hear the word as a living word and apply it to our own lives, is a bad idea. Such an application is essential. In fact, in Luke's Gospel we see Jesus himself doing this very thing. At the beginning of his public ministry Jesus stood up in the temple and read from the prophet Isaiah:

> "The Spirit of the Lord is upon me,
>   because he has anointed me
>   to bring glad tidings to the poor.
> He has sent me to proclaim liberty to captives
>   and recovery of sight to the blind,
>   to let the oppressed go free,
> and to proclaim a year acceptable to the Lord."
>   (Luke 4:18–19)

Then, instead of explaining these words in terms of Isaiah's call, Jesus applies the words to himself: "He said to them, 'Today this scripture passage is fulfilled in your hearing' " (Luke 4:21). We, as disciples of Jesus Christ, are to hear the word as a living word in our lives too.

However, this same method of interpretation can result, not in Spirit-filled wisdom, but in self-deception and misinterpretation. We can abuse scripture by using it to support ideas of our own that have nothing to do with the living word. Perhaps an example will illustrate the danger of misinterpretation. Imagine that a woman who was *breaking open the word* listens to this passage from Genesis 2:7: "...the Lᴏʀᴅ God formed man out of the clay of the ground and blew into his nostrils the breath of life, and so man became a living being." She is asked to name a word or phrase that stands out for her. She picks, "...and so man became a living being." When asked to share her thoughts on the phrase she says, "I think this passage supports abortion rights. Notice that man did not become a living being until after God breathed into his nostrils. A fetus does not breath through the nostrils. Therefore, a fetus is not a living being. Abortion is not depriving a living being of life."

Such a conclusion certainly cannot be supported by the biblical passage, and the conclusion is in direct opposition to the teaching of the Catholic Church. What should facilitators of faith sharing groups do when scripture is being misinterpreted? How is the facilitator to know? Facilitators of faith sharing groups need to know how to break open the Lectionary: they need to know the biblical context, as distinct from the Lectionary context, of the Lectionary readings. They need this knowledge, not to turn a faith sharing group into a Bible study group, but to be equipped to gently guide the discussion so that scripture is not abused. This book is written to provide facilitators of faith sharing groups with background information so that they can do just that. It will also be useful for lectors who will better be able to proclaim the word if they understand the meaning of the passage they are reading.

Breaking Open the Lectionary begins with a chapter that answers the following questions:

- What is the Lectionary?
- Why is familiarity with the Lectionary not familiarity with the Bible?
- What is a fundamentalist?
- What is the Catholic approach to scripture?
- How does this book, *Breaking Open the Lectionary,* help us avoid misinterpreting scripture?

As we respond to these questions the reader will see that knowledge of the biblical context of the Lectionary readings is essential for facilitators in the RCIA process and for those who proclaim the word. The remainder of the book will provide this essential background information by placing the Lectionary readings for each Sunday of the liturgical year in their biblical contexts and explaining how knowledge of these contexts truly does affect our ability to understand what the inspired authors intended to teach. As we will see, this knowledge will not inhibit those in faith sharing groups from applying the readings to their own lives; it will greatly enhance their ability to hear the living word in a way that is compatible with what the Bible actually teaches.

THE LECTIONARY AND SCRIPTURE

Those who facilitate *breaking open the word* in the RCIA process are helping catechumens hear the Lectionary readings as a living word that has meaning and power in the context of their individual lives. Lectors who proclaim the word are helping the gathered community hear the word both in the context of their own lives and in the context of their shared life with the community. However, it is not unusual for a person who is not familiar with the Bible to hear something that, in fact, is contradictory to what the Bible teaches. In order to be of service when a misinterpretation occurs, we each need some background knowledge so that we can gently and confidently contribute to the discussion in such a way that the Bible is not used to support something that is contrary to what the Bible actually teaches. In this chapter we will provide some of this background information by responding to five questions:

- What is the Lectionary?
- Why is familiarity with the Lectionary not familiarity with the Bible?
- What is a fundamentalist?
- What is the Catholic approach to scripture?
- How does this book, *Breaking Open the Lectionary*, help us avoid misinterpreting scripture?

We will close with a final note on how to use *Breaking Open the Lectionary*.

WHAT IS THE LECTIONARY?

The Lectionary is the book that contains the scripture readings that we read at Mass. The Lectionary contains an arrangement of readings, taken out of their biblical context, and put into the context of the liturgical year.

During the liturgical year we celebrate the great mysteries of our faith. The liturgical year begins with the Advent season, during which we spend four weeks preparing for the coming of Christ. Next is the Christmas season, which begins with the Christmas Vigil and continues through four Sundays, ending on the Sunday after the Epiphany when we celebrate the Baptism of the Lord. Between the great seasons we celebrate Ordinary Time. Ordinary Time begins on the Monday after the Baptism of the Lord and continues until Lent. Lent begins with Ash Wednesday and continues through six Sundays during which we prepare for the Easter Triduum (Holy Thursday, Good Friday, and Holy Saturday) and for the Easter season. The Easter season begins with the Easter Vigil and continues through seven weeks until the feast of Pentecost, after which we once more return to Ordinary Time. Ordinary Time starts again on the Monday after Pentecost Sunday and continues through the feast of Christ the King, the feast that precedes the First Sunday of Advent.

While we celebrate the same mysteries each year, we do not have the same readings. We have two cycles of readings for weekdays and three cycles of readings for Sundays. Our present Lectionary readings are the fruit of the Second Vatican Council's *Constitution on the Sacred Liturgy* (*Sacrosanctum Concilium*), which directed that the "treasures of the Bible are to be opened up more lavishly, so that a richer fare may be provided for the faithful at the table of God's Word" (no. 51).

This "richer fare" means that on Sundays we usually read passages from the Old Testament, the Psalms, the New Testament, and the Gospels. The passage from the Old Testament is chosen because it has some relation to the Gospel. The Gospel is, of course, the primary reading because Jesus Christ is the focus of the whole liturgy. (For this reason we have put an explanation of the Gospel in its biblical context first in our explanations of the readings for each Sunday.) The exception to this selection of readings for the Lectionary occurs during the Easter season, when the Old Testament reading is replaced with a reading from the Acts of the Apostles.

While we do not hear all of a Gospel during the liturgical year, we do have continuous readings of all four Gospels. During Year A we hear Matthew, during Year B, Mark, and during Year C, Luke. John is heard during Lent and Easter, and on five Sundays of Year B because Mark is short.

We also have continuous readings of many of the letters. During Year A we hear much of the first four chapters of 1 Corinthians, and readings from Romans, Philippians, and 1 Thessalonians. During Year B we hear readings from 1 Corinthians chapters 6–11, 2 Corinthians, Ephesians, James, and Hebrews chapters 1–10. During Year C we hear readings from 1 Corinthians chapters 12–15, Galatians, Colossians, Hebrews chapters 11–12, Philemon, 1 Timothy, 2 Timothy, and 2 Thessalonians. Unlike the Old Testament readings, the Epistles are not chosen because of their thematic connection to the Gospel readings.

It is evident, then, that during Advent, the Christmas season, Lent, and the Easter season, biblical passages are selected to be in the Lectionary because they emphasize a theme. During Ordinary Time passages are selected so that we can become better acquainted with a particular Gospel or Epistle. In every case we hear passages, not in their biblical context, but in the context of the liturgical year. Why is this fact important?

WHY IS FAMILIARITY WITH THE LECTIONARY NOT FAMILIARITY WITH THE BIBLE?

The Lectionary is not the Bible. Many adult Catholics who claim to be familiar with the Bible are familiar with the Lectionary, but have never read the Bible. While the Lectionary is made up of a collection of biblical readings placed in the context of the liturgical year, the Bible is made up of a collection of books; in fact, the word *Bible* means "books." Each book in the Bible has its own internal integrity and can be understood only if we read it from the beginning to the end. To begin by reading several paragraphs in chapter 13, then skipping back to read the first three paragraphs of chapter 2, and then skipping forward to reading the last three paragraphs of chapter 30 would make no sense at all. However, that is what we have done with the Bible if we have read only the Lectionary and never the books from which the Lectionary readings have been taken.

WHAT IS A FUNDAMENTALIST?

The meaning of the word *fundamentalist* has changed in the last hundred years, so it is important to define exactly what we mean when we use it. In this book the word *fundamentalist* is used to refer to those who believe that they are understanding what the Bible teaches when they take a biblical passage out of its biblical context, apply the words to the context of their own lives, and put the authority of scripture behind what they understand the words to mean in this new context. In other words, a fundamentalist is a person who interprets biblical passages without considering their biblical context.

A person who does consider the biblical context of a passage before trying to understand what the biblical author is teaching is called a contextualist. The Catholic Church teaches us to be contextualists.

Before we explain the contextualist approach, however, it might be helpful to name what fundamentalists and contextualists have in common. Both fundamentalists and contextualists believe that:

- the Bible teaches revealed truth

- the biblical authors are inspired

- the Bible is a living word that can speak to each of us directly and give us spiritual guidance and comfort

If contextualists didn't hold these beliefs then contextualists would see no value in *breaking open the word*.

However, a contextualist who *breaks open the word* is aware that the original inspired authors of scripture were teaching something to contemporary audiences and that the truths being revealed are related to what the authors intended to teach. It is an abuse of scripture to take a sentence out of context and use it to answer a question that is completely different from the question that the inspired author was addressing.

Does this mean that we cannot apply the truths of scripture to our own lives? After all, the original authors obviously knew nothing about the circumstances of our lives. Of course not. Scripture is meant to be applied to our lives. However, the truth that we apply to our own lives needs to be related to, or at least compatible with, what the Bible itself teaches.

What is the Catholic approach to scripture?

The Catholic Church teaches us that in order to understand what an inspired biblical author is teaching we must take into account such things as the time in history when the author lived, the relationship that the author had with his audience, and the literary form in which the author chose to write (see *Catechism of the Catholic Church*, para. 110). In other words, in order to discover the sacred authors' intention we must read the words of scripture in context. There are three important contexts to consider. The first one that we will discuss is *literary genre* or *literary form*.

The literary form

The Bible is not a book with chapters but a library with books. The books are written in many different literary forms. All of us have some familiarity with literary forms. We know that a front-page article in the newspaper is different from an editorial. We know that an article in an encyclopedia is different from a work of fiction. It is not difficult to distinguish one literary form from another. However, many adult Catholics are unaware that a variety of forms is present in the Bible and so they fail to take this fact into account.

A failure to consider literary form can result in misunderstanding what an inspired author is teaching on a subject, and it can result in completely misunderstanding the very subject being discussed. An example of each of these errors will make our point clear.

Failure to understand what the author teaches on a topic. One topic that several books of the Bible address is the problem of suffering. Would a loving, all-powerful God allow an innocent person to suffer? One book in the Bible that explores this question in depth is the Book of Job. The author explores all angles of the problem by having the characters in his story, Job, Eliphaz, Bildad, and Zophar, get into a debate on the issue. Some of what these characters have to say as they debate the issue turns out to be wrong. We know this because at the end of the debate God appears and says that they are wrong. The author obviously is teaching what the character God has to say on the subject.

Imagine that we are reading out of context a passage from the Book of Job, a passage from one of Eliphaz's speeches. We simply proclaim the passage, and at the end we say, "the word of the Lord." If those listening have never read the Book of Job as it appears in the Bible they may have no idea that the literary form of the book is a debate, and that the passage just heard is on the lips of a character with whom the inspired author disagrees. So they may understand the subject being discussed (the problem of suffering) but come away thinking Eliphaz's misunderstanding (that everyone who suffers must deserve it) is what the Bible actually teaches. This is not a message that we would want people to apply to their own lives because it is an error; it is contradictory to what the Bible actually teaches on the subject.

Failure to understand the topic being addressed. Those who ignore the question of literary form sometimes completely misunderstand the very topic that a particular passage or story is addressing. This happens often, but never more often than with the very first story in the Bible, the story of creation. The author of this story is teaching many things: that all that exists was created by a loving God, that all that God created is good, that human beings, male and female, are created in God's own image, that there is only one God (the sun and moon are not gods), that we should keep holy the Sabbath. We could discuss any of these truths as we break open the word and apply them to our own lives.

However, instead of discussing these topics, topics relevant to our relationship with God, some people use the story to argue against Darwin's theory of evolution, even to argue against the theory of evolution being taught in science classes in public schools. Darwin's theory is about the relationship of material forms to each other, not the relationship of the created order to God. Whether Darwin's theory is correct or incorrect, we cannot use the story of creation to argue against it because the author of the story of creation remains silent on the topic that Darwin was addressing. No biblical text can solve a scientific argument because no inspired biblical author addressed a scientific topic. To use biblical texts to argue for or against scientific theories is to abuse the biblical text. If those who are breaking open the word hear the creation story calling them to start a petition against teaching the theory of evolution in science classes, they are misunderstanding the passage. The Bible does not address that topic. The Bible teaches us what we need to know to be in right relationship with God, each other, and the earth—what we need to know for our salvation.

The beliefs of the time

In addition to considering the literary form in which a passage from the Bible appears, we must consider the beliefs of the time of the author. Inspired authors were inspired in the sense that they were gifted with spiritual insight, but they were not inspired in the sense that they had God's point of view and knew things about other topics that no one else in their generation knew. We can use the story of creation to illustrate this point too.

The author of the story of creation says, "Then God said, 'Let there be a dome in the middle of the waters, to separate one body of water from the other.' And so it happened: God made the dome, and it separated the water above the dome from the water below it. God called the dome 'the sky.' Evening came, and morning followed—the second day" (Gen 1:6–8).

As we read this passage we realize that the author lived during a time when everyone presumed that the earth was flat and that it had a dome over it. When we look at the sky, we know that the black part is space and the twinkly part is matter—stars. Had we lived in 450 BC we would have presumed just the opposite, that the black part was matter—the dome—and that the dome had holes in it. Because the author presumed that the earth was flat and had a dome over it, he pictured God making it that way. However, the shape of the earth is irrelevant to the truths that the author is teaching. Had the author lived after the scientific age and written a story to teach the same truths, he would have pictured God making the earth round. Either way, the shape of the earth is a presumption of the time, not one of the spiritual truths that the author intends to teach.

It can be dangerous to take a presumption of the time, or an application of a core truth to a particular social setting, and claim that this is a revealed truth. We know this from the way the Bible was used when people in the United States were arguing over the morality of slavery. Some people used a passage from Ephesians to support their idea that slavery was moral: "Slaves, be obedient to your human masters with fear and trembling, in sincerity of heart, as to Christ, not only when being watched, as currying favor, but as slaves of Christ, doing the will of God from the heart…" (Eph 6:5–6). They were unaware that the author of Ephesians said this because he was applying his core truth—God loves each of us so we must love each other—to the social setting of his audience, a setting in which both wives and slaves were considered to be the property of their husbands and masters. The author of Ephesians is not addressing the question, "Is it moral for one person to own another?" His words cannot be used to answer that question.

A process of revelation

The third context that we need to consider is a particular passage's place in the process of revelation. The Bible that we now have is the end result of a five-step process. This process started with events. The events occurred over a two-thousand-year period from the time of Abraham (1850 BC) to the end of the first century AD. People talked about the events. As time went on, the oral traditions about the events began to be written down. At various times in history people would go over the inherited oral and written traditions about the events and edit them. Finally, some of these edited texts became precious to the Spirit-filled community because they nourished that community and they taught what the community believed to be true. That is, some of the books became canonical.

Over the two thousand years during which the events were occurring, people were growing in their understanding of God, of themselves in relationship to God, and of what God would have them do to cooperate in the coming of God's kingdom. This means that some inspired authors were teaching a revealed truth, but their insight did not represent the fullness of revelation that became available to the community of faith after Jesus' public ministry, death, and resurrection. People who are unaware that the Bible reveals a two-thousand-year process of coming to knowledge about God's love sometimes take an early insight and present it as the fullness of revelation that the Bible contains on a given topic. This, too, is a way of abusing the Bible.

Again, an example will make our point clear. We spoke earlier about the debate over the problem of suffering that appears in the Book of Job. The author of Job addressed the question, "Is it possible that an innocent person would suffer?" The belief of his time (450 BC) was that an innocent person could not suffer; otherwise God was either not all-loving or not all-powerful. As Job's friends debate the issue they express the beliefs of the time, beliefs that the author is arguing against. The author believes that innocent people do suffer, and that their suffering must have a purpose other than punishment because everything in God's created order has a purpose. However, he does not know what that purpose might be.

The Gospel of Mark also deals with the question of suffering. Mark's audience is facing persecution and is asking, "Why should I suffer?" Mark holds Jesus up as a model and shows how Jesus' suffering led not to death but to eternal life. If those in Mark's audience will only remain faithful as Jesus did they too will conquer death and rise with Christ.

Why didn't the author of Job, an inspired author, point to life after death as part of his answer to the problem of suffering? He couldn't because he didn't know about life after death. This concept became part of Jewish thinking in the two hundred years before Jesus, but the author of Job lived several hundred years before that. In other words, the author of Job made a valuable contribution in the process of coming to knowledge about the meaning of human suffering, but his work does not represent the fullness of revelation that we have in Jesus Christ. To take an early insight of an inspired author and present it as the fullness of revelation is one more way to misrepresent what the Bible teaches.

How does this book help us avoid misinterpreting scripture?

Breaking Open the Lectionary will help those who *break open the word* avoid misinterpreting scripture because it will provide readers with the background information needed to recognize when the application of a particular passage to a person's life is faithful to the Bible and when it is not. *Breaking Open the Lectionary* is composed of short articles that place the Lectionary readings for each Sunday in their biblical contexts, as distinct from their contexts in the Lectionary. Armed with this knowledge, the reader will more readily recognize a misinterpretation when one occurs, and will be more able to contribute some valuable insights regarding the passage in question.

Breaking Open the Lectionary is not meant to challenge what we are doing when we *break open the word,* but to complement it. As the reader will discover, contextualists are all the more able to give witness to the truth that "the word of God is living and effective, sharper than any two-edged sword, penetrating even between soul and spirit, joints and marrow, and able to discern reflections and thoughts of the heart" (Heb 4:12).

A FINAL NOTE ON HOW TO USE THIS BOOK

Breaking Open the Lectionary puts the Lectionary readings for each Sunday in their biblical contexts. It functions as a companion to the Lectionary; it does not include the Lectionary readings. RCIA Breaking Open the Word groups, other faith sharing groups, and lectors should first read the Lectionary readings from the Lectionary or from a missal before reading *Breaking Open the Lectionary*. After reading the Lectionary or the missal one will know what Sunday in the Lectionary cycle is being celebrated and can look up that Sunday in the table of contents of *Breaking Open the Lectionary*. On some Sundays a Solemnity that displaces the Sunday readings will be celebrated. The readings for these Solemnities are not included in *Breaking Open the Lectionary* but can be found on the Paulist Press Web site at www.paulistpress.com.

On some feasts, such as Christmas and Easter, the Lectionary offers different readings for Masses said at different times of the day. On some feasts, such as the feast of the Holy Family and the Baptism of the Lord, the Lectionary offers alternate or optional readings. On these feasts we have simply selected one set of readings for which to provide a commentary. For instance, on Easter the Vigil Mass has been selected since that is the Mass at which those involved in the RCIA process will be celebrating.

On the third, fourth, and fifth Sundays of Lent Breaking Open the Word groups will be using Cycle A readings during all three cycles in order to celebrate the Scrutinies. Cycle A readings are included in all three volumes of *Breaking Open the Lectionary* and can be found in the table of contents.

In addition to putting the Lectionary readings in context, *Breaking Open the Lectionary* provides three sets of questions for small-group discussion or personal reflection: questions for Breaking Open the

Word groups in the catechumenate, questions for other faith sharing groups, and Bible study questions.

Questions for Breaking Open the Word groups are the same for each Sunday:

1. What word or phrase stands out for you? Why?

2. With whom in the readings do you most identify? Why?

3. Do you feel attracted to anything in today's readings? Do you feel resistant to anything? Do you know why?

At the end of each Sunday's commentary on the readings a page reference will remind you to refer back to this page for these questions.

Three questions have been provided for other faith sharing groups. However, these are offered merely as suggestions. The Lectionary readings, the homily at Mass, or the commentary on the readings may well raise questions that the participants in the groups prefer to discuss. Some of the questions suggested may be inappropriate, or even painful, for group members depending on their experiences. If the questions provided do not meet the needs of your group, you can always use a question such as "In what ways did today's readings affirm you?" "In what ways did they challenge you?" "What can you do to respond to this challenge?"

No matter what questions you use, remember that where two or three are gathered in Christ's name, Christ is with you.

ADVENT

First Sunday of Advent

Luke 21:25–28, 34–36 *in its biblical context*

Our Gospel on the first Sunday of Advent is the middle of a conversation. Therefore, in order to understand what Jesus is saying, we have to put today's passage in the context in which it appears in Luke's Gospel.

"Some people" have commented on "how the temple was adorned with costly stones and votive offerings" (Luke 21:5). Jesus tells them, "All that you see here—the days will come when there will not be left a stone upon another stone that will not be thrown down" (Luke 21:6). Jesus is warning the people of coming persecution. (In fact, the Romans did persecute Christians and destroy the temple in AD 70, some fifteen years before Luke's Gospel took its present form, around AD 85.)

On hearing of coming persecution the people ask, "Teacher, when will this happen? And what sign will there be when all these things are about to happen?" (Luke 21:7). While today's Gospel reading is part of Jesus' response to this question, it is not his first response. Before saying what we read in the Lectionary reading, Jesus gives further detail about their coming persecution: "... they will seize and persecute you, they will hand you over to the synagogues and to prisons, and they will have you led before kings and governors because of my name" (Luke 21:12).

In today's Lectionary passage, however, Jesus is describing not only the coming persecution but a final, culminating event, the coming of the *Son of Man*. It is much easier to understand what Jesus is saying if we know a little about what is called *apocalyptic* writing and *apocalyptic* imagery.

Apocalyptic writing is a kind of writing that was very popular in Israel for a period of four hundred years, from 200 BC to AD 200. It was always addressed to people facing persecution, and it always offered them hope. Here the hope Jesus offers is the coming of the "Son of Man" who will save the people. Jesus says, "And then they will see the Son of Man coming in a cloud with power and great glory. But when these signs begin to happen, stand erect and raise your heads because your redemption is at hand."

Apocalyptic writing often uses apocalyptic images, that is, cosmic images, to describe just how horrible, how *earth-shattering* the persecution will be. Jesus uses this kind of imagery when he says,

"There will be signs in the sun, the moon, and the stars, and on earth nations will be in dismay, perplexed by the roaring of the sea and the waves."

When Jesus describes the "Son of Man coming in a cloud with power and great glory," he is quoting another apocalyptic passage from the Book of Daniel. In that book Daniel has a vision in which God sends someone to save the people from persecution: "As the visions during the night continued, I saw

> One like a son of man coming,
>   on the clouds of heaven;
> When he reached the Ancient One
>   and was presented before him,
> He received dominion, glory, and kingship;
>   nations and peoples of every language serve him.
> His dominion is an everlasting dominion
>   that shall not be taken away,
>   his kingship shall not be destroyed. (Dan 7:13–14)

In its initial setting the author of the Book of Daniel was assuring his fellow Jews, who were suffering persecution under Antiochus Epiphanes (167 BC–164 BC), that God would send a "son of man" to save them. The phrase *son of man* became a messianic title, the only messianic title that Jesus uses in reference to himself in the Synoptic Gospels (Mark, Matthew, and Luke). Here Jesus is promising his followers that he himself will come to save them from persecution. When Jesus comes the people's redemption will be at hand.

After assuring the people that he will save them, Jesus cautions the people to be constantly vigilant for the coming of the Son of Man: "Be vigilant at all times and pray that you have the strength to escape the tribulations that are imminent and to stand before the Son of Man."

The Lectionary omits the verses that seem to say that Jesus' second coming will also be imminent: "Amen, I say to you, this generation will not pass away until all these things have taken place" (Luke 21:32). By the time Luke is writing, the second coming is already overdue. Since no one knows when exactly it will occur, the message for Luke's audience, and for us, is that we must always be ready. This message, always relevant, is particularly relevant during Advent when we not only recall Jesus' first coming, but also prepare for his daily coming into our lives.

Jeremiah 33:14–16 in its biblical context

Jeremiah was a prophet who offered hope to the people of Judah right before the Babylonian exile (587 BC–537 BC). The king at that time, Zedekiah, was not a good king because he was not faithful to Israel's covenant relationship with God. God had promised to protect Israel, but Zedekiah relied on political power for protection, not on fidelity to covenant love.

In the passage that we read today, Jeremiah is saying that even though Zedekiah is not faithful, God is faithful. God will keep God's promise to the house of David (Zedekiah is of the house of David). God "will raise up for David a just shoot; / he shall do what is right and just in the land." In other words, this future king will not act as Zedekiah has acted. "In those days Judah shall be safe / and Jerusalem shall dwell secure," unlike their present time when the Babylonians are threatening to destroy Jerusalem.

1 Thessalonians 3:12–4:2 in its biblical context

When we read Paul's First Letter to the Thessalonians we are reading the earliest writing in the New Testament, dating to AD 50, some fifteen years before our earliest Gospel (Mark, AD 65). As we can see in the passage selected for today, the people were expecting Jesus' second coming imminently. Paul urges the Thessalonians to "be blameless in holiness before our God and Father at the coming of our Lord Jesus with all his holy ones."

The Thessalonians are very interested in Jesus' "holy ones." They were concerned because, as they have waited for Jesus' second coming, some of their fellow Christians have died. They want to know if those who have died have missed out on Jesus' saving power, since they will not be there when Jesus comes. Paul assures them that those who have died have not missed out. Jesus can and will save them too; in fact, Jesus will save them first (see 1 Thess 4:16). So, at the second coming, the Thessalonians will be overjoyed to see not only Jesus, but Jesus' holy ones. Paul's prayer for the Thessalonians as they await the coming of the Lord is that they "increase and abound in love for one another and for all." We are to prepare for the coming of the Lord in exactly the same way, by growing in love, by growing in fidelity to our covenant relationship with God.

Questions for Breaking Open the Word groups are on page 13.

Questions for other faith sharing groups

1. What will you do this Advent to prepare for the coming of the Lord?

2. Do you think of Jesus' second coming as something to long for or something to dread? Do you know why you feel as you do?

3. Jesus tells the people to "stand erect" when he comes. Why do you think Jesus says this? What posture seems most appropriate to you? Why?

Bible study questions

1. What book is Jesus quoting when he describes the coming of the Son of Man?

2. What is Jesus promising his listeners when he talks about the coming of the Son of Man?

3. What does Jesus advise his followers to do while they wait?

4. What question was on the mind of the Thessalonians?

5. How does Paul respond to their concern?

SECOND SUNDAY OF ADVENT

Luke 3:1–6 in its biblical context

The Gospel reading selected for the second Sunday of Advent is the very beginning of Luke's account of Jesus' public ministry. Like Matthew, Luke begins his Gospel with stories surrounding Jesus' birth. In addition, Luke includes a story about Jesus when he was twelve years old (Luke 2:41–52). He then moves on to Jesus' public ministry, the place in the story where Mark, one of Luke's sources, begins his Gospel. All four Gospels, different as they are, begin their accounts of Jesus' public ministry by describing John the Baptist preparing the way for Jesus.

Notice that Luke begins his story with a wide lens by naming people in authority, both in civil and religious settings, many of whom will try to block Jesus' and John's ministries.

- Pontius Pilate, governor of Judea, will play a role in Jesus' crucifixion (see Luke 23:1–25).

- Herod Antipas, the tetrarch of Galilee, will arrest John because John criticized his relations with his brother's wife (see Luke 3:19–20 and Matt 14:3–12 for the rest of the story).

- Herod will kill John the Baptist and will want to kill Jesus. Luke tells us that when Jesus is informed of Herod's desire, Jesus responds, "Go and tell that fox, 'Behold, I cast out demons and I perform healings today and tomorrow, and on the third day I accomplish my purpose'" (Luke 13:32).

- The high priest, Caiaphas, was head of the Sanhedrin, the Jewish ruling council that will condemn Jesus and bring him to Pilate (Luke 22:66–23:1; Matt 26:57).

By introducing Jesus and John's ministries in the context of the reign of these leaders Luke is teaching that no authority, civil or religious, is so powerful that it can prevent God's chosen ones from accomplishing God's will. As Jesus says, despite Herod's opposition Jesus will accomplish his purpose "on the third day" (Luke 13:32).

Luke tells us that John "went throughout the whole region of the Jordan, proclaiming a baptism of repentance for the forgiveness of sins...." Luke then applies to John the Baptist words that were originally referring to the prophet we call Second Isaiah (Isa 40–55):

> *A voice of one crying out in the desert:*
> *"Prepare the way of the Lord,*
> *   make straight his paths...."*

In its original setting these words are part of Second Isaiah's call story. Second Isaiah lived during the time of the Babylonian exile (587 BC–537 BC). He was called by God to comfort the exiles and to assure them that God was accomplishing something wonderful and new through their suffering and that God would restore them to the promised land.

The Book of Isaiah describes Second Isaiah's call with these words:

> A voice cries out:
> In the desert prepare the way of the LORD!
> Make straight in the wasteland a highway for our God!
> Every valley will be filled in,
> every mountain and hill shall be made low;
> The rugged land shall be made a plain,
> the rough country, a broad valley.
> Then the glory of the LORD shall be revealed,
> and all mankind shall see it together. (Isa 40:3–5)

In the Book of Isaiah the *Lord* for whom the way is being prepared is God; in the Gospels the *Lord* is Jesus. By reinterpreting the words from Isaiah, Luke and the other evangelists are teaching that Jesus is God.

While all four evangelists use some part of Second Isaiah's call story as they describe the mission of John the Baptist, only Luke includes the line, "and all flesh shall see the salvation of God." Part of the hope Second Isaiah offered the exiles was that God would use their suffering to bring other nations to a knowledge of God. This theme is extremely important to Luke. Luke is writing to Gentiles. He wants his Gentile audience, who previously were not among God's chosen people, to understand that the hope that Second Isaiah offered the exiles has been fulfilled in Jesus. Through Jesus all nations will come to know of God's love for them.

Baruch 5:1–9 in its biblical context

The Book called Baruch is part of the Catholic canon (the word *canon* refers to the books included in the Bible because they are believed to be inspired and to teach revelation) but not part of the Jewish canon or the canon of other Christian denominations. The book is named after Jeremiah's scribe. The setting for the passage we read today is, like that of Second Isaiah, the time of the Babylonian exile.

During the Babylonian exile all of the upper-class Jews, along with their king, were ripped out of the holy land and transported to Babylon. Jerusalem was ravaged and the temple was destroyed. Baruch's words are words of hope offered to the exiles that Jerusalem will be returned to its former glory and the exiles will return:

> Jerusalem, take off your robe of mourning and misery;
> put on the splendor of glory from God forever....
> For God will show all the earth your splendor:

> look to the east and see your children....
>   Led away on foot by their enemies they left you:
>   but God will bring them back to you
>   borne aloft in glory as on royal thrones.

In describing how God will make the path clear for the exiles' return, Baruch uses words very similar to the words that our Gospel writers quoted from Isaiah and applied to John the Baptist:

> For God has commanded
>   that every lofty mountain be made low,
> and that the age-old depths and gorges
>   be filled to level ground,
>   that Israel may advance secure in the glory of God.

In Isaiah the path was being cleared for the coming of the Lord. In Baruch God is clearing the way for the return of the exiles.

Philippians 1:4–6, 8–11 in its biblical context

Paul, like our psalmist, knows from experience that God will save God's people. He is writing the Philippians, whom he visited on his second journey (Acts 16:11–40), from prison (Phil 1:12–13). You might think that Paul would be discouraged and would be asking God, "Why me?" Instead he is full of hope and confidence. Paul tells the Philippians that he is confident of this: "that the one who began a good work in you will continue to complete it until the day of Christ Jesus."

Paul's prayer for the Philippians is very similar to his prayer for the Thessalonians that we read last Sunday. Paul prays that as the Philippians wait for the coming of the Lord they will grow in love: "And this is my prayer: that your love may increase ever more and more in knowledge and every kind of perception, to discern what is of value, so that you may be pure and blameless for the day of Christ...."

Once more we learn that the way to prepare for the coming of the Lord is to grow in love.

Questions for Breaking Open the Word groups are on page 13.

Questions for other faith sharing groups

1. Have you ever been subjected to the decisions of duly appointed authority figures who have misused their authority? Explain. How do you think a Christian should respond to such a situation?

2. Do you believe that no human authority can thwart God's will and God's purpose? If so, do you have any experience that confirms this belief? Explain.

3. When have you "sown in tears" but "reaped in joy"?

Bible study questions

1. How do all four Gospels begin their accounts of Jesus' public ministry?

2. Why does Luke name specific people in positions of civil and religious leadership?

3. What did John the Baptist proclaim to the people?

4. How does Luke reinterpret the meaning of "Prepare the way of the Lord"? What is Luke teaching through this reinterpretation?

5. What hope does Baruch offer the exiles in Babylon?

THIRD SUNDAY OF ADVENT

Luke 3:10–18 in its biblical context

Last Sunday we read Luke's description of John the Baptist's role as

> *A voice of one crying out in the desert:*
> *"Prepare the way of the Lord...."*
> (Luke 3:4)

Between that reading and the reading for this third Sunday of Advent, Luke's Gospel tells us more about John's message. It is this message, omitted in the Lectionary, that causes the crowds, the tax collectors, and the soldiers in today's Gospel to ask, "What should we do?"

John the Baptist's preaching centers heavily on repentance and judgment. When the crowds come to hear John's message he calls them "a brood of vipers" (Luke 3:7) and warns them to change their lives: "Produce good fruits as evidence of your repentance.... Even now the ax lies at the root of the trees. Therefore every tree that does not produce good fruit will be cut down and thrown into the fire" (Luke 3:8a, 9). So when those in the crowd ask, "What should we do?" they are asking what they should do to produce good fruit so that they will avoid punishment when the Lord comes.

Notice that the people who are listening and responding to John's message are not the Pharisees and scribes, leaders in the community who were held in high esteem. Rather, Luke tells us that "tax collectors" and "soldiers" were anxious to mend their ways, those marginalized by their fellow Jews because they imposed Roman authority on a subject people. As we read Luke's Gospel we will notice over and over that he emphasizes inclusion. Those who are marginalized are sought out. This is part of Luke's theme: even Gentiles are now invited into a relationship of covenant love with God.

John the Baptist's response to the question "What should we do?" is important both for what he says and for what he fails to say. When those in the crowd ask, "What should we do?" John does not tell them to observe the law more scrupulously but to give generously to those in need. When the tax collectors ask, "What should we do?"

John does not tell them to stop collecting taxes but to collect only what is prescribed. When the soldiers ask, "What should we do?" John does not tell them to stop being soldiers but to carry out their duties with integrity: "Do not practice extortion, do not falsely accuse anyone, and be satisfied with your wages."

John the Baptist has such a powerful effect on the people that they begin to wonder if John himself might be the coming messiah. John clearly denies this possibility: "I am baptizing you with water, but one mightier than I is coming. I am not worthy to loosen the thongs of his sandals. He will baptize you with the Holy Spirit and fire." We will not learn more about the distinction between the two baptisms that John is making until we read the Acts of the Apostles, the second part of Luke's two-volume work.

In Acts we read that when Paul was in Ephesus he found some disciples and asked them, "Did you receive the holy Spirit when you became believers?" (Acts 19:2). When they replied that they had never heard of the holy Spirit Paul asked how they were baptized: "They replied, 'With the baptism of John.' Paul then said, 'John baptized with a baptism of repentance, telling the people to believe in the one who was to come after him, that is, in Jesus'" (Acts 19:3b–4). Paul then baptized the people in the name of "the Lord Jesus" (Acts 19:5b). In terms of experience, the difference between the two baptisms was power. The people were now able to speak in tongues and to prophesy.

In Luke's Gospel, John the Baptist is the one who announces the coming of Jesus, not only as Jesus' public ministry begins, but even while John is still in the womb (see Luke 1:44). For this reason you may find it puzzling that after hearing about Jesus' mighty acts from his own disciples, John sends messengers to Jesus to ask, "Are you the one who is to come, or should we look for another?" (Luke 7:19).

Scripture scholars suggest that perhaps even John was surprised that Jesus, as he taught the people, stressed mercy and forgiveness more than he stressed wrath and judgment. As today's reading comes to an end we see that John describes Jesus' ministry in harsher terms than those in which Jesus will live out that ministry: "His winnowing fan is in his hand to clear his threshing floor and to gather the wheat into his barn, but the chaff he will burn with unquenchable fire."

As we continue to read Luke's Gospel we will notice that instead of calling sinners "a brood of vipers," Jesus will try to have dinner with them.

Zephaniah 3:14–18a in its biblical context

The setting for our reading from the prophet Zephaniah is not the time of the Babylonian exile, the setting for last Sunday's Old Testament reading, but nearly one hundred years earlier, during the reign of King Josiah (640 BC–609 BC). Josiah was king of Judah, the southern kingdom, after Israel, the northern kingdom, had been defeated by the Assyrians (721 BC). For some years, Judah had been a vassal state of Assyria, a nation whose world power was diminishing as the power of the Babylonians was growing. King Josiah led a reform, partly to avoid a fate similar to that already suffered by the northern kingdom.

The prophet Zephaniah warned those living in the southern kingdom that a day of the Lord was approaching when God would destroy Judah for her sins as well as destroy Judah's political enemies. However, a faithful remnant, a small group of faithful survivors, would remain. The words that we read today are addressed to that remnant:

> Shout for joy, O daughter Zion!
> Sing joyfully, O Israel!
> Be glad and exult with all your heart,
> O daughter Jerusalem!
> The LORD has removed the judgment against you
> he has turned away your enemies....

Once God has cleansed the people Jerusalem need no longer fear, because God will renew the people in God's love. The Lord God will be in their midst:

> Fear not, O Zion, be not discouraged!
> The LORD, your God, is in your midst,
> a mighty savior;
> he will rejoice over you with gladness,
> and renew you in his love....

Philippians 4:4–7 in its biblical context

Paul, like Zephaniah and Isaiah, is urging the people to rejoice: "Rejoice in the Lord always. I shall say it again: rejoice!"

Why should the people rejoice? Because "the Lord is near." Knowing that the Lord is near, the people should have no anxiety at all, not because they have everything they need, but because they trust God's love and care for them: "Have no anxiety at all, but in everything, by prayer and petition, with thanksgiving, make your requests known to God."

The Philippians could give thanks as they ask for what they need rather than after they have received what they need only if they trust God's love. This kind of trust leads to peace: "Then the peace of God that surpasses all understanding will guard your hearts and minds in Christ Jesus."

In addition, as the Philippians wait for the coming of the Lord, their "kindness should be known to all."

Questions for Breaking Open the Word groups are on page 13.

Questions for other faith sharing groups

1. How do you respond to preachers who emphasize God's judgment over God's mercy? Do you know why you respond as you do?

2. Who is marginalized in your town? What could you do to reach out to them?

3. If you asked John the Baptist, "What should I do to prepare for the coming of the Lord?" what do you think he would tell you?

Bible study questions

1. On what does John the Baptist's preaching center?

2. Who is listening and responding to John's message?

3. How does this scene fit into the overall theme of Luke's Gospel?

4. What is the difference between John's baptism and Jesus' baptism?

5. According to Paul, why should the Philippians rejoice?

FOURTH SUNDAY OF ADVENT

Luke: 1:39–45 in its biblical context

On the fourth Sunday of Advent, for the first time in this liturgical year, we read one of the stories surrounding the birth of Jesus. To understand the full significance of the story we must know a little about birth narratives.

Birth narratives are stories about the birth of someone who later becomes very great. The story is composed, not to describe a birth exactly as it occurred, but to teach the significance of that person's birth as it is later understood in the light of subsequent events. The story of Mary visiting Elizabeth, referred to as *the visitation,* is a postresurrection story. It was written after the resurrection to teach what was understood about Jesus in the light of the resurrection. This story is not primarily about Mary or Elizabeth; it is primarily about Jesus. The story of the visitation is teaching that Jesus is divine.

In Luke's Gospel the story of the visitation follows immediately after the story of the annunciation, in which the angel Gabriel tells Mary that she will conceive a child through the Holy Spirit and that the child will be called "Son of the Most High" (Luke 1:32). Luke's Gospel is the only Gospel that brings Mary on stage for the annunciation, and the only Gospel to picture the visitation. Both stories are teaching Jesus' divinity.

As we read today's story of the visitation we already know the identity of the child in Mary's womb. However, Elizabeth does not know what the reader knows. The fact that Elizabeth, and even the child in her womb, recognize that they are in the presence of their Lord is attributed to the Holy Spirit. "...Elizabeth, filled with the Holy Spirit, cried out in a loud voice and said, 'Blessed are you among women, and blessed is the fruit of your womb. And how does this happen to me, that the mother of my Lord should come to me?' "

By picturing Elizabeth greeting Mary with these words, Luke is alluding to an Old Testament passage. When we recognize the allusion, Luke's teaching becomes even clearer. In 2 Samuel we read how the ark of the covenant, the symbol of God's presence with God's people, was recaptured from the Philistines and brought back to Jerusalem. David, in awe of the Lord's power, says, "How can the ark of the LORD come to me?" (2 Sam 6:9). By having Elizabeth echo David's words, Luke is picturing Mary as the new ark of the covenant and Jesus as the God who has come to dwell with God's people. That is why John the Baptist leaps in his mother's womb. He too recognizes the presence of the Lord.

While the story of the visitation is primarily about Jesus' identity, the story also teaches us something very important about Mary and about why the church honors Mary as we do. Elizabeth says to Mary, "Blessed are you who believed that what was spoken to you by the Lord would be fulfilled."

Why does Elizabeth call Mary *blessed?* One reason is that Mary believed the words of the angel as they affected her personally. Mary's faith-filled response to the angel's announcement of Jesus' birth was, "May it be done to me according to your word" (Luke 1:38).

However, when we read Mary's response to Elizabeth's words (not included in this week's reading; see Luke 1:46–56), we see that Mary understood God's promises to her in a much wider context than her own personal life. Mary says,

> "He has helped Israel his servant,
>   remembering his mercy,
> according to his promise to our fathers,
>   to Abraham and to his descendants forever."
>   (Luke 1:54–55)

Through Mary's response Luke is teaching that Jesus is the fulfillment of all of God's covenant promises to Israel.

Micah 5:1–4a in its biblical context

While the prophet Micah lived in Judah in the eighth century, the words we read today from the Book of Micah date to the time of the Babylonian exile (587 BC–537 BC). It was not unusual for a prophet's words to be edited and expanded upon by later generations. The setting of the Babylon exile is explicitly named earlier in Micah:

> To Babylon shall you go,
>   there shall you be rescued.

> There shall the LORD redeem you
> from the hand of your enemies.
>   (Mic 4:10)

The prophecy that we read today was offering hope to those in exile by reminding them that God had made promises to King David, promises that God will keep. Micah is referring to a future king of David's line when he pictures the Lord saying:

> You, Bethlehem-Ephrathah,
>   too small to be among the clans of Judah,
> from you shall come forth for me
>   one who is to be ruler in Israel;
> whose origin is from of old,
>   from ancient times.

This is a reference to David and to David's line for two reasons: First, David came from Bethlehem. As we read in 1 Samuel: "David was the son of an Ephrathite named Jesse, who was from Bethlehem in Judah" (1 Sam 17:12). In addition, Bethlehem was the place where the Lord sent Samuel to anoint David king: "I am sending you to Jesse of Bethlehem, for I have chosen my king from among his sons.... Samuel, with the horn of oil in hand, anointed him [David] in the midst of his brothers; and from that day on, the spirit of the LORD rushed upon David" (1 Sam 16:1, 13). Micah is assuring those in exile that a future king in the line of David will come forth.

The hope expressed in today's reading from Micah rests on a promise that God made to King David that his line would be secure forever: "Your house and your kingdom shall endure forever before me; your throne shall stand firm forever" (2 Sam 7:16). Like Mary, the prophet believed that God would fulfill God's promises to Israel.

This future king of David's line, in contrast to some of the their past kings, will be faithful.

> He shall stand firm and shepherd his flock
>   by the strength of the LORD,
>   in the majestic name of the LORD, his God;
> and they shall remain, for now his greatness
>   shall reach to the ends of the earth;
>   he shall be peace.

By proclaiming this prophecy from Micah during Advent the church is expressing our belief that all the hopes of Israel and all of God's promises have been fulfilled in Jesus.

Hebrews 10:5–10 in its biblical context

In today's reading the author of Hebrews places the words of Psalm 40:7–9 on Jesus' lips as Jesus comes into the world. Psalm 40 says:

> Sacrifice or oblation you wished not,
>   but ears open to obedience you gave me.

Holocausts or sin-offerings you sought not;
 then said I, "Behold I come;
 in the written scroll it is prescribed for me.
To do your will, O my God, is my delight,
 and your law is within my heart!"

(Ps 40:7–9)

The author of Psalm 40 is teaching that God prefers obedience to sacrifice.

By quoting Psalm 40 the author of Hebrews is teaching that Jesus' sacrifice is far superior to any sacrifice that was offered previously. Jesus did not offer holocausts instead of obedience. Rather, Jesus first offered obedience—he did the will of his Father. That obedience led to Jesus' passion, death, and resurrection. By Jesus' obedient sacrifice, we have been saved: "By this 'will' [Jesus' obedience to his Father's will], we have been consecrated through the offering of the body of Jesus Christ once for all."

Because Jesus' sacrifice was the perfect sacrifice there is no longer any need to offer the kind of holocausts that the old law required.

We proclaim this reading from Hebrews on the fourth Sunday of Advent to remind ourselves that we are to follow Jesus in doing God's will. Mary is the preeminent example of a person who has done just that.

Questions for Breaking Open the Word groups are on page 13.

Questions for other faith sharing groups

1. Do you have a devotion to Mary? If so, why?

2. Do you have difficulty saying to God, "Be it done unto me according to thy word"? Why or why not?

3. Whom in your life, that you know personally, do you consider most blessed? Why?

Bible study questions

1. What is the purpose of a birth narrative?

2. What two stories in which Mary appears are unique to Luke's Gospel?

3. What are these stories teaching?

4. Why does Elizabeth call Mary *blessed?*

5. In what two contexts did Mary believe that the words spoken to her would be fulfilled?

The Christmas Season

Christmas (During the Day)
Cycles A, B, and C

John 1:1–18 in its biblical context

There are four Lectionary selections for Christmas Masses: the Christmas Vigil Mass, the Mass at midnight, the Mass at dawn, and the Mass during the day. The Gospel for the Vigil Mass is Jesus' genealogy at it appears in Matthew's Gospel. The Gospels for the midnight and dawn Masses are selections from Luke's infancy narratives. However, the Gospel of John has no infancy narrative. For the Mass during Christmas day we read the beginning of John's Gospel, in which John speaks not of a child conceived by Mary through the Holy Spirit, but of a preexistent Word that became flesh. From the very beginning, John's is a high-Christology Gospel.

To say that a Gospel is "high Christology" is to say that it emphasizes Jesus' divinity rather than Jesus' humanity. John emphasizes Jesus' divinity throughout his Gospel because he wants his readers to understand that the risen Christ is alive and in their midst. John's Gospel was written toward the end of the first century AD, sometime after the expected second coming. John's audience is asking, "Where is the risen Christ?" Their expectations of Jesus' returning on the clouds of heaven had not yet been fulfilled. John responds to this question by presenting the story of Jesus Christ in such a way that his divinity is constantly apparent. John wants his audience to know that the Word who became flesh and lived among them is still among them through the church and through the sacraments. John, of course, does not use the word *sacrament,* but we have come to use that word to refer to those mighty effective signs, such as baptism and Eucharist, through which the risen Christ is still dwelling with his people.

As John begins his Gospel he takes us to a time before creation, "In the beginning," when the Word, who was with God and who was God, already existed. John tells us that, "He was in the beginning with God. / All things came to be through him, / and without him nothing came to be."

We see, then, that each of our four Gospels, as each is progressively more distant from Jesus' passion, death, and resurrection, tells the good news of Jesus Christ in a larger context. Mark has no story of Jesus' origins at all but begins with Jesus' public ministry. Matthew, through the genealogy that goes back to Abraham, puts the saving acts of Jesus Christ in the context of Jewish salvation history. Luke, through a genealogy that goes back to Adam, puts Jesus' saving acts in the context of the whole human race. John's picture is even bigger: John presents Jesus as the preexistent Word through whom all else that exists came into being.

Having identified the Word with the transcendent God, John tells us that

> . . . the Word became flesh
> and made his dwelling among us. . . .

John intends the word *flesh* to be shocking. The transcendent God, who is the source of all life, took on human flesh in order to dwell among the people. Why would God do such a thing? Why would God lower Godself and become mucked up in human flesh? John tells us that this was done in order to reveal God to us: "No one has ever seen God. The only Son, God, who is at the Father's side, has revealed him." Through God's self-revelation we have all received grace and truth.

In all four Gospels John the Baptist gives testimony to Jesus Christ by making it clear that one greater than he is coming. However, in John's Gospel, John the Baptist refers to Jesus' preexistence: "The one who is coming after me ranks ahead of me because he existed before me."

John the Baptist came to testify to the light, to Jesus, "the true light, which enlightens everyone." The world as a whole did not know or accept this light. However, the Gospel author claims that those who did accept him "saw his glory." To see Jesus' glory is to recognize Jesus' divinity. John is writing his Gospel so that his end-of-the-century audience (and we) will realize that the risen Christ still dwells among them and so that they too will see his glory.

Isaiah 52:7–10 *in its biblical context*

Today we read the beautiful words of Second Isaiah offering hope to the exiles in Babylon.

> How beautiful upon the mountains
>   are the feet of him who brings glad tidings,
> announcing peace, bearing good news,
>   announcing salvation, and saying to Zion,
> "Your God is King!"

The salvation being announced to the exiles is that God will send someone to defeat their political enemies and allow them to return to their homeland, to Zion. They have lost their land and their king from David's line, but God is still king. God still loves the Israelites and will keep all the promises of covenant love.

> Break out together in song,
> O ruins of Jerusalem!

For the LORD comforts his people,
he redeems Jerusalem.

The Lord is comforting the people through the words of Second Isaiah and is assuring them that they still belong to God. That their relationship of covenant love is still secure is emphasized by the words *your* and *his*. It is not just "God is King," but "*your* God is king." God comforts "*his* people." The exiles still belong to God, and God still belongs to them. God's promise to protect them remains true even during these most difficult times of exile.

When we read Second Isaiah in the context of our liturgy, the glad tidings becomes the good news of Jesus Christ, the God who is King is Jesus, and the redemption offered is redemption from sin. The prophet's words take on a second layer of meaning in the light of Jesus' life, death, and resurrection.

Hebrews 1:1–6 in its biblical context

The author of Hebrews shares John's high Christology, announcing immediately that God spoke to us "through the Son, whom he made heir of all things and through whom he created the universe...." After Jesus redeemed the human race, "he took his seat at the right hand of the Majesty on high, as far superior to the angels as the name he has inherited is more excellent than theirs."

The author of Hebrews then supports his statement that Jesus is higher than the angels by referring to a number of Old Testament texts that he applies to Jesus. "You are my son; this day I have begotten you" is from Psalm 2:7, a royal psalm that originally celebrated the king of Judah. "I will be a father to him, and he shall be a son to me," is from 2 Samuel 7:14. As we saw in our Old Testament reading last week, it is part of the Lord's promise to David that his heirs, the future kings of the Davidic line, would be secure. "Let all the angels of God worship him" is an allusion to Deuteronomy 32:43 as it appears in the Septuagint (the Greek translation of the Old Testament) calling on the angels to glorify God. By applying these texts to Jesus, the author of Hebrews is doing what we did when we read the passage from Second Isaiah in the context of our liturgy. He is finding an additional level of meaning in the words of the Old Testament authors in the light of the death and resurrection of Jesus Christ.

One final note on our reading from Hebrews: notice that the author of Hebrews refers to Jesus as "the firstborn into the world." This is a high-Christology title for Jesus (see Col 1:15). You undoubtedly will remember that in Luke's account of Jesus' birth Luke says, "and she gave birth to her firstborn son" (Luke 2:7). This often puzzles those who believe that Mary did not have additional children, since the word *firstborn* might be taken to imply that she did. Scripture scholars suggest that Luke, like the authors of Colossians and Hebrews, is using the word *firstborn* to refer to Jesus' divinity.

As we see from our readings, our Christmas celebration is not simply a celebration of Jesus' birth many years ago, but a celebration of Jesus' whole role in salvation history and a celebration of the fact that the risen Christ still dwells with his people. As we celebrate the birth of Jesus, we encounter the risen Christ in his word proclaimed, in his eucharistic presence, and in each other.

Questions for Breaking Open the Word groups are on page 13.

Questions for other faith sharing groups

1. How do you think of Jesus? Do you prefer to emphasize his divinity or his humanity? Why?

2. Who has been a John the Baptist in your life, announcing the presence of Jesus? Explain.

3. Who has been a Second Isaiah in your life, offering hope? Explain.

Bible study questions

1. What question is on the mind of John's audience?

2. How does John's Gospel respond to the question on the mind of his audience?

3. What did today's passage from Second Isaiah mean to the exiles in Babylon?

4. What additional level of meaning does today's reading from Second Isaiah have for Christians?

5. What did the word *firstborn* mean for the authors of Hebrews and Colossians?

Holy Family

Luke 2:41–52 in its biblical context

Today, on the feast of the Holy Family, we read a story about Jesus, Mary, and Joseph that appears only in Luke's Gospel. As was true of the story of the visitation that we read on the fourth Sunday of Advent, today's story is written from a postresurrection point of view to teach what was understood only after the resurrection.

Luke tells us that "each year Jesus' parents went to Jerusalem for the feast of Passover." This means that Mary and Joseph were faithful Jews who observed the pilgrimage feast of Passover by going up to the temple in Jerusalem to celebrate for seven days. Now that Jesus was twelve he accompanied his parents on the trip. "After they had completed its days, as they were returning, the boy Jesus remained behind in Jerusalem, but his parents did not know it." Mary and Joseph did not realize that Jesus was missing for a whole day. On discovering his absence they returned to Jerusalem, but still did not find him for two more days. "After three days they found him in the temple."

This detail of the story foreshadows the ending of Luke's Gospel when Jesus will again go to Jerusalem and again will be "lost" for three days. This trip too will be at the time of Passover, which will be Jesus' last meal with his disciples before they lose him. After three days they will find Jesus in his postresurrection appearances.

While Mary and Joseph have been looking for Jesus, Jesus has not been looking for them. Jesus was "sitting in the midst of the teachers, listening to them and asking them questions, and all who heard him were astounded at his understanding and his answers."

Notice that Luke does not let us hear what Jesus said to the teachers in the temple. In fact, so far in Luke's Gospel, Jesus has not said a single word. We know Jesus' identity because we have been told by an angel, by Elizabeth, and by Simeon. But we have yet to meet Jesus ourselves. Jesus' first words will be in response to his mother's question, "Son, why have you done this to us? Your father and I have been looking for you with great anxiety." Jesus replies, "Why were you looking for me? Did you not know that I must be in my Father's house?"

Many people, on reading these words, think they sound rude. Why didn't Jesus at least apologize for frightening his parents? Luke's point rests on the word *must*. In both his Gospel and in his Acts of the Apostles Luke uses this word to describe actions that must be done in order to carry out God's will. For instance, when Jesus describes his preaching mission he says, "To the other towns also I must proclaim the good news of the kingdom of God, because for this purpose I have been sent" (Luke 4:43). The same wording appears when Jesus talks about his suffering: "The Son of Man must suffer greatly and be rejected by the elders, the chief priests, and the scribes, and be killed and on the third day be raised" (Luke 9:22). Jesus' response to his mother is revealing that Jesus' main relationship in life is with his heavenly Father. He must do his heavenly Father's will.

Notice that Luke tells us that Jesus' parents "did not understand what he said to them." This detail is surprising if one thinks of a Gospel as similar to a novel where one scene builds on another. Why wouldn't Mary understand, given the annunciation and the visitation? This obvious "seam" between stories, a certain inconsistency from one story to another, is a sign that the stories grew up independently of each other. Luke is collecting stories that he has inherited from oral and written tradition. Luke tells us that this is what he is doing as he begins his Gospel (see Luke 1:1–4). Mary and Joseph's lack of understanding is parallel to the lack of understanding that will occur at the end of Luke's Gospel when the disciples do not understand why Jesus had to do his Father's will and go through his passion and death.

Luke does not present Jesus as a son who had no regard for his parents' wishes. Rather, Luke tells us that Jesus "went down with them and came to Nazareth, and was obedient to them." Jesus advances "in wisdom and age and favor before God and man" under Mary and Joseph's care.

Mary, like Jesus, continues to be obedient to God's will. Although she does not understand Jesus' words, instead of arguing with him, Mary "kept all these things in her heart." As we know from the annunciation, Mary's posture before God is the same as her son's: "May it be done to me according to your word" (Luke 1:38).

Sirach 3:2–6, 12–14 in its biblical context

The Book of Sirach (also called Ecclesiasticus) is considered canonical by the Catholic Church, but not by Protestant churches. It is part of a body of literature called wisdom literature, which dates to after the Babylonian exile (587 BC–537 BC). The experience of the Babylonian exile forced the Israelites to question many of their treasured beliefs. In wisdom literature the authors arrive at conclusions based on reason rather than on their reflections about God's powerful acts in history (such as the exodus).

Sirach was originally written in Hebrew by Ben Sirach during the first part of the second century BC (200 BC–175 BC) but was translated into Greek by the original author's grandson. The author extols the traditions of his Israelite ancestors for his contemporaries who have embraced the Greek culture.

In the passage that we read today the author teaches his audience what kind of family relationships please God. God gives parents authority over their children. Therefore, to honor one's parents is to live in right relationship not only with parents, but with God. Honor to parents is required throughout one's lifetime, even when parents reach old age. God will be attentive to the prayers of those who honor their parents.

Fidelity in relationships, then, becomes the theme of both our Gospel and our reading from Sirach. Just as Jesus is faithful to both his heavenly Father and his earthly parents, so must we be faithful to God and to each other, especially in our family relationships.

Colossians 3:12–21 in its biblical context

The Lectionary introduces the reading from Colossians with the words, "A reading from the Letter of Saint Paul to the Colossians." The letter itself begins, "Paul, an apostle of Christ Jesus by the will of God..." (Col 1:1). However, many scripture scholars do not think that Paul wrote Colossians. During the first century AD there was a literary convention called *pseudonymity*. If an author were a disciple of a great teacher and writing in the tradition of that teacher he would attribute his writing to the teacher rather than to himself. This was not a dishonest act, but a way of honoring one's intellectual and spiritual predecessor.

The author of this letter is reminding the Colossians that they have been chosen by God, and that they are "holy" and "beloved." These facts have profound ramifications on how they must treat each other.

They must treat each other with "compassion, kindness, humility, gentleness, and patience...."

Notice that the author tells wives to be subordinate to their husbands, and children to obey their parents. Today's reading stops at chapter 3, verse 21. Verse 22 says, "Slaves, obey your human masters in everything...." These are parallel ideas. Both slaves and wives are to be obedient to their husbands/masters because they are understood to be the property of their husbands/masters. Right order would therefore demand obedience.

Colossians 3:22 was used to support slavery during the Civil War. Today some people use Colossians 3:18 to support the idea that wives are not partners in marriage, but are more like children. Their role is to be subordinate. This passage from Colossians reminds us that one context in which we must place every biblical text is the context of the beliefs of the times. We must separate the core teaching of the author from what is an application of that teaching for the author's specific historical audience (see chapter 1 for a thorough discussion of this context).

In this passage the core teaching is that because God has chosen us, and because we are holy and beloved, we must treat each other as beloved children of God. Because we are Christians, we are acting in Christ's name: "Whatever you do, in word or in deed, do everything in the name of the Lord Jesus." The application of this truth to the social setting of the Colossians is that wives and slaves, who are property, should respect that order and treat their husbands/masters accordingly. The core truth is just as applicable to our society as it was to the Colossians; the specific application is not.

Questions for Breaking Open the Word groups are on page 13.

Questions for other faith sharing groups

1. Have you had to disappoint a loved one in order to follow your understanding of God's will? Explain.

2. In what ways do you think Mary suffered throughout her life? Is Mary a model for you in this regard? Explain.

3. Have you had the experience of "letting go" of a child as the child grows up and follows his or her own interests? Did you find this difficult? In what way might today's Gospel help a parent in such a situation?

Bible study questions

1. What does Jesus' being lost for three days foreshadow?

2. What point is Luke making about Jesus in the first words that Jesus speaks in Luke's Gospel?

3. How does Mary's posture before God compare to her son's?

4. What is the author teaching in today's passage from Sirach?

5. What is the core teaching in our passage from Colossians?

JANUARY 1: SOLEMNITY OF MARY, MOTHER OF GOD
CYCLES A, B, AND C

Luke 2:16–21 in its biblical context

Our reading today begins with the shepherds going in haste and finding Mary, Joseph, and the infant lying in the manger. "When they saw this, they made known the message that had been told them about this child." Obviously we cannot understand this passage unless we know the message that the shepherds had received.

Only in Luke's Gospel do we read the annunciation of Jesus' birth to the shepherds:

> Now there were shepherds in that region living in the fields and keeping the night watch over their flock. The angel of the Lord appeared to them and the glory of the Lord shone around them, and they were struck with great fear. The angel said to them, "Do not be afraid; for behold, I proclaim to you good news of great joy that will be for all the people. For today in the city of David a savior has been born for you who is Messiah and Lord. And this will be a sign for you: you will find an infant wrapped in swaddling clothes and lying in a manger." (Luke 2:8–12)

After receiving this message the shepherds go in haste to Bethlehem "to see this thing that has taken place, which the Lord has made known" to them (Luke 2:15). When the shepherds arrive and see exactly what they had been told to expect—an infant lying in a manger—they tell everyone, including Mary and Joseph, about the angels' message.

To understand the full significance of the angels' message we must know something about the literary form *infancy narrative*. An infancy narrative is a story that describes a person's birth not to re-create events exactly as they occurred, but to tell the reader how great that person became. Both Matthew and Luke have infancy narratives. The core of the two stories is the same: Mary is engaged to Joseph. Mary conceives Jesus through the power of the Holy Spirit. Jesus will be a savior. But the details differ. Matthew tells us of magi who follow a star to seek out the infant savior. Luke tells us of shepherds who receive the good news from the angels and rush to Bethlehem to discover that the message they received is true. They find the "sign" for which they are looking: an infant wrapped in swaddling clothes and lying in a manger. Why is an infant wrapped in swaddling clothes a sign? What does the sign signify?

Luke has used a teaching device common at the time called *midrash*. Luke winds Old Testament allusions around New Testament events to teach the significance of the New Testament events. To describe Jesus as "wrapped in swaddling clothes and lying in a manger" is to teach, through allusions, that Jesus is both human and divine.

The description of Jesus "wrapped in swaddling clothes" is an allusion to the Book of Wisdom, in which King Solomon is described as "a mortal man, the same as all the rest" (Wis 7:1).

> In swaddling clothes and with constant care I was nurtured.
> For no king has any different origin or birth.... (Wis 7:4–5)

The description of Jesus lying in a manger is an allusion to Isaiah in which God bemoans the fact that Israel does not recognize her Lord.

> Hear, O heavens, and listen, O earth,
>   for the LORD speaks:
> Sons have I raised and reared,
>   but they have disowned me!
> An ox knows its owner,
>   and an ass, its master's manger,
> But Israel does not know,
>   my people has not understood.
>   (Isa 1:2–3)

With Luke's story of the shepherds this situation is reversed. When told of the infant wrapped in swaddling clothes and lying in a manger, the shepherds believe the good news. They hurry to Bethlehem to see the sign. They find Jesus in the manger (a feeding trough) because Jesus has come to be nourishment for his people, to dwell with his people. The shepherds do recognize their Lord.

Today we honor Mary as the mother of God. This title was given Mary not so much to say something about Mary as to say something about Jesus: Jesus is one person, divine and human, and Mary is the mother of that one person. Today's reading teaches the same truth about Jesus but instead of using theological language it uses biblical allusions. Jesus is wrapped in swaddling clothes (fully human) and lying in a manger (the Lord who has come to nourish the people): he is both human and divine, God dwelling with God's people.

The infancy narratives, too, are written not to teach about Mary but to teach about Jesus. At the same time, in today's reading and in the scene in which Jesus is lost and then found in the temple, Luke tells us that Mary "kept all these things, reflecting on them in her heart" (Luke 2:19, 3:51). In Luke, Mary is presented as the preeminent disciple, allowing the Word to take flesh in her and pondering events as they unfold in her life.

Numbers 6:22–27 *in its biblical context*

The Book of Numbers gets its name from the fact that it begins and ends with a census (see chapters 1 and 26). The setting for the book is the desert during the exodus experience from the time that the Israelites left Mount Sinai until the time when they reached the Jordan. The point of view of those gathering and arranging the inherited material, however, dates to after the Babylonian exile. These priestly editors were very concerned with the role of priests in the life of the people.

Our reading begins: "The LORD said to Moses: 'Speak to Aaron and his sons and tell them: This is how you shall bless the Israelites.'" Aaron and his sons are of the priestly class. The blessing that they are told to give to the people is God's response to the ways in which the Israelites have committed themselves to act so that they remain pure in preparation for the holy war that will follow (see chapters 5 and 6).

The first sentence of the blessing is, "The LORD let his face shine upon you, and be gracious to you!" If the Lord's face is shining upon you, that means that the Lord is with you. When one feels the absence of the Lord, the Lord is said to be hiding the Lord's face, as in Psalm 44:

> Awake! Why are you asleep, O LORD?
>   Arise! Cast us not off forever!
> Why do you hide your face,
>   forgetting our woe and our oppression?
>   (Ps 44:24–25)

This blessing from Numbers could not be more appropriate for today's feast because our Gospel reading is describing the fulfillment of God's granting this blessing: the sign of the infant lying in the manger. The Lord's face is shining upon the people: God has come to dwell with the people.

The second line of the blessing is, "The LORD look upon you kindly and give you peace!" The peace for which Aaron and his sons were praying is the peace that comes with the absence of war, for which they were preparing. When we read this blessing in the context of today's liturgy, the peace for which we are praying is that peace which Jesus came to give us: peace not only in our world, but peace in our relationships with God, with others, and with ourselves.

Galatians 4:4–7 in its biblical context

In his Letter to the Galatians, Paul is arguing against a teaching introduced by some missionaries who taught the Galatians after Paul had left them: that in addition to having faith in Jesus Christ, one must obey the law to be saved. Paul tells the Galatians that the law is no longer binding, that Jesus has ransomed the human race from the law: "But when the fullness of time had come, God sent his Son, born of a woman, born under the law, to ransom those under the law, so that we might receive adoption." Paul assures the Galatians that they are no longer slaves to the law, but are adopted children and heirs of God. Using this same metaphor, we are also children of the woman who gave birth to Jesus. The church honors Mary not only as the preeminent disciple, the one after whom we model ourselves, and as the mother of God, but as our own mother.

Questions for Breaking Open the Word groups are on page 13.

Questions for other faith sharing groups

1. Does Mary play a role in your prayer life? Explain.

2. Why do you think Mary is considered a model disciple? What about her most appeals to you?

3. Do you think of yourself as a beloved child of God? What ramifications does this belief have in your life?

Bible study questions

1. What do Matthew's and Luke's infancy narratives have in common? How do they differ?

2. What is *midrash?*

3. To what Old Testament passages is Luke alluding when he describes the infant wrapped in swaddling clothes and lying in a manger?

4. What theological concept is being taught through these allusions?

5. What false teaching is Paul arguing against in his Letter to the Galatians?

SECOND SUNDAY AFTER CHRISTMAS
CYCLES A, B, AND C

John 1:1–18 in its biblical context

Of the four canonical Gospels, that is, the Gospels that became part of the Bible, John's was written last, probably toward the end of the first century AD. John's audience had lived well beyond the expected second coming of the Son of Man on the clouds of heaven. By this time people were asking, "Where is Jesus Christ? We expected his return long before now."

In order to respond to this question, John writes a Gospel that differs in many ways from the other three Gospels (called the Synoptic Gospels because of their similarity to each other). John's theme, which he introduces in the opening poem that we read today, is that the Word has become flesh and dwells among us. Instead of looking back to the time when the historical Jesus lived on earth or to a future time when the Son of Man would return, John wants to help his audience see that the risen Christ is alive and in their midst.

John does not begin his story with Jesus' baptism, as does Mark, or with Jesus' conception, as do Matthew and Luke. John starts before time and before the existence of the created order. John's first words are an allusion to the Book of Genesis, which begins: "In the beginning, when God created the heavens and the earth, the earth was a formless wasteland, and darkness covered the abyss, while a mighty wind swept over the waters" (Gen 1:1–2). John's setting precedes the creation described in Genesis. John says,

> In the beginning was the Word,
>   and the Word was with God,
>   and the Word was God.
> He was in the beginning with God.
> All things came to be through him,
>   and without him nothing came to be.

John introduces us to a preexistent Word, who was *with* God and who *was* God.

In Genesis we read that on each day God said, "Let there be . . ." and through the power of God's word what God named came into existence. John tells us that it was through the preexistent Word that all things came to be, and "without him nothing came to be." This is a very high Christology, a Christology that claims Jesus' divinity not by describing Jesus as having been conceived by Mary through the Holy Spirit, but as a preexistent Word that became flesh and dwelt among us.

> And the Word became flesh
>   and made his dwelling among us,
>   and we saw his glory,
>   the glory as of the Father's only Son,
>   full of grace and truth.

To say that we "saw his glory" is to say that people recognized Jesus as divine. In fact, John presents John the Baptist as having a post-resurrection understanding of Jesus' divinity from the very beginning. In today's Gospel John the Baptist says, "This is he of whom I said, 'The one who is coming after me ranks ahead of me because he existed before me.'" Far from having to send his disciples to ask Jesus, "Are you the one who is to come, or should we look for another?" (Luke 7:19; Matt 11:3), John the Baptist is pictured as referring to Jesus' preexistence.

John's Gospel tells us that John the Baptist gave testimony to the "true light, which enlightens everyone." John will continue the theme of Christ as the light of the world throughout his Gospel. Those who do not yet recognize Christ are presented as being in the dark or as coming to Jesus at night (see Nicodemus in John 3:3; Mary of Magdala in John 20:1). By telling the story of Jesus Christ in the unique way in which he does, John is trying to help his audience see the light, that is, understand that Jesus is in their midst. All they have to do is learn to recognize that the Word has become flesh and dwells among us in the church.

Sirach 24:1–2, 8–12 in its biblical context

The Book of Sirach is one of the books that is included in the canon of Roman Catholic Bibles but not in the canon of Protestant Bibles. Catholics call such books *deuterocanonical* while Protestants call them *apocryphal*. The foreword of Sirach explains that the book was originally written in Hebrew but was translated into Greek by the original author's grandson in the second century BC. In some tables of contents the book is called Ecclesiasticus.

Sirach was written to extol the wisdom of Judaism in a world that had become Hellenized, that is, increasingly being influenced by the Greek culture. In fact, the book contains two poems that praise wisdom, one in its opening chapter and one in chapter 24, parts of which we read today.

Notice that in the poem wisdom is personified, that is, wisdom is described as though she were a person.

> Wisdom sings her own praises and is honored in God,
>> before her own people she boasts;
> in the assembly of the Most High she opens her mouth,
>> in the presence of his power she declares her worth....

As the poem continues, the author specifically places God's wisdom in Israel rather than in the Greek culture by having personified wisdom say:

> "The Creator of all commanded and said to me,
>> and he who formed me chose the spot for my tent,
> saying, 'In Jacob make your dwelling,
>> in Israel your inheritance,
>> and among my chosen put down your roots.'"

Just as in John's Gospel the Word became flesh and dwelt among us, so in Sirach Wisdom is told by God to pitch her tent, that is, to dwell in Israel.

Wisdom, too, claims to have existed before the rest of creation.

> "Before all ages, in the beginning, he created me,
>> and through all ages I shall not cease to be."

However, there is no claim that wisdom is God. God created wisdom and selected Israel as the nation with whom wisdom was to dwell.

Ephesians 1:3–6, 15–18 in its biblical context

In his Letter to the Ephesians, Paul is also praising God for the great gifts God has given God's people: "Blessed be the God and Father of our Lord Jesus Christ, who has blessed us in Christ with every spiritual blessing in the heavens, as he chose us in him, before the foundation of the world...." In Psalm 147 the psalmist understood that God had given to Israel what God had not given to any other nation. However, by the time Paul is living the followers of Jesus

Christ have come to realize that God's love extends to every nation. It has been God's loving plan since "before the foundation of the world" to include the Ephesians in God's redemptive plan.

The Ephesians have responded in love to God's saving plan: "Therefore, I too, hearing of your faith in the Lord Jesus and of your love for all the holy ones, do not cease giving thanks for you, remembering you in my prayers...." As Paul prays for the Ephesians he prays that "the God of our Lord Jesus Christ, the Father of glory, may give you a spirit of wisdom and revelation resulting in knowledge of him," and that "the eyes of your hearts be enlightened." Like Sirach, Paul wants the Ephesians to let God's wisdom find a home in them. Like John, Paul wants them to see the light of Christ so that they can continue to experience Christ's redemptive presence in their midst.

Questions for Breaking Open the Word groups are on page 13.

Questions for other faith sharing groups

1. In what ways do you experience Christ as in our midst?

2. Do you feel grateful for having been taught "God's ordinances"? What difference has this made in your life?

3. Do you believe that God wants everyone to respond to God's love? What practical ramifications does this belief have in your life?

Bible study questions

1. How does John's Gospel begin? How does this differ from the other Gospels?

2. What is John's theme? Why is this John's theme?

3. In John's Gospel, when does John the Baptist recognize Jesus' true identity?

4. What is a *deuterocanonical* book? What do Protestants call these same books? Why?

5. What does Paul pray for when he prays for the Ephesians?

THE EPIPHANY OF THE LORD

Matthew 2:1–12 in its biblical context

Today's Gospel is the wonderful story of the magi coming to pay homage to the Christ child. We have probably all acted out this story either as children in costume or by assembling a crib set. It is very likely that in all of our enactments the magi arrived at the manger, a combination of images that does not appear in the Gospels. The magi appear only in Matthew; the manger only in Luke.

The fact that Matthew and Luke both tell stories of Jesus' birth, but that their stories differ in details, is evidence that both Matthew and Luke were using the literary form of *infancy narrative*. (We discussed infancy narratives briefly in the Gospel commentary on the Feast of the Holy Family.) Infancy narratives teach not what was known about a child at the time of the child's birth but what was known after the person became great.

In order to teach his postresurrection message about Jesus, Matthew winds Old Testament images around his account of New Testament events. Alluding to Old Testament passages in this way was a teaching technique of the time called *midrash*. We will better understand Matthew's teaching if we are familiar with the Old Testament passages to which he refers.

When the magi arrive at Herod's palace they ask, "Where is the newborn king of the Jews? We saw his star at its rising and have come to do him homage." This is an allusion to Numbers 24:15–17a.

> The utterance of Balaam, son of Beor
>   the utterance of the man whose eye is true,
> The utterance of one who hears what God says,
>   and knows what the Most High knows,
> Of one who sees what the Almighty sees,
>   enraptured and with eyes unveiled:
> I see him, though not now;
>   I behold him, though not near:
> A star shall advance from Jacob,
>   and a staff shall rise from Israel....

In the Book of Numbers these words appear on Balaam's lips. This scene takes place while the Israelites are camped on the plains of Moab across the Jordan from Jericho. They have not yet crossed the Jordan to claim the promised land. Balak, the king of Moab, is afraid that the Israelites will conquer his people. He asks Balaam to curse the Israelites so that they will no longer be a threat. Balaam explains that he cannot say anything that God would not have him say. When Balaam speaks, he blesses the Israelites rather than curses them.

When Balaam says, "A star shall advance from Jacob, / and a staff shall rise from Israel," he is speaking of King David, who did later conquer the holy land. The setting of this scene precedes David, but the person telling the story lived after David. The story in Numbers is teaching that David's reign was ordained by God. Matthew uses Balaam's words to teach not about David, but about Jesus.

In Matthew's story, when Herod assembles the chief priests and scribes to ask where the Christ was to be born, they reply,

> "In Bethlehem of Judea,
> for thus it has been written through the prophet:
> *And you, Bethlehem, land of Judah,*
>   *are by no means least among the rulers of Judah;*

since from you shall come a ruler,
  who is to shepherd my people Israel."

This passage, largely based on Micah 5:1, is also a reference to King David. Micah was a prophet to the southern kingdom in the eighth century BC. He is reminding the people that King David, who was the greatest king they ever had, was from Bethlehem. Bethlehem is the source of the Davidic dynasty to whom God has promised fidelity. Micah is offering the people hope that future kings will also come from the Davidic line and will be faithful to God.

Still a third Old Testament passage that Matthew uses in his story appears as our Old Testament reading: Isaiah 60:1–6.

Isaiah 60:1–6 in its biblical context

Our reading from Isaiah is from Third Isaiah (chapters 56–66), the post-Babylonian exile prophet who offered hope to the returned exiles that, despite great hardship, they could rebuild the temple and Jerusalem. Today's reading begins:

> Rise up in splendor, Jerusalem! Your light has come,
>   the glory of the Lord shines upon you.

The life of the returned exiles was extremely difficult:

> See, darkness covers the earth,
>   and thick clouds cover the peoples....

However, God is still with God's chosen people:

> ...but upon you the LORD shines,
>   and over you appears his glory.

Third Isaiah reiterates the hope offered by Second Isaiah (Isa 40–55) that God would use the suffering of the exiles to bring other nations to a knowledge of God:

> Nations shall walk by your light,
>   and kings by your shining radiance....

> Caravans of camels shall fill you,
>   dromedaries from Midian and Ephah;
> all from Sheba shall come
>   bearing gold and frankincense,
>   and proclaiming the praises of the LORD.

Matthew pictures the magi going to the house where they find Jesus and Mary: "On entering the house they saw the child with Mary his mother. They prostrated themselves and did him homage. Then they opened their treasures and offered him gifts of gold, frankincense, and myrrh." In Third Isaiah the recipient of the kings' attention and gifts is the nation Israel, God's instrument of revelation to the nations. In Matthew, Jesus is the recipient of the magi's homage and gifts. Matthew is teaching that Jesus is the fulfillment of God's promises to the Israelites. Jesus is the light to all nations. Other nations have come to recognize their Lord.

Ephesians 3:2–3a, 5–6 in its biblical context

The author of the Letter to the Ephesians teaches in plain words what Matthew has taught through his dramatization of the magi coming to pay Jesus homage: Jesus is light to all nations. Ephesians says, "... the Gentiles are coheirs, members of the same body, and copartners in the promise in Christ Jesus through the gospel." This is obviously surprising news. Previous generations did not know that the covenant would be opened to Gentiles: "It was not made known to people in other generations as it has now been revealed to his holy apostles and prophets by the Spirit."

The author, purportedly Paul (Ephesians may be attributed to Paul rather than written by Paul), learned this mystery through revelation and now passes it on to the Ephesians because he learned it for their benefit: "You have heard of the stewardship of God's grace that was given to me for your benefit, namely, that the mystery was made known to me by revelation."

For nearly two thousand years the Israelites had understood themselves as being especially called and chosen to be in a relationship of covenant love with God. Now, after Jesus' resurrection, the invitation to covenant love is understood to have been extended to all. Matthew's audience is primarily Jewish. Through his story of the magi Matthew is teaching his Jewish contemporaries, and us, that the promises made to the Israelites have been fulfilled in Jesus. The Israelites have become God's instrument of revelation to the nations. All nations now adore their Lord.

Questions for Breaking Open the Word groups are on page 13.

Questions for other faith sharing groups

1. In what ways has Jesus been light for you personally?
2. In what ways has Israel been a light to other nations?
3. As a disciple of Jesus, what responsibility do you have to be a light to your family? To your workplace?

Bible study questions

1. What do infancy narratives teach?
2. What is *midrash*?
3. To what Old Testament passage is Matthew alluding when he includes the star in his account? When he refers to Bethlehem?
4. What hope did Third Isaiah offer his audience?
5. What teaching do Matthew's infancy narrative and our passage from Ephesians have in common?

ORDINARY TIME: SUNDAYS 1–9

THE BAPTISM OF THE LORD
(FIRST SUNDAY IN ORDINARY TIME)

Luke 3:15–16, 21–22 in its biblical context

On the first Sunday of Ordinary Time (that time in the liturgical year when we are not celebrating a special season like Advent or Christmas) we celebrate Jesus' baptism. The first part of today's reading, in which John the Baptist denies that he is the messiah, we read on the third Sunday of Advent:

> "I am baptizing you with water,
>   but one mightier than I is coming.
> I am not worthy to loosen the thongs of his sandals.
> He will baptize you with the Holy Spirit and fire."

We discussed the distinction between John's baptism and Jesus' in the commentary for that Sunday.

Our Lectionary reading then omits John's description of Jesus' ministry as one in which Jesus will be primarily a judge: "His winnowing fan is in his hand to clear his threshing floor and to gather the wheat into his barn, but the chaff he will burn with unquenchable fire" (Luke 3:17). Luke also tells us that Herod has had John imprisoned.

It is after Jesus has been baptized and is praying that the Spirit descends upon Jesus and the voice from heaven speaks: "After all the people had been baptized and Jesus also had been baptized and was praying, heaven was opened and the Holy Spirit descended upon him in bodily form like a dove. And a voice came from heaven, 'You are my beloved Son; with you I am well pleased.'" By picturing the voice saying these words, Luke is once more alluding to Old Testament passages in order to teach the significance of New Testament events. When we recognize the allusions we will understand the teaching.

The words "You are my beloved Son" are an allusion to Psalm 2. Psalm 2 is a messianic psalm, that is, it speaks of the messiah, the anointed one (the word *messiah* means "anointed") whom God would send to save God's people. The Israelites understood their kings to be God's anointed. This psalm would have been sung over the centuries to honor the king.

In Psalm 2 God affirms that God has appointed Israel's king:

> "I myself have set up my king
> on Zion, my holy mountain."
>
> (Ps 2:6)

Then the king speaks:

> I will proclaim the decree of the LORD:
> The LORD said to me, "You are my son;
> this day I have begotten you.
> Ask of me and I will give you
> the nations for an inheritance
> and the ends of the earth for your possession.
>
> (Ps 2:7–8)

By alluding to this psalm Luke is once more teaching what he has already taught in his story of the annunciation to Mary: Jesus is God's son, begotten of God.

The words "with you I am well pleased" are an allusion to the Book of Isaiah and are part of our Old Testament Lectionary reading for this First Sunday in Ordinary Time. As we will soon see, by alluding to this passage Luke is foreshadowing Jesus' passion and death and teaching that Jesus is God's suffering servant whose passion and death redeemed all nations.

Isaiah 42:1–4, 6–7 in its biblical context

Today's reading is from Second Isaiah (chapters 40–55 of Isaiah), the prophet who spoke words of hope to those suffering in exile in Babylon (587 BC–537 BC). When Second Isaiah says, "Thus says the LORD: / Here is my servant whom I uphold, / my chosen one with whom I am pleased," the servant about whom he is speaking is the nation Israel. Second Isaiah's words are very good news indeed because God calls Israel *my* servant. The exile was a terribly troublesome time for the Israelites, not just because they had lost their kingdom and their temple but because these losses made them question their whole understanding of their covenant relationship with God. God had promised that David's kingdom and David's line would be secure forever. Now David's kingdom was no more. Had the Israelites misunderstood their relationship with God? Were they God's chosen people?

Second Isaiah responds to these questions with a resounding "yes." Israel is God's servant whom God upholds. The exiles' suffering is not a sign that God has deserted them. Rather, God has a purpose in their suffering. Through their suffering the Israelites will bring other nations to a knowledge of God.

> I, the LORD, have called you for the victory of justice,
> I have grasped you by the hand;
> I formed you, and set you
> as a covenant of the people,
> a light for the nations. . . .

This passage from Isaiah is one of four *suffering servant songs*. Since the songs speak of a suffering servant, they were not originally thought of as songs about the hoped-for messiah, because the messiah was not expected to suffer. However, after Jesus did suffer and then rise from the dead the suffering servant songs were used to probe the mystery of a suffering messiah. When Luke pictures God speaking of Jesus as his beloved son with whom God is well pleased, Luke is reminding his audience of Second Isaiah's servant songs. He is teaching that the suffering servant who opens the eyes of the blind and brings prisoners out from confinement is now understood to be Jesus Christ.

Acts 10:34–38 in its biblical context

As we join the story in Acts, Peter is speaking to those gathered in the house of Cornelius. This is obviously the middle of the story. Extremely important events have preceded this scene. During Jesus' life on earth the disciples understood that their mission was to the Israelites. After the resurrection they came to understand that God was inviting everyone into a relationship of covenant love. This revelation came about as a result of a dream that Peter had, combined with a summons to come to the house of Cornelius.

In Peter's dream he saw a sheet lowered from heaven, and on it were all kinds of animals. A voice said to Peter, "Slaughter and eat." Peter refused to take and eat because, according to Jewish law, some of the animals were unclean. The voice said, "What God has made clean, you are not to call profane" (Acts 10:15).

Peter did not know what this dream meant. Soon after, however, Peter was summoned to the house of Cornelius, a Gentile. Under normal circumstances Peter would not have entered the home of a Gentile. However, as Peter explains, "God has shown me that I should not call any person profane or unclean. And that is why I came without objection when sent for" (Acts 10:28–29). Cornelius then explains to Peter that an angel asked him to summon Peter and told him that all in the house are ready to listen to what Peter has to say. Today's reading is the beginning of Peter's response. Notice that Peter begins by referring to Jesus' baptism: "You know…what has happened all over Judea, beginning in Galilee after the baptism that John preached, how God anointed Jesus of Nazareth with the Holy Spirit and power." Jesus' anointing "with the Holy Spirit and power" resulted in Jesus going about doing good. The baptism that Jesus gives us, a baptism of the Holy Spirit, enables us to go about doing good as Jesus did, in his name.

Questions for Breaking Open the Word groups are on page 13.

Questions for other faith sharing groups

1. Are you baptized? If so, when and where were you baptized? What does your baptism mean to you?

2. Do you think of Jesus primarily as a judge? If so, why? If not, how do you think of Jesus?

3. In what ways have you experienced the power of the Spirit in your life?

Bible study questions

1. To what Old Testament text is Luke alluding when the voice from heaven says, "You are my beloved Son . . . "? What is Luke teaching through this allusion?

2. To what Old Testament text is Luke alluding when the voice says, " . . . with you I am well pleased"? What is Luke teaching through this allusion?

3. Why were songs about a suffering servant not originally understood to be messianic songs?

4. For what purpose did early Christians use Second Isaiah's suffering servant songs?

5. What did Peter learn from his dream of the sheet lowered with all the animals?

Second Sunday in Ordinary Time

John 2:1–11 in its biblical context

In order to understand the full meaning of John's story of the wedding at Cana it will be helpful to know a little about John's contemporaries, the question that is on their minds, and John's method of responding to that question.

John's Gospel dates to near the end of the first century, probably about AD 90. Jesus was expected to return in glory on the clouds of heaven long before that time. So John's audience is asking, "Where is he?" John is trying to help his audience understand that the risen Christ is in their midst, through the church and through the sacraments.

In order to help his contemporaries, and us, recognize Christ in our midst John uses a kind of writing called *allegory*. An allegory has two levels of meaning—a literal level that is evident immediately, and a second level of meaning that is hidden at first. We understand this second level of meaning, called the allegorical or the intentional meaning, when we realize that the plot elements in the literal level of the story stand for something else. In an allegory the author's teaching is found at this second level of meaning.

John's story of the wedding at Cana is an allegory. John gives us many hints to look for a deeper level of meaning. For one, John calls this story, and six other stories in his Gospel, *signs*. Our reading today ends with this statement: "Jesus did this as the beginning of his signs at Cana in Galilee and so revealed his glory, and his disciples began to believe in him." As you know, a sign is something that points to something else. Remember, too, that John's audience is looking for a particular sign that will reveal Jesus' glory, Jesus' coming in glory on the clouds of heaven. Through his Gospel John is teaching his contemporaries to see other signs of Jesus' presence and glory so that they, like the disciples in the story, will believe in Christ.

In order to understand John's teaching, then, we must "translate" the symbols in the literal story line. Jesus stands for the risen Christ. The disciples stand for John's contemporaries and every generation of believers ever since, including us. Jesus is at a wedding. A wedding, in both the Old Testament and the New, stands for God's relationship with God's people. We will see this metaphor used in today's Old Testament reading from Isaiah, in which God's people are called God's bride. So the story, at the allegorical level, is about the risen Christ's relationship with God's people.

Jesus' mother is at the wedding. Notice that she is never named. This is another signal from John that we should look for an allegorical meaning. Mary is functioning as a symbol and not only as a person. Jesus calls his mother "woman." This, too, is a clue to look for allegory. On the literal level Jesus' words sound rude. On the allegorical level, by picturing Jesus calling his mother "woman" John is alluding to the woman in Genesis, the woman who is called Eve because she is the mother of all the living. The woman in John's story is the mother of all the living in a spiritual sense. Jesus' mother stands for the church.

Notice that it is the woman who mediates between Jesus and the needs of the guests. She says to Jesus, "They have no wine." Jesus responds, "Woman, how does your concern affect me? My hour has not yet come." On the literal level Jesus is telling his mother that his hour to show his glory has not yet come. In John's Gospel the hour in which Jesus shows his glory is the hour when Jesus is raised up— Jesus' crucifixion and resurrection. On the allegorical level the risen Christ is telling the church that his hour to return on the clouds in glory has not yet come. This is a partial response to the question on the minds of John's audience: "Where is Jesus?"

Next Jesus' mother, who stands for the church, says to the servers, "Do whatever he tells you." God's people are to be obedient to Christ. There are six empty ablution jars. Ablution jars were used for ritual cleansing, required by the law. The jars are empty. This means that the old way of relating to God, through the law, is now ineffective. At Jesus' instruction, the servants fill the empty ablution jars with water that becomes wine. Water and wine, of course, stand for baptism and Eucharist, what we have come to call the sacraments of initiation.

Shortly after the wedding at Cana, in a dialogue not included in today's reading, John pictures Jesus in conversation with Nicodemus. Jesus tells Nicodemus that "no one can enter the kingdom of God without being born of water and Spirit" (John 3:5). This too is a pattern in John: In addition to teaching something through an allegorical story (the wedding at Cana), John will teach the same truth through a dialogue (Jesus' conversation with Nicodemus). Both the story of the wedding at Cana and the conversation with Nicodemus are teaching that Jesus has initiated a new spiritual order. One enters this spiritual order through the sacraments of baptism and Eucharist.

We see, then, that there is an allegorical level of meaning to the story of the wedding at Cana. Through the story John is responding to the question "Where is the risen Christ?" At the allegorical level John is teaching that the risen Christ is already present to his people through the church and through the sacraments.

Isaiah 62:1–5 in its biblical context

The setting for our reading from Third Isaiah (Isa 56–66) is the time after the Babylonian exile, when the people are rebuilding their ravaged holy land and temple. The exile had been a terrible time of suffering for the Israelites, not only because they had lost their kingdom and their temple, but because the loss of these things made them question their relationship with God. After all, God had promised to protect them. During the exile a prophet we call Second Isaiah urged the people to have hope. God would send someone to save them.

The exile ended when God sent Cyrus, a Persian, who conquered the Babylonians and allowed the Israelites to return home. Third Isaiah is referring to their rescue from exile and being allowed to return when he says that the Israelites have been vindicated; they have been vindicated for putting their hope in God and for believing that they were in a covenant relationship with God.

> For Zion's sake I will not be silent,
>   for Jerusalem's sake I will not be quiet,
> until her vindication shines forth like the dawn
>   and her victory like a burning torch.

Now that the exile is over, other nations will no longer think of the Israelites as defeated and banished:

> No more shall people call you "Forsaken,"
>   or your land "Desolate,"
> but you shall be called "My Delight,"
>   and your land "Espoused."

Third Isaiah then continues using marriage as a metaphor for the relationship between God and Gods' people:

> As a young man marries a virgin,
>   your Builder shall marry you;
> and as a bridegroom rejoices in his bride
>   so shall your God rejoice in you.

John builds upon this traditional imagery when he chooses a wedding as the setting for the first of his stories, his signs, through which he teaches us that the risen Christ is already present in our midst.

1 Corinthians 12:4–11 in its biblical context

In our reading from 1 Corinthians Paul is teaching that there is one Spirit who gives people different kinds of spiritual gifts for the benefit of the community. "There are different kinds of spiritual gifts but the same Spirit.... To each individual the manifestation of the Spirit is given for some benefit." Among the gifts given are wisdom, knowledge, faith, healing, mighty deeds, prophecy, discernment of spirits, speaking in tongues, and interpreting tongues.

The Spirit gives gifts not just to those in leadership, but to everyone: The gifts are given "to each individual." The Spirit produces all of these gifts, "distributing them individually to each person as he wishes."

The inspired author of the Gospel according to John was full of the Spirit. We too need to open ourselves to the Spirit in order to be able to understand John's good news about Jesus Christ and to recognize the presence of the risen Christ in our midst.

Questions for Breaking Open the Word groups are on page 13.

Questions for other faith sharing groups

1. Do you think marriage is a good metaphor for the relationship between God and God's people? Why or why not? What truths do you think are being taught by this metaphor?

2. In what way is the church the mother of all the living in the new spiritual order? Has the church been a mother to you? Explain.

3. What spiritual gifts do you think you have received? How do you put these gifts at the service of the community?

Bible study questions

1. What is an *allegory?*

2. What hints does John give us that we should look for a deeper meaning to his story?

3. At the allegorical level, what is the story of the wedding at Cana teaching?

4. What is Paul's main point in our reading from 1 Corinthians?

5. For what purpose are people given gifts?

THIRD SUNDAY IN ORDINARY TIME

Luke 1:1–4; 4:14–21 in its biblical context

Today's reading begins with the first verses of Luke's Gospel. These verses are very important because Luke is the only person who tells us how he went about writing his Gospel. His description helps us understand the nature of his Gospel as well as what we are claiming when we claim that a biblical author is inspired.

Luke tells us that he is not the first to write about the events concerning Jesus, nor is he an eyewitness to the events: "Since many have undertaken to compile a narrative of the events that have been fulfilled among us, just as those who were eyewitnesses from the beginning and ministers of the word have handed them down to us. . . . " Certainly Luke is claiming that there were events. Jesus was a historical person, and there were eyewitnesses to the events surrounding Jesus' life, death, and resurrection. Those eyewitnesses passed on accounts of the events orally—they were "ministers of the word." This means that they were not historians. Luke received the oral tradition, not from people who were responding to the question, "What happened?" but from people who were responding to the question, "What is the significance of what happened in our lives?"

Luke is not the first to write down the oral tradition. Many before Luke had "undertaken to compile a narrative of events." Luke, too, has decided to write "an orderly sequence." This means that Luke is editing the inherited oral and written traditions about the events that have been handed down in the community. Luke is not doing this for future generations, but for a contemporary audience. He addresses that audience as "Theophilus." His interest is not to teach history but to build faith: He is writing his orderly account so that Theophilus "may realize the certainty of the teachings you have received."

Certainly the Christian community claims that Luke was inspired. Otherwise Luke's work would not be included in the canon (those books included in the Bible). However, we are not claiming that Luke went into some kind of a trance and received his information directly from God. Neither are we claiming that Luke was an eyewitness and passed on exactly what he personally knew from experience. Rather, we are claiming that Luke depended on the work of other inspired teachers—those who passed on the stories orally and in writing before Luke started his Gospel. Luke was dependent on the work of the Holy Spirit in the community, on the community witness. The community, as well as Luke, was inspired.

After giving us this introduction, our Lectionary reading skips over the stories of Jesus' birth, baptism, and temptation and picks up the story again with Luke's first description of Jesus' public ministry. Remember, at Jesus' baptism the Spirit descended upon him. Now Jesus returns "to Galilee in the power of the Spirit."

Jesus goes to the synagogue in his hometown of Nazareth and, according to Luke, reads a passage from the Book of Isaiah. Actually

Luke has woven several passages from Isaiah together: Isaiah 61:1–2 and Isaiah 58:6. In chapter 61 the prophet is describing his own call:

> The spirit of the Lord GOD is upon me,
>   because the LORD has anointed me;
> He has sent me to bring glad tidings to the lowly,
>   to heal the brokenhearted,
> To proclaim liberty to the captives
>   and release to the prisoners,
> To announce a year of favor from the LORD.
>
> (Isa 61:1–2a)

In chapter 58 the prophet is describing what God considers a true fast:

> This, rather, is the fasting that I wish:
>   releasing those bound unjustly,
>   untying the thongs of the yoke;
> Setting free the oppressed,
>   breaking every yoke. (Isa 58:6)

Luke has omitted some of Third Isaiah's call story and has inserted into the call story the quotation about setting free the oppressed. The effect of Luke's editing is to universalize the group who is to be served—it is no longer just Israel (see Isa 61:3a)—and to emphasize the marginalized condition of those included in Jesus' ministry: the oppressed. The "year of favor from the Lord" mentioned by Isaiah and Jesus ("a year acceptable to the Lord") is a jubilee year. A jubilee year was held every fifty years. During a jubilee year the people were to let the ground lie fallow, free slaves, forgive debts, redistribute property, and have a great feast.

After reading the scroll Jesus says to those gathered in the synagogue, "Today this Scripture passage is fulfilled in your hearing." By picturing Jesus applying Isaiah's words to himself Luke is teaching that the covenant promises that God made to the Israelites are being fulfilled in Jesus. This theme of fulfillment, of God's promises being kept through Jesus, will reappear often in Luke's Gospel.

Notice also that for Jesus scripture was a living word that spoke directly to him about his own relationship with God. We too believe that scripture is a living word that can speak directly to us. It is this belief that underlies our practice of *breaking open the word* and of meeting in faith sharing groups to listen to the word and share our insights about how the living word is speaking to each one of us personally.

Nehemiah 8:2–4a, 5–6, 8–10 *in its biblical context*

In today's Old Testament passage from the Book of Nehemiah we read about Ezra proclaiming the law to the whole community of Israel. Both Nehemiah and Ezra were leaders after the Babylonian exile when the people had to rebuild their ravaged land and temple.

Nehemiah, after whom the book is named, was a layman who oversaw the physical rebuilding of the holy land. Ezra was a priest who helped the people reestablish their spiritual lives.

In today's reading we see that Ezra is like Moses, except that instead of delivering the law from a mountain, Ezra delivers it from "a wooden platform that had been made for the occasion." The people listen attentively to Ezra, rising when he opens the scroll, as we do when we listen to the Gospel, and committing themselves to obey the law with their response, "Amen, amen!"

As the people hear the law read they weep, evidently in sorrow over past disobedience. However, the law is a great gift. It is the social extension of the people's covenant relationship with God. So Ezra tells the people not to be sad and weep, but, "Go, eat rich foods and drink sweet drinks, . . . for today is holy to our LORD . . . rejoicing in the LORD must be your strength." There is no greater joy than being in right relationship with God.

1 Corinthians 12:12–30 in its biblical context

Today's reading is a continuation of last Sunday's reading in which Paul is stressing the unity of Christ's body, the church. This unity, coming from the one Spirit, is so strong that it unites Jews and Greeks, slaves and free. The body is made up of different parts, each with its own gifts, given for the good of the whole. One person in the church cannot say to another person in the church, "I do not need you," any more than the head can say to the feet, "I do not need you."

The parts of the body must have concern for one another. There should never be competition among the members: "If one part suffers, all the parts suffer with it; if one part is honored, all the parts share its joy." Paul makes it clear that he is not discussing abstract concepts, but words that the Corinthians should take to heart: "Now you are Christ's body, and individually parts of it." We too are invited to take Paul's words to heart and to work for the visible unity of Christ's body, the church.

Questions for Breaking Open the Word groups are on page 13.

Questions for other faith sharing groups

1. In what ways do you depend on the wisdom of the community to arrive at truth?

2. If we were to proclaim "a year acceptable to the Lord," what about the way we live do you think would have to be changed in order to make our way of living acceptable to the Lord?

3. Have you experienced pain from the divisions that exist in Christ's body, the church? Explain. What could you do personally to help heal these divisions?

Bible study questions

1. What three stages in the development of the Gospel preceded Luke's writing of his Gospel?

2. To what question were those who passed on the oral tradition responding?

3. For what purpose does Luke write his Gospel?

4. What is Luke teaching by picturing Jesus applying Isaiah's words to himself?

5. Why can one person in the church not say to another person, "I do not need you"?

FOURTH SUNDAY IN ORDINARY TIME

Luke 4:21–30 in its biblical context

Today's Gospel repeats the last sentence of last Sunday's reading: "Today this Scripture passage is fulfilled in your hearing." As we pointed out, the theme of fulfillment, that God's covenant promises to the Israelites have been fulfilled in Jesus, is very important to Luke. Equally important is Luke's theme of the universal nature of Christ's saving acts. Luke is writing to Gentiles and teaching them that they too are now invited into a covenant relationship with God. As we will see, Luke's theme of universalism is present in today's reading.

The first words of the Lectionary reading, "Jesus began speaking in the synagogue, saying..." are not in scripture. We know that today's reading is not the beginning of Jesus' talk to those in the synagogue. He has just finished reading from the scroll of Isaiah, the scripture passage to which he is referring when he says, "this Scripture passage is fulfilled in your hearing." The crowd's reaction to Jesus' remarkable statement is positive: they speak highly of him. However, they also ask, "Isn't this the son of Joseph?"

By having the people ask this question, Luke is creating what is called *dramatic irony* between the readers of the Gospel and the characters in the story. Dramatic irony occurs when the author and audience share information that the characters in the story know nothing about. Luke and the readers of the Gospel know that Jesus is God's own son. This has been made clear in the infancy narratives and in the genealogy. In the genealogy Luke begins by saying, "When Jesus began his ministry he was about thirty years of age. He was the son, as was thought, of Joseph..." (Luke 3:23). The reader knows that Jesus is not actually the son of Joseph. In today's reading, too, when the people say, "Isn't this the son of Joseph?" the reader knows that the people do not know Jesus' true identity.

The fact that the people are mistaken in their understanding about his identity makes Jesus' reaction to them more understandable. Jesus speaks as if he knows that he will be rejected by his own. He says,

"Amen, I say to you, no prophet is accepted in his own native place." Jesus then gives his fellow townspeople two examples from their own history in which Gentiles rather than Israelites benefited from the ministry of the Israelite's prophets.

The first example comes from 1 Kings. As Jesus says in today's reading, because of a drought and a severe famine, the great prophet Elijah was sent to a poor widow who provided for his needs. That widow did not live in Israel, but in Sidon. While Elijah was under her care the woman's son "fell sick, and his sickness grew more severe until he stopped breathing" (1 Kgs 17:17). In response to her cries for help Elijah begged God to give life back to her son. "The Lord heard the prayer of Elijah; the life breath returned to the child's body" (1 Kgs 17:22). Elijah then returned the son to his mother.

The second example is from 2 Kings. In this story Naaman, a leper who was an army commander of the king of Aram, sought a cure from the prophet Elisha. Elisha told Naaman to wash seven times in the Jordan and his leprosy would be healed. At first Naaman refused to follow Elisha's directions, but on the urging of his servant he did as he was instructed: "So Naaman went down and plunged into the Jordan seven times at the word of the man of God. His flesh became again like the flesh of a little child, and he was clean" (2 Kgs 5:14).

The point Jesus is making, and Luke is emphasizing, is that others may benefit from Israelites' prophets more than they themselves benefit. This is good news for the Gentiles, Luke's audience, but bad news for Jesus' own people. As we see, they are very angered by Jesus' words. "When the people in the synagogue heard this, they were all filled with fury. They rose up, drove him out of the town, and led him to the brow of the hill on which their town had been built, to hurl him down headlong."

By describing the angry response of the people and the fact that they want to kill Jesus, Luke is foreshadowing Jesus' future passion and death as he introduces Jesus' public ministry. However, the crucifixion will not end with death but with life. This story, too, ends with life: "But Jesus passed through the midst of them and went away." Luke is teaching that no amount of opposition can thwart God's power to save not only the Israelites, but the Gentiles as well.

Jeremiah 1:4–5, 17–19 in its biblical context

Our reading from Jeremiah is part of Jeremiah's call and commissioning to be a prophet. Call stories have a traditional form: God calls, the prophet offers some objection, God responds to the objection. Today's Lectionary reading gives us the initial call: "Before I formed you in the womb I knew you, / before you were born I dedicated you, / a prophet to the nations I appointed you." Our reading does not include the prophet's objection or God's response. Jeremiah's objection is: "Ah Lord God!... / I know not how to speak; I am too young" (Jer 1:6). God's response is, "Say not, 'I am too young.' / To whomever I send you, you shall go; / whatever I command you, you shall speak. / Have no fear before them, / because I am with you to deliver you, says the LORD" (Jer 1:7b–8).

Even in God's response to Jeremiah's objection we can tell that Jeremiah will be met with resistance. Nevertheless, Jeremiah is told to "gird your loins; / stand up and tell them / all that I command you." The "them" to whom Jeremiah is to stand up is "Judah's kings and princes, / against its priests and people." What has Judah done? The nation's offense is named in a passage not included in the Lectionary. God says that Judah's wickedness rests in

> . . . forsaking me,
> And in burning incense to strange gods
> and adoring their own handiwork.
> (Jer 1:16)

Judah is guilty of idolatry.

Although Jeremiah will face resistance, he will prevail. God will take care of Jeremiah:

> "Be not crushed on their account,
>   as though I would leave you crushed before them. . . .
> They will fight against you but not prevail over you,
>   for I am with you to deliver you, says the LORD."

Like Jesus, Jeremiah will not be defeated by his enemies because no earthly power can thwart God's will and God's plan to save God's people.

1 Corinthians 12:31–13:13

Again today's reading from 1 Corinthians is a continuation of our reading from the last two Sundays. It is one of the most beloved passages in the New Testament: Paul's description of the greatest gift of all, which is love.

The other gifts that Paul has named amount to nothing unless they are accompanied by love. If we speak in tongues but do not have love, we are "a resounding gong or a clashing cymbal." If we have faith so as to move mountains but do not have love, we are nothing. If we give away all that we own, but without love, we gain nothing.

Next Paul describes this greatest of all gifts: "Love is patient, love is kind. It is not jealous, it is not pompous, it is not inflated, it is not rude, it does not seek its own interests. . . ." Paul tells us that love "bears all things, believes all things, hopes all things, endures all things."

As we read Paul's description of love we realize that Jesus was full of love. Jesus endured his passion and death in order to redeem the whole human race, including us.

Questions for Breaking Open the Word groups are on page 13.

Questions for other faith sharing groups

1. Are you resistant to advice, even good advice, from certain people? If so, who are these people? Why are you resistant?

2. Have you ever, through no effort of your own, been the recipient of something that "belonged" to another, such as an inheritance? If so, what was your reaction to this event? Do you see any relationship between this question and your spiritual life? Explain.

3. Why do you think that all other gifts are as nothing without love?

Bible study questions

1. What two themes are very important in Luke's Gospel?

2. What two examples does Jesus give the people of non-Israelites receiving the benefits of a prophet's ministry?

3. What is Luke teaching?

4. What is the greatest gift of all?

5. What characteristics will a person who has received this gift exhibit?

FIFTH SUNDAY IN ORDINARY TIME

Luke 5:1–11 in its biblical context

Last week we read Luke's account of Jesus' rejection in his hometown of Nazareth. This week we read Luke's version of the call of Simon Peter. Luke's Gospel has several stories that the Lectionary has skipped. Most are stories of Jesus' mighty power: the cure of a demoniac in Capernaum, the cure of Simon's mother-in-law, the cure of many sick people, and the rebuking of some demons who shout, "You are—the Holy One of God" (Luke 4:31–41). One story not included in the Lectionary is the one in which Jesus states the purpose of his ministry. Having experienced many healings, the crowds do not want Jesus to leave them. Jesus says, "To the other towns also I must proclaim the good news of the kingdom of God, because for this purpose I have been sent" (Luke 4:43). Our Lectionary reading picks up the story at this point.

Today's reading begins with Jesus doing just what he said he was sent to do: preach "the word of God." The crowd is so responsive that Jesus is pressed for room. He sees two boats by the lake, the fishermen having returned from an unsuccessful fishing trip. Jesus gets into Simon Peter's boat and teaches the crowd from there. From this point on, the characters on center stage in this story are Jesus and Peter. Near the end of the story those who are in the other boat will be named, but for now the spotlight is definitely on Peter. The preeminence given Peter is typical of Luke's two-volume work, his Gospel and the Acts of the Apostles.

When we discussed Luke's Gospel on the third Sunday in Ordinary Time we noted that Luke is editing the inherited oral and written traditions of the community. One of the written sources that Luke uses in writing his Gospel is the Gospel of Mark. It is interesting, therefore, to compare Luke and Mark's accounts of the call of Peter (see Mark 1:16–20). In Mark there is no marvelous catch, and Jesus heals Simon Peter's mother-in-law after he is called, not before. The marvelous catch story is familiar to us, not because it is part of a call story in another Gospel but because it is part of a postresurrection appearance story in John's Gospel (see John 21:1–14). We see then that Luke has combined his sources in a unique way. What is Luke trying to teach by telling the story as he does?

Because of the order in which Luke has arranged the stories, Peter knows and has faith in Jesus before Jesus calls him. Jesus has already cured his mother-in-law. So Jesus is not getting into the boat of a stranger when he teaches from Simon Peter's boat; Simon Peter has already witnessed Jesus' power firsthand.

After Peter and the crowd listen to Jesus preach the word of God, Jesus says to Simon Peter, "Put out into deep water and lower your nets for a catch." Simon Peter is hesitant to do this. He speaks to Jesus with deep respect, calling him "Master," and explains that he and his partners have worked hard all night and caught nothing. Then Peter says, "…but at your command I will lower the nets." Peter already has faith in Jesus because Jesus has cured Peter's mother-in-law. Faith is necessary for discipleship.

After doing as Jesus directed, Peter's nets are so full that he needs help from the other boat that is still accompanying them. Notice that those on the other boat are still unnamed. Luke clearly wants our concentration to be on Peter. When Peter sees that they have caught so many fish that their boats are close to sinking he falls at the knees of Jesus and says, "Depart from me, Lord, for I am a sinful man." Jesus is no longer "Master," but "Lord."

In John's Gospel the marvelous catch of fish is the reason that the disciples recognize who Jesus is (see John 21:1–14). Here Peter's recognition of Jesus as Lord causes Peter to profess his unworthiness. As we learned last week, a call story often involves an objection on the part of the one called. In response to Peter's objection that he is a sinful man Jesus says, "Do not be afraid; from now on you will be catching men." Peter, like Jesus, will become an evangelizer, one who preaches the word of God.

As he concludes his call story Luke finally names Simon's fishing partners and soon to be fellow disciples, James and John, the sons of Zebedee. He does not yet name Andrew, Peter's brother, who, in

Mark, is called at the same time as Peter (Mark 1:16–20). Luke concludes by telling us, "When they brought their boats to the shore, they left everything and followed him." Again the wholehearted response necessary for discipleship is emphasized. They do not just follow Jesus, but Jesus becomes the center of their lives. They leave everything to follow him.

Isaiah 6:1–2a, 3–8 in its biblical context

Today's passage from Isaiah is part of the story of Isaiah's call and commissioning as a prophet. As Isaiah describes his call he places himself in a historical setting, "the year King Uzziah died," that is, 742 BC. Isaiah has a vision of God's heavenly courtroom. God is presented as a king on a lofty throne with seraphim (a choir of angels) giving God homage. The seraphim cry to one another:

> "Holy, holy, holy is the LORD of hosts!
> All the earth is filled with his glory!"

The seraphim's cry about God's holiness is undoubtedly familiar to you because it has been incorporated into the eucharistic prayer at Mass. We join Isaiah in proclaiming God most holy. Isaiah's language, Hebrew, did not have the comparative and superlative degree of words (e.g., fast*er;* fast*est*). Therefore, to express the superlative the word was repeated three times. Isaiah is in total awe of God, who is most holy. Earthquake and fire are common symbols of God's theophany, God's self-revelation; thus "the frame of the door shook and the house was filled with smoke."

As typical in call stories, Isaiah now offers an objection. "Then I said, 'Woe is me, I am doomed! For I am a man of unclean lips, living among a people of unclean lips; yet my eyes have seen the King, the Lord of hosts!'" Isaiah says that he is "doomed" because it was believed that no one could see the face of God and live. In Exodus, when Moses is receiving instructions from God, Moses says, "'Do let me see your glory!' [God] answered, 'I will make all my beauty pass before you. . . . But my face you cannot see, for no man sees me and still lives'" (Exod 33:18–19a, 20). In addition, Isaiah realizes that he is not worthy to be in the presence of the most holy because he is a man of "unclean lips."

The response to the objection comes from one of the seraphim. "Then one of the seraphim flew to me, holding an ember that he had taken with tongs from the altar. He touched my mouth with it, and said, 'See, now that this has touched your lips, your wickedness is removed, your sin purged.'" Isaiah does not become worthy by his own power or effort. Rather, God has called and prepared Isaiah so that he is able to do the work to which he has been called. Isaiah's whole person has been made clean, and his lips have been prepared to speak God's word to God's people.

Now that Isaiah has been cleansed he is ready to respond to the call. When the voice of the Lord asks, "Whom shall I send? Who will go for us?" Isaiah can respond wholeheartedly: "Here I am . . . send me!"

1 Corinthians 15:1–11 in its biblical context

In this Sunday's reading we move forward several chapters in our readings from 1 Corinthians. We join Paul as he is arguing against some Corinthians who do not believe in the resurrection of the body. That this is the subject Paul is addressing is made clear immediately after our Lectionary selection. "But if Christ is preached as raised from the dead, how can some among you say there is no resurrection of the dead?" (1 Cor 15:12).

Paul insists that Jesus did rise from the dead. Not only did he rise, but he appeared to Cephas (Peter), then to the Twelve, to more than five hundred brothers at once, to James, to all the apostles, and finally to Paul himself. Paul knows from personal experience that his testimony about the resurrection is true. Although Paul did not meet Jesus until after Jesus died and rose, Paul counts himself among the apostles: "For I am the least of the apostles, not fit to be called an apostle, because I persecuted the church of God. But by the grace of God I am what I am." It is urgent for Paul that the Corinthians believe in Christ's resurrection because he wants the Corinthians to be saved: "I am reminding you, brothers and sisters, of the gospel I preached to you. . . . Through it you are also being saved. . . ."

Questions for Breaking Open the Word groups are on page 13.

Questions for other faith sharing groups

1. If you were choosing disciples, what qualities would you be looking for? Do you yourself have these qualities?

2. Are you willing to say to God, "Here I am. Send me!"? Why or why not?

3. Do you believe in the resurrection of the body? What significance does this belief have in your life?

Bible study questions

1. What Gospel is a source for Luke?

2. How does Luke's story of Peter's call differ from that of his source?

3. What does Isaiah see in his vision?

4. Why is the word *holy* repeated three times?

5. About what is Paul arguing with the Corinthians?

SIXTH SUNDAY IN ORDINARY TIME

Luke 6:17, 20–26 in its biblical context

Last week we read the call of Simon Peter. This week's Lectionary selection begins with the words, "Jesus came down with the Twelve...."
This is a reference to the preceding passage in Luke in which we are
told that Jesus departed to a mountain to pray. After spending the
night in prayer, Jesus "called his disciples to himself, and from them
he chose Twelve, whom he also named apostles" (Luke 6:13). Only
Luke's Gospel depicts Jesus giving the name *apostle* to the Twelve. As
was evident in last week's reading from 1 Corinthians, in which Paul
referred to himself as an apostle, the word *apostle* does not always
refer to one of "the Twelve."

After coming down from the mountain Jesus addresses not just
"the Twelve" but "a great crowd of his disciples and a large number
of the people from all Judea and Jerusalem and the coastal region of
Tyre and Sidon," people who, presumably, were considering becoming Jesus' disciples. Luke tells us that before Jesus began to speak he
raised "his eyes toward his disciples." This is Luke's way of telling
us that the words Jesus is speaking to this crowd are about discipleship. If we keep this context in mind the meaning of Jesus' words will
become clear.

Jesus begins by saying,

> "Blessed are you who are poor,
>   for the kingdom of God is yours.
> Blessed are you who are now hungry,
>   for you will be satisfied."

Is Jesus talking about one's socioeconomic status, saying that it is
a blessing to lack the necessities of life? If that were Jesus' message
then he would not be so insistent that his disciples give to the poor
in order to relieve them of their miserable situation (see Luke 18:22).
Jesus would not encourage his disciples to relieve someone of a source
of blessing.

The disciples' socioeconomic status is not Jesus' main interest;
Jesus is interested in the disciples' relationship to the "kingdom of
God" and to the "Son of Man." He says as much when he says that
the poor are blessed because "the kingdom of God" is theirs, and
that those who suffer "on account of the Son of Man" are blessed.
A poor disciple is not necessarily one who has no resources at all. A
poor disciple is one who does not depend on his or her own wealth,
but on God's providence.

Jesus doesn't promise such people that after a miserable life they
will reach heaven, so that in the end it will all be worth it. Rather,
Jesus says, "the kingdom of God *is* yours." A disciple enters the kingdom of God and lives in the kingdom of God once he or she starts
to "be poor," to depend on God's providence. Disciples own nothing
because they know that they are stewards of God's property and are

required to see that God's resources are used to relieve the poverty of those who are poor and hungry.

Seen in the context of discipleship, the "woes" directed at the disciples and at those in the crowd who are considering becoming disciples become understandable. When Jesus says, "Woe to you who are rich," he is describing people whose lifestyle is so comfortable that they do not want to respond to a call to discipleship. To respond might mean a less comfortable life than they have now. Rather than relying on God's providence, they choose to rely on themselves. When Jesus says, "Woe to you when all speak well of you," he is describing people who act to please others rather than to please God. Such people fail to speak up when they see a wrong; they fail to act for justice. A true prophet, one who speaks for God, will always antagonize those who are acting unjustly but do not want to change. False prophets are much more popular than true prophets because they do not challenge people to conversion and a new way of life.

We know from the call stories that to become a disciple of Jesus one must "leave everything" to follow him. Luke's "sermon on the plain," in which Jesus teaches the beatitudes ("Blessed are you" statements), is teaching much the same thing. Disciples become poor: they put their entire trust in God so that they no longer are concerned about their material well-being or their reputation.

Jeremiah 17:5–8 in its biblical context

Instead of a beatitude and a woe, our reading from Jeremiah gives us a beatitude and a curse. The beatitude is teaching what Jesus taught his disciples: "Blessed is the one who trusts in the LORD...." A person who trusts in the Lord is like a tree planted by water. When heat comes, or a drought, the tree is fine because its roots reach to the stream.

The curse teaches what Jesus taught his disciples through his woes:

> Cursed is the one who trusts in human beings,
> who seeks his strength in flesh,
> whose heart turns away from the LORD.

People like this are so comfortable that they resist a call to conversion. They trust in themselves rather than in God. They are like a bush in the desert with its roots in a lava waste. They will not be able to bear fruit.

Notice that the reading begins, "Thus says the LORD: / Cursed is the one...." This strikes us as strange because we know that God is love, so we do not picture God as cursing anyone. In the Old Testament, when God is described as cursing someone, the author is simply picturing God using the same modes of expression that human beings used. When an author describes God as though God were a human being we say that the author has used an *anthropomorphic* description of God. Even so, a curse in ancient times was not used to cause evil but to prevent evil from prevailing. Curses were pronounced with the same solemnity as were blessings and were believed to be effective.

1 Corinthians 15:12, 16–20 in its biblical context

Our reading from Corinthians is a continuation of last week's reading in which Paul is arguing against the idea that there is no resurrection of the dead. Paul says, "If Christ is preached as raised from the dead, how can some among you say there is no resurrection of the dead?" To doubt the resurrection of the dead is to doubt Christ's resurrection. In fact, it is to say that the faith Christians have is in vain. Instead of being redeemed, we would still be in our sins. It would also mean that those who have already died, those who we believe are with Christ, have perished rather than entered eternal life. If there is no resurrection of the dead then Christians "are the most pitiable people of all."

Paul insists, however, that Christ has been raised from the dead. He is "the firstfruits of those who have fallen asleep." In other words, since Christ has risen from the dead, we have been freed from our sins, and our beloved relatives who have died have not perished. What God has done for Jesus, the firstfruit, God will do for those who put their faith in Jesus. Those who are Jesus' disciples on earth will be raised with him to eternal life.

Questions for Breaking Open the Word groups are on page 13.

Questions for other faith sharing groups

1. If a beloved adult child asked you, "What must I do to be a faithful disciple of Christ?" how would you respond? Do you think your response would be similar to the one Jesus would give? Why or why not?

2. What role do you think wealth plays in discipleship? Do you think wealth can be a detriment rather than a blessing to a "blessed" life?

3. If you were to act for justice in your church or community, what issue would you want to address? What might be the ramifications of your taking action?

Bible study questions

1. Does Jesus want people to go without the necessities of life? How do you know?

2. What is Jesus teaching through the beatitudes?

3. What is Jeremiah teaching through his beatitude?

4. If one believes that Jesus rose from the dead, what other Christian beliefs follow?

5. What does Paul mean when he refers to Jesus as *firstfruits?*

SEVENTH SUNDAY IN ORDINARY TIME

Luke 6:27–38 in its biblical context

Today we continue the sermon begun in last Sunday's Gospel. Jesus has come down from the mountain (this sermon is often called the sermon on the plain), and has been speaking to the newly appointed Twelve, a large group of disciples, and a crowd who are probably discerning whether or not to become disciples.

Notice that Jesus begins, "To you who hear I say...." Jesus isn't referring just to one's ability to hear sound, but to one's ability to comprehend, to take something to heart, and to act upon it. People will have to listen very carefully to Jesus to understand what he is saying because, on the surface, Jesus' advice doesn't seem to be good advice at all.

Jesus tells the crowd, "...love your enemies, do good to those who hate you, bless those who curse you, pray for those who mistreat you." It is extremely hard not to feel resistant to this teaching because it seems to go against human nature. Our enemies are the last people on earth we want to love. If a person strikes us, we want to hit that person back, not offer the other cheek. If a person takes our coat we want to get it back, not offer him our sweater as well. If people ask us for something, we think about whether or not they deserve to have it. We wouldn't want some lazy person to have a free handout. If someone takes what is ours without asking, the last thing we are going to do is let that person keep what has been stolen. Jesus' advice seems way off the mark. Don't we have a right, maybe even a duty, to protect ourselves and our property?

Jesus seems to understand that the crowd is feeling resistant. Jesus points out that it isn't at all difficult to act lovingly toward another if we expect some benefit to ourselves. If, as disciples of Jesus Christ, we love only those who love us, and we lend only to those who can pay us back, we are not distinguishing ourselves from sinners. There is no particular virtue in acting generously only for the sake of being repaid.

Then Jesus returns to his original instruction: "...love your enemies and do good to them, and lend expecting nothing back; then your reward will be great and you will be children of the Most High...." If we love our enemies we will receive a reward after all. However, this reward will be a spiritual, not a material reward: we will become children of the Most High.

Why is becoming God's children the fruit of loving one's enemies? Because when we love our enemies we are acting like our heavenly Father acts, who is "kind to the ungrateful and the wicked." We are to give others an experience of God's love by the way we treat them. We are to "be merciful, just as your Father is merciful."

Jesus then teaches his disciples that the way we treat others is the way we ourselves will be treated: "Stop judging and you will not be judged. Stop condemning and you will not be condemned. For-give and you will be forgiven." If we do not hear and follow Jesus' instructions, instead of entering a new and deeper relationship with God we will experience what it is like to be treated as we treat others, in a judgmental and unforgiving manner.

Now, after originally telling the disciples not to act with the hope of reward, Jesus tells them that if they love their enemies their reward will be great. "Give, and gifts will be given to you; a good measure, packed together, shaken down, and overflowing, will be poured into you lap." Those who become Jesus' disciples, who hear and follow his instructions, will be all the more open to receive God's bountiful love, love that God pours out even on our enemies.

1 Samuel 26:2, 7–9, 12–13, 22–23 in its biblical context

As we join the story of Saul and David in 1 Samuel Saul is searching for David, not because he loves him but because he has begun to fear David and wants to kill him: "In those days, Saul went down to the desert of Ziph with three thousand picked men of Israel, to search for David in the desert of Ziph."

The reason that Saul wants to kill David is that he has become jealous of David and fears that David will replace him as king. Saul was the first king of Israel, and David was Saul's soldier. After battles, when David had performed splendidly, David and Saul would return to heroes' welcomes. But the people would shout,

> "Saul has slain his thousands,
>   but David his ten thousands."
>   (1 Sam 18:7 or 21:12)

Saul's son, Jonathan, loved David with all his heart. Saul's daughter also loved David and became his wife. This gave David a possible claim to the throne. "Therefore Saul feared David all the more [and was his enemy ever after]" (1 Sam 18:29).

David's behavior toward Saul is a model of the kind of behavior that Jesus is trying to teach his disciples: David treats his enemy lov-ingly. Although Saul is hoping that he can kill David, instead David has the opportunity to kill Saul. "So David and Abishai went among Saul's soldiers by night and found Saul lying asleep within the barri-cade, with his spear thrust into the ground at his head. . . ." Abishai wants to take advantage of the situation. He asks David's permission to kill Saul.

David has a religious motive for not killing Saul. He understands Saul to be God's *anointed*, that is, God's *messiah*. David says to Abishai, "Do not harm him, for who can lay hands on the LORD's anointed and remain unpunished?" It was part of the Israelites' under-standing of covenant love that God would send an anointed one to save the people when they were in political difficulty. God sent Moses to save the people from the Egyptians. Now God has sent Saul to save the people from the Philistines. It is God who has appointed Saul king. David will not harm Saul.

David tries to use the occasion to prove to Saul that David wishes him no harm and is not trying to replace him as king. He removes the spear and water jug from their place at Saul's head. Then, from a distance, he shouts back at Saul and Saul's soldiers. "Today, though the Lord delivered you into my grasp, I would not harm the Lord's anointed."

Our Lectionary selection does not tell us Saul's reaction. Saul says, "I have done wrong. Come back, my son David, I will not harm you again, because you have held my life precious today. Indeed, I have been a fool and have made a serious mistake" (1 Sam 26:21). At least for a short while, David's love of enemy resulted in his no longer being persecuted.

1 Corinthians 15:45–49 in its biblical context

Paul is still convincing the Corinthians that there is a resurrection of the body. In today's reading Paul tells the Corinthians that just as we bear the image of Adam in that we have an earthly body, so we bear the image of Jesus who, since his resurrection, has a spiritual body. The earthly body comes first, then the spiritual body. We have earthly bodies now, but after death, we too will have spiritual bodies. "Just as we have borne the image of the earthly one [that is, we have earthly bodies like Adam], we shall also bear the image of the heavenly one [that is, we will have spiritual bodies like Christ]." Paul wants the Corinthians to be assured that their beloved dead, and they too, will follow Christ through death to eternal life.

Questions for Breaking Open the Word groups are on page 13.

Questions for other faith sharing groups

1. Do you think the advice Jesus gives his disciples in today's Gospel is good advice? Why or why not?

2. Have you ever tried to love an enemy? If so, how did things turn out?

3. Do you know any way to teach people that they are lovable other than by loving them? If not, what ramifications does this fact have?

Bible study questions

1. How does Jesus teach us to treat our enemies?

2. What will we become if we love our enemies?

3. Why does David not kill Saul?

4. What is Saul's reaction?

5. What argument does Paul use to convince the Corinthians that there is a resurrection of the body?

EIGHTH SUNDAY IN ORDINARY TIME

Luke 6:39–45 in its biblical context

The sermon on the plain continues. Remember, the context is discipleship. Jesus has taught his brand new disciples that the poor and the hungry are blessed, and that his disciples must love their enemies. These are very hard teachings. Jesus' contemporaries would have presumed just the opposite: that the rich are blessed and that their enemies are God's enemies too. Last week, as we read Jesus' teaching that we must love our enemies, we acknowledged that we might feel resistant to Jesus' teaching. Jesus' words in today's Gospel suggest that those listening to Jesus were feeling resistant too.

Today's Lectionary reading begins, "Jesus told his disciples a parable...." What follows does not seem to be a parable at all, but a question: "Can a blind person guide a blind person? Will not both fall into a pit?" We will have a great deal to say about parables as we read Luke's Gospel. For now we will simply notice that the word *parable* is used in Luke's Gospel not only to describe developed stories; it is also used, as it is here, to name a short, proverbial saying. This distinction will become important in later discussions.

Jesus' question, "Can a blind person guide a blind person?" addresses the resistance his disciples may be feeling to his teachings. If they are resistant it is because they have a blind spot; they cannot *see* the truth of Jesus' teaching. Until the disciples can see the truth, they are not ready to lead others. If they were to teach others now they would simply teach others their own misunderstandings. That would be the blind leading the blind. The disciples and those they are leading would both fall into the pit. Before leading others the disciples need to spend time with Jesus so that they can learn the truth. Jesus then tells them that "when fully trained, every disciple will be like his teacher." In other words, disciples become like their teacher when, instead of resisting the truth that their teacher is teaching, they understand and embrace it.

Jesus then asks, "Why do you notice the splinter in your brother's eye, but do not perceive the wooden beam in your own?" When Jesus speaks of a "wooden beam" in his disciple's eye he is again describing spiritual blindness. This blindness leads one to be judgmental about the behavior of others while, at the same time, failing to notice what is wrong in one's own behavior. Jesus insists that if his disciples want to judge someone they should judge themselves: "Remove the wooden beam from your eye first; then you will see clearly to remove the splinter in your brother's eye."

Jesus wants his disciples to bear good fruit. However, they will not be able to bear good fruit until they become disciples, listen to their teacher, stop being judgmental about others, recognize and repent of their own failings, and understand Jesus' new teaching. Once they have accomplished this they will bear good fruit. "A good tree does not bear rotten fruit, nor does a rotten tree bear good fruit. For every tree is known by its own fruit."

One of the effects of Jesus' teachings about the poor, about enemies, and about judging others is that as his disciples respond to Jesus' teachings they will become more loving. "A good person out of the store of goodness in his heart produces good, . . . for from the fullness of the heart the mouth speaks." When the disciples are fully trained they will be like their teacher. Like Jesus, they will act out of love rather than acting out of ignorance.

Sirach 27:4–7 in its biblical context

The Book of Sirach, also called Ecclesiasticus, is in the Catholic canon but not in the Jewish or Protestant canons. Such books are called *deuterocanonical* books by Catholics, *apocryphal* books by Protestants. All of the deuterocanonical books, including Sirach, date to the last few hundred years before Jesus Christ. The Book of Sirach was translated from Hebrew into Greek by the original author's grandson. In the foreword of the book he states his reason for making his grandfather's wisdom available to Greek-speaking people: "Many sleepless hours of close application have I devoted in the interval to finishing the book for publication, for the benefit of those living abroad who wish to acquire wisdom and are disposed to live their lives according to the standards of the law."

The selection that we read today is typical of the kind of wisdom that is taught in the Book of Sirach. The author would agree 100 percent with what Jesus taught his disciples in the Gospel. Sirach says,

> The fruit of a tree shows the care it has had;
>   so too does one's speech disclose the bent of one's mind.

Jesus, too, warned the disciples that if they want to bear good fruit they must refrain from speaking until proper care has been taken, until they themselves have learned the truth. Only good trees bear good fruit.

Sirach teaches his readers that their speech reveals their inner character:

> When a sieve is shaken, the husks appear;
>   so do one's faults when one speaks.

Likewise, Jesus taught the disciples that when the mouth speaks, one's fullness of heart, one's store of goodness, is revealed. Good speech is produced out of the store of goodness in one's heart.

In fact, speech is so revealing that Sirach advises that we judge no one favorably until we have heard that person speak:

> Praise no one before he speaks,
>   for it is then that people are tested.

1 Corinthians 15:54–58 in its biblical context

Paul continues to emphasize for the Corinthians the importance of the resurrection of the body. Because Jesus has risen from the dead, and because we who are his disciples will also rise from the dead, Jesus has conquered death: "Death is swallowed up in victory." In Christ, the corruptible body "clothes itself with incorruptibility and this which is mortal clothes itself with immortality."

When Paul says that "the sting of death is sin," he is saying that sin is the way death infiltrates itself into human beings. Sin does not lead to resurrection, but to death. When Paul says that "the power of sin is the law," he is pointing out that the law defines sin but the law has no power to save people from sin. So the law does not lessen sin's power. Only Christ frees us from the power of sin. "But thanks be to God who gives us the victory through our Lord Jesus Christ."

Because being a disciple of Jesus Christ will lead to eternal life, Paul encourages the Corinthians to "be firm, steadfast, always fully devoted to the work of the Lord, knowing that in the Lord your labor is not in vain." If the Corinthians remain faithful disciples of Jesus Christ, they will bear good fruit in this life and they will inherit eternal life.

Questions for Breaking Open the Word groups are on page 13.

Questions for other faith sharing groups

1. Why is it is a good idea to ask yourself, "Do I feel resistant to anything in today's Gospel?" If you do feel resistant, what does that tell you about yourself?

2. What is so dangerous about being blind to one's own faults? What can you do to prevent this from happening to you?

3. In what area of your life do you most want to bear good fruit? Since good fruit depends on the health of the tree, what can you do to bear better fruit in this area?

Bible study questions

1. What is Jesus teaching the disciples about themselves when he talks about the blind leading the blind?

2. What will the disciples have to do in order to bear good fruit?

3. What does Paul mean when he says "the sting of death is sin"?

4. What does Paul mean when he says that "the power of sin is the law"?

5. In what way has Jesus conquered death?

Ninth Sunday in Ordinary Time

Luke 7:1–10 *in its biblical context*

As we read Luke's story of Jesus healing the centurion's servant, we want to remember Luke's audience and theme. Luke is writing Gentiles who have been newly invited into a relationship of covenant love with God. Luke is constantly emphasizing the universal nature of Jesus' saving power. This story will have special importance for such an audience.

Today's Gospel does not follow immediately after last Sunday's reading. The Lectionary has not included the conclusion to Jesus' sermon on the plain. As Jesus ends his sermon to his disciples and the crowd, he challenges those who might listen to his teaching but not follow it. Jesus says, "Why do you call me, 'Lord, Lord,' but not do what I command? I will show you what someone is like who comes to me, listens to my words, and acts on them" (Luke 6:46–47). Jesus then compares such a person to one who digs a deep foundation for his house and builds it on rock, rather than on ground without a foundation. Floodwaters cannot shake the house built on rock. Just so, nothing can shake the person who becomes Jesus' disciple, and who not only listens but acts on Jesus' words.

Luke then moves to the story we hear today, in which we meet a most unlikely person to have heard and acted on Jesus' words. The centurion in today's Gospel had never met Jesus; others had told him about Jesus. "When he [the centurion] heard about Jesus, he sent elders of the Jews to him, asking him to come and save the life of his slave." The centurion is not Jewish. Like those in Luke's audience, he is a Gentile. The fact that he is a centurion means that he is an officer in the Roman army stationed in Capernaum to help keep the peace. Remember, the Jews did not have self-rule during Jesus' lifetime. Theirs was an occupied country.

Even though the centurion is not Jewish, the Jews in Capernaum urge Jesus to respond to his request. Notice that they think in terms of earning rather than in terms of gift. The Jews tell Jesus, "He deserves to have you do this for him, for he loves our nation and built the synagogue for us." The presumption behind this statement is that Jesus' ministry would normally be for the Jews. It would be an exception for Jesus to go out to a non-Jew. This is a completely accurate presumption. We know from reading the Acts of the Apostles that it was not until after Jesus' resurrection that the apostles realized that the covenant was open to everyone. In Acts Peter learns this from events and from the Holy Spirit. The events involve another centurion, Cornelius, who asks that Peter come to his home (see Acts 10).

The centurion in today's story does not invite Jesus to his home. He gives as his reason his own unworthiness: "Lord, do not trouble yourself, for I am not worthy to have you enter under my roof." In addition, the centurion undoubtedly knows that if Jesus were to enter his home, the home of a Gentile, Jesus would be made ritually unclean for worship. This centurion is a thoughtful person, not only in regard to his ill servant and to his Jewish neighbors, but to Jesus himself. Jesus shows no sign of being concerned about his ritual cleanliness, however.

The centurion has such faith in Jesus that he believes Jesus can simply "say the word" and his servant will be healed. As a soldier he knows all about authority. If he is told to do something, he does it. If someone subject to him is given an order, that person obeys it. He believes that Jesus has authority over sickness. If Jesus orders the sickness to leave, his servant will be well again.

Luke tells this story in such a way as to emphasize the man's faith more than the healing. Jesus remarks with amazement, not on the centurion's worthiness or lack of it, but on his faith: "I tell you, not even in Israel have I found such faith." The centurion has not earned this healing by his generosity to the Jews or by his thoughtfulness for others. Rather, his faith has made him able to receive the gift of Jesus' healing power. Almost as an afterthought, Luke tells us that when "the messengers returned to the house, they found the slave in good health."

By telling the story as he does Luke is teaching his Gentile audience that Jesus' healing power is a gift freely given, not something that anyone has earned. The centurion is an example of a person who has heard Jesus' words and acted on them. In other words, he believed, and therefore acted on what he heard. In addition, the fact that he was a Gentile did not exclude him from Jesus' healing power. The same is true of Luke's audience. Gentiles are now invited to place their faith in Jesus and to receive the gift of Jesus' redemptive power.

1 Kings 8:41–43 in its biblical context

The setting for our reading from 1 Kings is the dedication of the newly built temple. Solomon, David's son, is now king. David had recaptured the ark of the covenant, God's dwelling place, from the Philistines and brought it to Jerusalem. Shortly before this dedication the ark has been placed in the temple: "The priests brought the ark of the covenant of the LORD to its place beneath the wings of the cherubim in the sanctuary, the holy of holies of the temple.... When the priests left the holy place, the cloud filled the temple of the LORD so that the priests could no longer minister because of the cloud, since the LORD's glory had filled the temple of the LORD" (1 Kgs 8:6, 10–11).

Now that God's glory has filled the temple Solomon, in his dedicatory speech, prays that God will be responsive to the prayers of those who come to the temple, including the prayers of foreigners.

> "To the foreigner, who is not of your people Israel,
>   but comes from a distant land to honor you....

> when he comes and prays toward this temple,
> listen from your heavenly dwelling...."

Solomon prays that God will listen even to the prayers of foreigners, because this will be a way for all peoples of the earth to come to know God's name:

> "...Do all that foreigner asks of you,
> that all the peoples of the earth may know your name...."

Solomon's prayer has been fulfilled in Jesus. Through Jesus the whole world has come to know the God of Israel.

Galatians 1:1–2, 6–10 *in its biblical context*

As you can tell from reading the selection from today's letter, Paul is upset with the Galatians. Notice that he interrupts his usual greeting to defend himself: "Paul, an apostle not from human beings nor through a human being but through Jesus Christ and God the Father who raised him from the dead...." Paul had earlier visited the Galatians and had preached the good news to them. Later some agitators had come and questioned both Paul's authority to teach and the content of his teaching. Here Paul is defending his authority. Paul's authority did not come from any human being but from Jesus Christ and from God the Father.

Paul then expresses his deep disappointment that the Galatians are so foolish as to listen to these agitators. "I am amazed that you are so quickly forsaking the one who called you by the grace of Christ for a different gospel—not that there is another." Paul uses the strongest language to warn the Galatians against false preachers: "...if anyone preaches to you a gospel other than what you have received, let that one be accursed!"

Paul insists that there is only one gospel, one good news, for the whole world, and that is the good news of Jesus Christ. The centurion in today's Gospel heard and acted on that good news. Luke wants his Gentile audience, including us, to do the same.

Questions for Breaking Open the Word groups are on page 13.

Questions for other faith sharing groups

1. Has your understanding of God's will grown over the years? How?

2. Is there anyone whom you consider outside of God's love and desire to save? If your answer is "no," what ramifications does this belief have in your life?

3. In what ways is your life built on rock? In what ways is it built on sand? What can you do to improve the foundation upon which you are building?

Bible study questions

1. What about the centurion amazes Jesus?
2. What is Luke teaching by the way he tells this story?
3. For whom does Solomon pray?
4. Why is Paul upset with the Galatians?
5. On what does Paul insist?

LENT

First Sunday of Lent

Luke 4:1–13 in its biblical context

On the first Sunday of Lent in all three liturgical cycles we read the story of Jesus' temptation in the desert. Many people have difficulty thinking of Jesus as being tempted because they believe that Jesus is God. They think of this story as a story about the devil *trying* to tempt Jesus, but not as a story in which Jesus actually *experiences* temptation. However, the Synoptic Gospels—that is, Mark's, Matthew's, and Luke's Gospels—all present Jesus as a human being who is tempted just as we are. Only John, who emphasizes Jesus' divinity, omits this story.

Today's reading begins: "Filled with the Holy Spirit, Jesus returned from the Jordan and was led by the Spirit into the desert for forty days, to be tempted by the devil." This is, of course, a reference to Jesus' baptism. In Luke's Gospel, Jesus is praying after his baptism in the Jordan River when "the holy Spirit descended upon him in bodily form like a dove. And a voice came from heaven, 'You are my beloved Son; with you I am well pleased'" (Luke 3:22). Between the baptism scene and the temptation Luke gives us Jesus' genealogy (see Luke 3:23–37), which affirms that Jesus is God's Son and the fulfillment of God's promises to the people.

Notice the emphasis on the presence of the Spirit. Jesus is tempted, but Jesus is filled with the Holy Spirit and is led by the Spirit into the desert (not into temptation). The Spirit will help Jesus, as the Spirit helps us, overcome temptation. The temptation, in all three instances, is to misuse his power. Everyone who met Jesus experienced him as a person of power both in word and deed. Now, before Luke tells us how Jesus used his power for good in the service of the kingdom of God, Luke pictures him overcoming temptation to use that power for any purpose other than the purpose for which it has been granted.

The first temptation that Jesus experiences is to use his power to serve his own needs rather than to spread the good news of the kingdom of God. Jesus is hungry because he has been fasting for forty days. The devil says, "If you are the Son of God, command this stone to become bread." Jesus responds, "It is written, *One does not live on bread alone.*" Jesus is quoting the Book of Deuteronomy. In Deuteronomy Moses is speaking to the Israelites about their experience at Mount Horeb. After reminding the people of the commandments and admonishing them to observe them, Moses describes God's care for the people in the past: "[God] therefore let you be afflicted with hunger, and then fed you with manna, a food unknown to you and your fathers, in order to show you that not by bread alone does man live, but by every word that comes forth from the mouth of the LORD" (Deut 8:3).

Jesus does not need to abuse his power to take care of himself. He knows that his Father will take care of all his needs as he did the needs of the Israelites during their time in the desert. Jesus will again be tempted to use his power to save himself on the cross. The rulers will taunt him, saying, "He saved others, let him save himself if he is the chosen one, the Messiah of God" (Luke 23:35). The soldiers, too, will taunt Jesus: "If you are King of the Jews, save yourself" (Luke 23:37). Jesus does not abuse his power by using it to satisfy his own needs.

The second temptation that the devil offers Jesus is to use his power for political purposes. Showing him all the kingdoms of the world, the devil says, "I shall give to you all this power and glory; for it has been handed over to me, and I may give it to whomever I wish. All this will be yours, if you worship me." Jesus again quotes Deuteronomy: "It is written: *You shall worship the Lord, your God, and him alone shall you serve.*" Jesus is quoting one of the commandments about which Moses reminded the people: "The LORD, your God, shall you fear; him shall you serve..." (Deut 6:13). Jesus overcomes the temptation to use his power to gain political influence.

Finally, the devil tempts Jesus to use his power merely for show—to do something spectacular. Notice that the devil, too, quotes scripture. When the devil says, "...for it is written: *He will command his angels concerning you, to guard you,* and: *With their hands they will support you, lest you dash your foot against a stone,*" the devil is quoting Psalm 91:

> For to his angels he has given command about you,
>   that they guard you in all your ways.
> Upon their hands they shall bear you up,
>   lest you dash your foot against a stone.
>
> (Ps 91:11–12)

As Jesus responds he again quotes Deuteronomy: "It also says, *You shall not put the Lord, your God, to the test.*" Again, the setting for this passage is Moses reminding the people of the commandments and the necessity of obedience. Moses says, "You shall not put the LORD, your God, to the test, as you did at Massah. But keep the commandments of the LORD, your God, and the ordinances and statutes he has enjoined on you" (Deut 6:16–17).

When Jesus speaks of not putting God to the test, he means that he does not want to disobey his Father and use his powers for anything other than to build up God's kingdom. From the reader's point of view, however, these words have a double meaning. Luke has already told us that Jesus is God's own Son, a divine person. By tempting Jesus, the devil is putting "the Lord, your God" (the divine Jesus) to the test. Once more, Jesus does not succumb to temptation. He proves he is the Son of God, not by disobeying his Father, as the devil tempts him to do, but by obeying.

Today's reading ends on an ominous note: "When the devil had finished every temptation, he departed from him for a time." The devil is not gone for good, nor is Jesus done with temptation. Like every other human being, Jesus experienced temptation throughout his life, but, unlike other human beings, Jesus did not sin.

Deuteronomy 26:4–10 in its biblical context

The whole Book of Deuteronomy takes place in the plains of Moab after the people have wandered for forty years in the desert and before they cross the Jordan River to the holy land. As we saw in the passages that Jesus quoted during his temptations, Moses is reminding the people of all that they have already experienced and is admonishing them to be faithful to Yahweh when they reach the promised land across the Jordan. In today's Lectionary selection Moses is telling the people how to thank God, both for saving them from the Egyptians and for giving them their land.

The people are to have a yearly ceremony in which they offer to God the firstfruits of their crops. First the people will present the priest with a basket containing their gifts, and the priest will place it before the altar of the Lord. The people will then remember the mighty acts of God's saving power that they experienced in the past: how when they became slaves in Egypt they called out to God, and God responded to their call. God "brought us out of Egypt with his strong hand and outstretched arm, with terrifying power, with signs and wonders; and bringing us into this country, he gave us this land flowing with milk and honey." Out of gratitude for both saving the people from slavery in Egypt and for giving them the land the Israelites now offer the firstfruits of their produce: "Therefore, I have now brought you the firstfruits of the products of the soil which you, O LORD, have given me." After making their offerings the people will bow down in the presence of their Lord.

Both our Gospel and our Old Testament readings describe desert experiences: Jesus' for forty days and the Israelites' for forty years. A desert experience is symbolic of times of trial when we feel alone and know that we cannot help ourselves. We cry out to God with confidence that, just as God has saved the people in the past, so will God save us now. Like Jesus, we are never in the desert alone. The Holy Spirit is with us to help us overcome obstacles and remain faithful to God.

Romans 10:8–13 in its biblical context

Just as the Israelites had confidence that God had and would save them, so does Paul assure the Romans that Jesus will save them. In order to teach this truth Paul quotes Isaiah. Isaiah says:

> Therefore, thus says the Lord GOD:
>   See, I am laying a stone in Zion,
>   a stone that has been tested,
> A precious cornerstone as a sure foundation;
>   he who puts his faith in it shall not be shaken.
>
> (Isa 28:16)

Isaiah is warning the people against putting their faith in political alliances rather than in God. Isaiah pictures God telling the people that they should put their faith in God and the sure foundation that God has built in Zion. Paul understands that Isaiah's words have been fulfilled in Jesus. Jesus is the cornerstone. All who put their faith in Jesus, Jews as well as Greeks, will be saved.

Questions for Breaking Open the Word groups are on page 13.

Questions for other faith sharing groups

1. Why do you think many people experience the temptation to abuse power that is legitimately theirs? Can you give some example of the abuse of power?

2. In our culture, what are we tempted to *worship* other than God?

3. Moses explains to the people that God used their adversity in the desert to teach them about God's loving care. Have you experienced God's care in adversity? Explain.

Bible study questions

1. In all three instances, what temptation does the devil offer Jesus?

2. What two levels of meaning are in the sentence, "You shall not put the Lord, your God, to the test"?

3. How does Luke tell us that Jesus continues to experience temptation throughout his life?

4. For what two things do the Israelites express their thanks to God?

5. What is Paul teaching the Romans in today's reading?

SECOND SUNDAY OF LENT

Luke 9:28b–36 in its biblical context

On the second Sunday of Lent, in all three liturgical cycles, we read the story of the transfiguration. The connection between this story and Lent may not be immediately apparent. Notice, however, that Luke tells us that Jesus, Moses, and Elijah were discussing Jesus' "exodus that he was going to accomplish in Jerusalem." This is a reference to Jesus' crucifixion. The story of the transfiguration addresses a question that was very much on the mind of postresurrection followers of Jesus: Would God have allowed his only-begotten Son to die an ignominious death on a cross, or did the fact that Jesus died on a cross mean that he was not God's Son after all?

It is hard for us to realize just how scandalous Jesus' death on the cross was. Crucifixion was the most shameful way to die. It was reserved for the worst of the worst. In addition, the law put a curse on anyone who died in the manner Jesus did. In Deuteronomy we read: "If a man guilty of a capital offense is put to death and his corpse hung on a tree, it shall not remain on the tree overnight. You shall bury it the same day; otherwise, since God's curse rests on him who hangs on a tree, you will defile the land which the LORD, your God, is giving you as an inheritance" (Deut 21:22–23). If Jesus were really God's Son, would God have allowed such a shameful death to occur?

The story of the transfiguration responds to this question. First, it makes clear that Jesus is God's Son, and that Jesus is divine. Luke tells us that while Jesus was praying, "his face changed in appearance and his clothing became dazzling white." Then we are told that the apostles "saw his glory." To see Jesus' glory is to see Jesus' divinity. Finally, "a cloud came and cast a shadow over them [Peter, James, and John]. . . . Then from the cloud came a voice that said, 'This is my chosen Son; listen to him.'" Jesus is definitely God's divine Son. The crucifixion does not negate that fact.

In addition, the crucifixion, despite its appearance, was not a defeat. It certainly seemed like a defeat to the apostles at the time it occurred. However, in the story of the transfiguration Jesus is talking with Moses and Elijah about "his exodus that he was going to accomplish in Jerusalem." The word *exodus* is, of course, an allusion to God's mighty intervention on Israel's behalf when the Israelites escaped from slavery in Egypt. Jesus is not going to endure this exodus; he is going to "accomplish" it. What will Jesus accomplish in Jerusalem through his crucifixion? Jesus will accomplish his Father's will: the salvation of the human race. Human beings will be freed from slavery to sin and death.

A second postresurrection question that the story of the transfiguration addresses is whether or not you must become Jewish in order to become a disciple of Jesus Christ. We know from reading the Acts of the Apostles that this was a much-debated question in the early years of the church. The question was answered definitively at the Council of Jerusalem (see Acts 15:5–29), where it was decided that a person would not have to obey all of the Jewish laws in order to become a follower of Christ.

This question is addressed in the story of the transfiguration through the presence of Moses and Elijah, the lawgiver and the prophet, who are speaking with Jesus about his coming crucifixion. Peter wants to put up three tents. In other words, he wants Moses and Elijah, as well as Jesus, to dwell with them. A tent is the place where a person dwells. When Israel describes God's presence in their midst, God is described as pitching his tent in Israel. In fact, the word *tabernacle* and the word *tent* both mean a dwelling place. Peter's idea is not accepted. Luke tells us that "he did not know what he was saying."

Moses and Elijah are not to tent, to remain with the people. When the voice from the cloud speaks it says, "This is my chosen Son; listen to him." In other words, the people are no longer to give Moses and Elijah, the law and the prophets, the same authority that they give Jesus. The apostles are to listen to Jesus. After the voice speaks Jesus is found alone.

After the transfiguration Luke tells us that the apostles "fell silent and did not at that time tell anyone what they had seen." In Mark's and Matthew's accounts we are told that Jesus instructed Peter, James, and John not to tell anyone until after the Son of Man had risen from the dead (Mark 9:10; Matt 17:9). Peter, James, and John do not tell anyone "at that time" about their experience because they do not yet understand it themselves. After the resurrection they will understand that this experience helped prepare them for the crucifixion. The church proclaims this story during Lent because it helps prepare us for the crucifixion too.

Genesis 15:5–12, 17–18 in its biblical context

Today's reading from Genesis describes the ceremony that ratified the covenant agreement between God and Abraham. Our reading begins with God promising Abram descendants. However, in the Book of Genesis God first promises Abram protection. God says,

> "Fear not, Abram!
>   I am your shield;
>   I will make your reward very great."
>   (Gen 15:1b)

In response Abram complains about being childless. "But Abram said, 'O Lord GOD, what good will your gifts be, if I keep on being childless and have as my heir the steward of my house, Eliezer?'" (Gen 15:2).

It is in response to Abram's complaint that God makes the promise about descendants that we read today: "Look up at the sky and count the stars, if you can. Just so . . . shall your descendants be." It was no easy thing for Abram to put his faith in the Lord, given his childless state. The Lord "credited it to him as an act of righteousness."

Next God promises Abram land. This time Abram asks for a sign: "O Lord GOD . . . how am I to know that I shall possess it?" In response to this request, God gives Abram directions for the covenant ceremony. God instructs Abram to set things up as they would be set up to ratify a solemn agreement between two human beings. In a covenant ceremony animals were cut in half, and the two contracting partners each walked between the cut halves. This was to signify the seriousness of their mutual agreement. Each would rather be cut in half like these animals than break the agreement. Abram did as he was instructed.

After it was dark, "there appeared a smoking fire pot and a flaming torch, which passed between those pieces." The smoking fire pot and the flaming torch represent God's presence. This is the same way God will make his presence known during the exodus—as a pillar of fire (see Exod 14:15–31). That the fire passed through the cut halves of the animals signifies that God became a partner in the covenant agreement. This was Abram's sign. God was now bound forever to Abram and to his descendants. Abram believed that God would keep God's promises.

Philippians 3:17–4:1 in its biblical context

Our passage from Philippians is part of Paul's impassioned plea to the Philippians not to be influenced by false teachers who are telling them that they must obey the Jewish law and be circumcised in order to be saved. The third chapter of Philippians begins, "Beware of the dogs! Beware of the evil-workers! Beware of the mutilation!" (Phil 3:2). Paul is upset by these false teachers because by their teaching they are denying the efficacy of Jesus' saving acts. We are redeemed by Christ, not by obedience to the law.

Instead of imitating these people Paul wants the Philippians to imitate him and his fellow Christians. They conduct themselves as people whose citizenship is in heaven. They await Jesus Christ, who "will change our lowly body to conform with his glorified body by the power that enables him also to bring all things into subjection to himself." Paul wants the Philippians to "stand firm in the Lord" so that they can experience the grace of Jesus' redemptive power.

Questions for Breaking Open the Word groups are on page 13.

Questions for other faith sharing groups

1. Have you ever questioned why God would let some particular thing happen? What were the circumstances? Did you arrive at an answer that you found satisfactory? Explain.

2. Is there any sort of death that you associate with shame? Explain. Do you think it is possible that a good person could die this way? Why or why not?

3. What do you think Jesus "accomplished" through the crucifixion?

Bible study questions

1. What two postresurrection questions does the story of the transfiguration address?

2. What does the story teach in response to these two questions?

3. What does God promise Abram?

4. What is the meaning of cutting the animals in half?

5. Why is Paul upset as he writes the Philippians?

Third Sunday of Lent

(RCIA groups use Cycle A readings on page 97)

Luke 13:1–9 in its biblical context

Our Gospel reading today does not follow last week's reading from Luke. Rather, it was selected for this third Sunday of Lent because it teaches us the urgency of repentance. The reading gives us two very good reasons to repent: The first is that sin causes suffering. The second is that we do not know how long we will have to repent, so we should repent now.

Our reading begins with some people telling Jesus about an atrocity Pilate committed: Pilate had persecuted and killed some Galileans. Then, after killing them, he mixed their blood with the sacrifice they were offering. As Jesus responds he is arguing against a presumption that was held by many people—that all suffering is punishment for sin. Jesus asks the people, "Do you think that because these Galileans suffered in this way they were greater sinners than all other Galileans? By no means!" Here Jesus is teaching that suffering is not punishment for sin.

Jesus gives a second example of people suffering, but not as punishment for sin. He reminds the people about a tower that had fallen in Siloam and killed eighteen people. Jesus asks, "...do you think they were more guilty than everyone else who lived in Jerusalem? By no means!" We are not told why the tower fell. Was it faulty construction? We do not know. But we do know that those who were killed were not being punished for their sins.

After both of these examples, however, Jesus calls the people to repentance and seems to threaten them with similar suffering. After hearing of Pilate's atrocity Jesus says, "But I tell you, if you do not repent, you will all perish as they did!" After speaking of the tower at Siloam Jesus says exactly the same words again, "But I tell you, if you do not repent, you will all perish as they did!" Obviously, Jesus is trying to emphasize something. What is he trying to teach?

While Jesus does not want people to think that suffering is punishment for sin, at the same time he does want them to know that sin does cause suffering. Sin causes suffering not because God is mean and punishing, but because suffering is the inevitable outcome of sin. When we sin we bring suffering upon ourselves and upon others. In order to avoid the suffering that results from sin Jesus urges his listeners to repent. Why should they cause themselves the same kind of suffering that other people have endured from Pilate's atrocities and from the falling tower?

After calling the people to repentance Jesus tells them a parable. A person who owns an orchard has lost patience with a fig tree that is not bearing fruit. He wants to cut it down. However, the gardener wants to give the fig tree more time to bear fruit. He says, "Sir, leave it for this year also, and I shall cultivate the ground around it and fertilize it; it may bear fruit in the future. If not you can cut it down." Any unrepentant person in Jesus' audience is like that fig tree. That person is not bearing fruit. The time to bear fruit is now. No one knows how long he or she has to repent and bear fruit in this life. Therefore the lesson is, repent now while there is still time.

One last comment on the passage and the parable: Some people misinterpret today's reading and see in it a mean and punishing God. Jesus came to reveal that God is love. In today's passage Jesus is arguing against the idea that a loving God would think the kind of suffering endured by the Galileans was punishment for sin. In doing this Jesus is following in the footsteps of his inspired Jewish predecessors. The theme of the Book of Job is that suffering is not necessarily punishment for sin.

Also in today's parable, the man who owns the garden and wants to cut down the fig tree does not stand for God. To understand the message being taught through a parable we compare the characters in the story to the audience, and draw the lesson from this comparison, as we have done. The story is not an allegory, so nobody in the story stands for God.

Exodus 3:1–8a, 13–15 in its biblical context

Today's Old Testament reading is one of the most famous passages in all of scripture—the story of Moses at the burning bush. As we read last week, God first appeared to Abram and entered into a covenant relationship with him. However, God did not reveal God's name to Abram. Notice that as God identifies Godself to Moses he says, "I am the God of your fathers...the God of Abraham, the God of Isaac, the God of Jacob."

The Book of Genesis contains the story of Abraham and the three generations after him: Isaac, Jacob, and Joseph. As we saw, God promised Abraham protection, land, and descendants. When Genesis ends, Joseph has gone to Egypt because of a famine in the holy land. Now, as we read Exodus, we have skipped forward some five hundred years, to 1250 BC. The Israelites are not in the holy land. Rather, they are slaves in Egypt.

The story that was started in Genesis continues in Exodus with God fulfilling his promises to Abraham and his descendants: "I have witnessed the affliction of my people in Egypt and have heard their cry of complaint against their slave drivers, so I know well what they are suffering. Therefore I have come down to rescue them from the hands of the Egyptians and lead them out of that land into a good and spacious land, a land flowing with milk and honey." The Israelites are God's people. God will lead them to the promised land.

In a passage not included in our Lectionary reading, God then calls Moses to lead the people. God says, "Come, now! I will send you to Pharaoh to lead my people, the Israelites, out of Egypt" (Exod 3:10). Moses objects to his call, but God persists. God says, "I will be with you; and this shall be your proof that it is I who have sent you: when you bring my people out of Egypt, you will worship God on this very mountain" (Exod 3:12).

It is at this point that our Lectionary reading picks up the story again. Moses has a second objection. Why would the people believe that he speaks for God? He doesn't even know God's name. So Moses asks, "But when I go to the Israelites and say to them, 'The God of your fathers has sent me to you,' if they ask me, 'What is his name?' what am I to tell them?" In response to Moses' question God enters into a new level of intimacy with God's people. God tells Moses that his name is "I am who am. . . . This is what you shall tell the Israelites: I AM sent me to you."

Scripture scholars have debated for years the full meaning of God's name. In Hebrew the revelation of God's name, a form of the verb "to be," consists of four letters: YHWH. Since the name was so holy, the Israelites refrained from pronouncing it, saying, "Adonai" (i.e., Lord) instead. Even to add the vowels "a" and "e" to YHWH so that it becomes "Yahweh" is to begin to interpret the meaning. The name suggests a number of meanings simultaneously: "I cause to be all that exists," "I cause to be all that happens," "I am always with you."

This reading from Exodus complements our Gospel reading. In both readings God is presented as a loving God who wants to save the people from their suffering. It is because Jesus wants to save people from suffering that he urges everyone to repent.

1 Corinthians 10:1–6, 10–12

In this reading, Paul is urging the Corinthians to avoid the kind of behavior that the Israelites engaged in during the exodus. As Paul holds up the story of the exodus as an example, he uses what scripture scholars call *typology*. This was a common way to interpret the Old Testament in Paul's time. Old Testament people and events were seen as types, or foreshadows, of New Testament people and events. Here Paul sees the exodus as a type for the journey of Christians. He sees parallel journeys in that the Israelites were led by God (under the cloud), passed through the sea, and were fed with spiritual food (manna) and drink (water from the rock). Christians too are led by God, pass through the sea of baptism, and are fed with spiritual food, the Eucharist. The rock from which the Israelites drank water is seen as a type of Christ, who gives us living water.

Some of the Israelites desired evil things and grumbled against God. They are an example of what happens when one sins: not all of them made it to the holy land. Some died in the desert. True, God is merciful and forgiving. However, God's people must respond to God's love in order to receive God's gifts. The first step in responding is to repent.

Questions for Breaking Open the Word groups are on page 13.

Questions for other faith sharing groups

1. Do you agree that sin always causes suffering both for the sinner and for those with whom the sinner is in relationship? Why?

2. Why is repentance an urgent matter?

3. Do you think that God hears the cry of those in distress? In what ways can you help God respond to that cry?

Bible study questions

1. What presumption is Jesus arguing against in today's Gospel?

2. What is Jesus teaching through the parable in today's Gospel?

3. What three meanings might God's name have?

4. What comparison does Paul make using typology in today's reading?

5. What is Paul teaching the Corinthians through this comparison?

FOURTH SUNDAY OF LENT

(RCIA groups use Cycle A readings on page 101)

Luke 15:1–3, 11–32 in its biblical context

Often when the Lectionary reading includes a parable from the Gospels, the selection does not name the audience to whom Jesus tells the parable. This makes it difficult to interpret the parable, because the lesson of a parable is drawn from a comparison between the story and the audience. In this Sunday's reading, however, the Lectionary tells us to whom Jesus is speaking when he tells the parable of the prodigal son: "Tax collectors and sinners were all drawing near to listen to Jesus, but the Pharisees and scribes began to complain, saying, 'This man welcomes sinners and eats with them.' So to them Jesus addressed this parable."

After naming this audience and before telling us the parable of the prodigal son, Luke's Gospel includes two other stories through which Jesus tries to teach the critical Pharisees and scribes that God loves even sinners. First he tells them the story of the lost sheep and then the story of the lost coin. Both stories illustrate the fact that when that which has been lost is found there is great rejoicing. "In just the same way, I tell you, there will be rejoicing among the angels of God over one sinner who repents" (Luke 15:10). While each of these stories teaches the scribes and Pharisees that Jesus has been sent to seek out sinners, neither teaches them that they are among the sinners whom Jesus welcomes and with whom he eats. The parable of the prodigal son, however, calls these self-righteous and judgmental people to self-knowledge and conversion.

As the parable of the prodigal son begins, the younger son is the obvious sinner. He has no respect for his father. He asks his father to give him "the share of your estate that should come to me." Then he packs up all his belongings, moves to a distant country, and squanders his inheritance "on a life of dissipation." As Jesus describes this younger son tending swine, the Pharisees could only have felt superior. They are nothing at all like this irresponsible and disobedient younger son. He is the epitome of a sinner.

In time the younger son realizes that he is worse off than his father's servants, so he decides to return home and apologize. His father sees him coming from a distance and runs out to greet him. He embraces and kisses the son and tells the servants to prepare a great party. "Then let us celebrate with a feast, because this son of mine was dead, and has come to life again; he was lost, and has been found." If Jesus simply wanted to teach the Pharisees and scribes what he had taught through the previous two stories, he could have stopped here. So far the story illustrates that there is great rejoicing when that which has been lost is found. Jesus wants to do more than that, however. Jesus loves the Pharisees and scribes too. He wants them to see that they, too, are sinners.

Enter the older brother. This son has been completely responsible. When he describes himself to his father he says, "Look, all these years I served you and not once did I disobey your orders." This son is just like the Pharisees and scribes. They, too, are very careful about obeying the law. As with the older brother, their obedience to the law has made them feel superior to those who have not been so obedient. Just as the older brother resents his father's welcoming his brother back and preparing a banquet to celebrate, so do the Pharisees resent Jesus' welcoming sinners and eating with them.

As the story continues, we can see that it is the older brother who is now the sinner. He is incapable of loving his own brother. When he hears from a servant that his brother has returned and that his father is rejoicing, he becomes angry and refuses to enter the house. The father loves both sons. Just as he came out to meet the younger son on his return, so does he now go out to meet with his angry and unloving older son. He begs him to join the celebration. " . . . But now we must celebrate and rejoice, because your brother was dead and has come to life again; he was lost and has been found." The Pharisees and scribes, of course, know how the older brother feels because they have the same faults as the older brother. As the story corrects the older brother, so does it correct the Pharisees.

Through this story Jesus is calling the Pharisees to self-knowledge and conversion. We do not learn whether the father persuades his older son to join the party or not. If the older brother is excluded it will be because he is incapable of loving his brother, his fellow sinner, and so he will exclude himself. The same is true of the Pharisees. If they remain self-righteous and judgmental, they will be excluding themselves from the kingdom of God, a kingdom to which Jesus is inviting them along with other sinners.

Joshua 5:9a, 10–12 in its biblical context

The Book of Joshua is named after Moses' successor, Joshua. Today's reading begins with the Lord saying to Joshua, "Today I have removed the reproach of Egypt from you." What has preceded this statement is that the Israelites have crossed the Jordan River and have camped in Gilgal. As they crossed the Jordan, God dried up the water for them so that they could cross on dry land, just as God had done when they escaped slavery in Egypt. Upon arriving in Gilgal Joshua circumcised those who had not been circumcised in the desert. Now the "reproach of Egypt," their time of slavery and wandering in the desert, is completely over.

After arriving in Gilgal the Israelites celebrate Passover, that is, they celebrate God's mighty acts on their behalf in freeing them from slavery in Egypt. The word *Passover* is a reminder that before they left Egypt the angel of death passed over the houses of the Israelites so that their children did not die during the last plague. The last plague enabled them to escape. While they were in the desert God fed them with manna. Now they no longer have need of manna because they are in the land that God promised them, a land flowing with milk and honey. They can eat from the produce of the land.

This story is teaching that God is faithful to God's promises even when the people sin, as they did in the desert during the exodus. The land that they are now entering is the land that God promised their ancestors. While they were in need in the desert God fed them with manna. They need have no fear about their future because God will continue to be faithful to them even though they sinned.

2 Corinthians 5:17–21 in its biblical context

Paul, too, assures the Corinthians that God does not count our trespasses against us but calls us to reconciliation. " . . . God was reconciling the world to himself in Christ, not counting their trespasses against them and entrusting to us the message of reconciliation." Paul is reminding the Corinthians that they are to be ministers of reconciliation because Paul needs to be reconciled to some of the Corinthians himself. Evidently some Corinthians are using standards to measure their ministers, standards that do not leave Paul in good stead. Paul describes those with whom he is at odds as "those who boast of external appearance rather than of the heart" (2 Cor 5:12).

We who have been made new in Christ are now called to continue Christ's ministry of reconciliation to all the world. The Pharisees and scribes did not understand this. They did not want those whom they regarded as sinners to be forgiven. Nor did they realize that because they were not ministers of reconciliation, as was Jesus, they were themselves sinning.

Questions for Breaking Open the Word groups are on page 13.

Questions for other faith sharing groups

1. When you hear the parable of the prodigal son do you find yourself agreeing with the older brother? Why or why not?

2. When you sin do you think that God withdraws from you or that you withdraw from God? Explain.

3. In what ways are you a minister of reconciliation? In what ways could you be a minister of reconciliation?

Bible study questions

1. Why is it important to know the audience to whom Jesus tells a parable?

2. What is Jesus teaching through the stories of the lost sheep and the lost coin?

3. What is Jesus teaching the Pharisees and scribes through the parable of the prodigal son?

4. What is the story from the Book of Joshua teaching?

5. About what is Paul assuring the Corinthians?

Fifth Sunday of Lent

(RCIA groups use Cycle A readings on page 104)

John 8:1–11 in its biblical context

We move now from Luke's Gospel to John's. However, today's reading focuses on the same theme that we had last week: Jesus is trying to get the scribes and Pharisees to stop judging others and to start judging themselves. The scribes and Pharisees need to learn that they too are sinners and have need of repentance.

Jesus is teaching a crowd in the temple area when the scribes and Pharisees bring in a woman who has been caught in adultery. They say to him, "Teacher, this woman was caught in the very act of committing adultery. Now in the law, Moses commanded us to stone such women. So what do you say?" John then adds, "They said this to test him, so that they could have some charge to bring against him."

In other words, even though they call Jesus "teacher," the scribes and Pharisees are not trying to learn from him. They are trying to trap him.

If Jesus says that the scribes and Pharisees should stone the woman he will be contradicting Roman law; the Jews do not have the right, under Roman occupation, to inflict the death penalty. On the other hand, if Jesus says that they should not stone the woman, he is virtually saying that they should disobey the law of Moses. In the Book of Deuteronomy we read, "If within the city a man comes upon a maiden who is betrothed, and has relations with her, you shall bring them both out to the gate of the city and there stone them to death: the girl because she did not cry out for help though she was in the city, and the man because he violated his neighbor's wife. Thus shall you purge the evil from your midst" (Deut 22:23–24). No matter what Jesus says, the scribes and Pharisees will have something against him.

Initially Jesus says nothing in response to the scribes' and Pharisees' question. Instead, "Jesus bent down and began to write on the ground with his finger." What was Jesus writing? We are not told. Some guess that Jesus was merely doodling in order to give himself time to think. Others suggest that Jesus wrote, "Where is the man?" After all, the woman was caught "in the very act of committing adultery," and the law calls for stoning for both the man and the woman. Why did the scribes and Pharisees bring only the woman?

As Jesus writes, the scribes and Pharisees continue to ask him whether or not they should stone the woman. Jesus finally answers by saying, "Let the one among you who is without sin be the first to throw a stone at her." Then Jesus bends down and starts writing again. John tells us that "in response, they went away one by one, beginning with the elders." This description has led to the suggestion that Jesus was writing down the sins of the scribes and Pharisees. Because Jesus pointed out their sins to them they were not able to throw the first stone. We do not know what Jesus was writing, but we do know that every one of the woman's accusers leaves. The scribes and Pharisees, so intent on obeying the law, are not able to trap Jesus into antagonizing either his fellow Jews by dismissing the law or the Roman authorities by obeying it.

Now Jesus is left alone with the woman. He asks her, "Woman, where are they? Has no one condemned you?" The woman replies, "No one, sir." Jesus then says, "Neither do I condemn you. Go, and from now on do not sin any more." Notice that with these words Jesus is obviously not condemning the woman; he puts treating her with love above the observance of the law, the very thing that the scribes and Pharisees are unable to do. However, Jesus does name her action as a sin. By warning the woman not to sin anymore Jesus is reminding her, and us, that part of repentance is the firm intention to refrain from sinning in the future.

Isaiah 43:16–21 in its biblical context

The original setting for the words from Second Isaiah (Isa 40–55) that we read today is the time of the Babylonian exile (587 BC–537 BC). This was a terrible time, not only because the Israelites were no longer in the holy land, but because the loss of the holy land made them wonder if God had deserted them. After all, God had promised Abraham and his descendants that the holy land would be theirs. God had promised King David that his line and his nation would be secure forever. What did it mean that the land had been devastated and that the king, along with all the upper-class Israelites, were now living in exile in Babylon? Were the Israelites still God's chosen people or not? What was the meaning of their suffering?

As Second Isaiah pictures God speaking to the exiles he reminds them of God's mighty acts in saving the people from slavery in Egypt. God opened

> …a way in the sea
> and a path in the mighty waters.

God defeated the Egyptians'

> …chariots and horsemen,
>   a powerful army,
> till they lie prostrate together, never to rise,
>   snuffed out and quenched like a wick.

What God did at that time God can do now. God then speaks. God says,

> Remember not the events of the past,
>   the things of long ago consider not;
> see, I am doing something new!

God is not telling the exiles to forget the events of the exodus but to forget the suffering that preceded their defeat at the hands of the Babylonians and the fact that they were conquered and led into exile. They should let go of the painful past and focus on the present, because God is doing something new:

> In the desert I make a way,
>   in the wasteland, rivers…
> for I put water in the desert
>   and rivers in the wasteland
>   for my chosen people to drink,
> the people whom I formed for myself,
>   that they might announce my praise.

In this passage Second Isaiah is responding both to the question about whether or not the exiles are still God's chosen people, and to the question concerning the purpose of their suffering. The exiles are still God's people. God calls them "my chosen people" and "the people whom I formed for myself." God has formed these people and will save them now as God has in the past, so that "they might announce my praise." As Second Isaiah continues, he will teach the exiles that their suffering will be God's way of making God known to all the nations (see Isa 52:12–53:12). Far from deserting the exiles, God still loves them and is accomplishing something wonderful and new through them.

Philippians 3:8–14 in its biblical context

In our reading from Philippians we see that Paul learned the very lesson that Jesus is trying so hard to teach the scribes and Pharisees. Paul understands that a person does not earn a right relationship with God through obedience to the law. Paul realizes that he does not have "any righteousness of my own based on the law but that which comes through faith in Christ, the righteousness from God...." Paul also realizes that he is far from perfect and that he will be growing in his ability to live as Christ would have him live all of his life: "It is not that I have already taken hold of it [i.e., the righteousness from God] or have already attained perfect maturity, but I continue my pursuit in hope that I may possess it, since I have indeed been taken possession of by Christ Jesus."

Paul also learned the lesson that Second Isaiah was teaching the exiles: that suffering has a purpose. Paul says that he has accepted "the sharing of [Christ's] sufferings by being conformed to his death, if somehow I may attain the resurrection from the dead." Just as Jesus' suffering and death led to resurrection and new life, so, Paul believes, will his suffering and death lead to eternal life.

Our readings on this fifth Sunday of Lent call us to self-reflection, to the acknowledgment that we are sinners, and to repentance. However, we need have no fear, because Christ does not condemn sinners. Rather, Christ offers us eternal life.

Questions for Breaking Open the Word groups are on page 13.

Questions for other faith sharing groups

1. Are there some laws with which you disagree because you think they require you to act in a way that is unloving? What are they? Do these laws affect your personal choices? How?

2. Do you find it difficult to condemn an act but not a person? Why or why not?

3. Do you "examine your conscience"? If so, how do you go about doing it? Has your method changed over the years? Explain.

Bible study questions

1. What is Jesus teaching the scribes and Pharisees in today's Gospel?

2. What two questions did the experience of the Babylonian exile raise in the minds of the Israelites?

3. How does our reading from Second Isaiah respond to these questions?

4. What lesson did Paul learn that the scribes and Pharisees failed to learn?

5. What did Paul learn that Second Isaiah was teaching the exiles?

PALM SUNDAY, PASSION

Luke 22:14–23:56 in its biblical context

All four Gospels tell the story of Jesus' suffering and death on a cross. However, each Gospel writer tells the story of Jesus' passion and death in his own unique way in order to be responsive to the needs of his audience. Luke is writing Gentiles, teaching them that the invitation to covenant love is now open to everyone. As Luke tells the story of Jesus' last meal with the apostles, his agony in the garden, his trials, and his crucifixion, Luke does not paint as stark a picture of the apostles' failures as we read in other Gospels. In addition, Luke includes details that emphasize Jesus' healing forgiveness.

While Luke does not deny that the apostles abandon Jesus in his hour of need, he does soften the picture of the apostles' failure. In Luke we realize that the failure will be temporary. After listening to the apostles argue about which of them is the greatest, and teaching them to be servant leaders, Jesus praises the apostles: "It is you who have stood by me in my trials; and I confer a kingdom on you, just as my Father has conferred one on me, that you may eat and drink at my table in my kingdom; and you will sit on thrones judging the twelve tribes of Israel."

Peter's failure, too, is clearly a temporary lapse. Jesus says to Peter, "Simon, Simon, behold Satan has demanded to sift all of you like wheat, but I have prayed that your own faith may not fail; and once you have turned back, you must strengthen your brothers." Peter will deny Jesus, but he will learn from this experience, and afterward he will be a faithful and strong leader for the others.

Even as Luke pictures Jesus complimenting and comforting the apostles he does not hide the fact that they continue to misunderstand. Jesus reminds them of the instructions he has given them. They were to go "forth without a money bag or a sack or sandals." He specifically asks if they wanted for anything, and they say, "No, nothing." Jesus then asks them if they are going to disobey those instructions now that he, and they, will be facing persecution. He ironically suggests that now they should disobey all his instructions and even arm themselves. "But now one who has a money bag should take it, and likewise a sack, and one who does not have a sword should sell his cloak and buy one." The apostles misunderstand the irony and say, "Lord, look, there are two swords here." Jesus shows just a little exasperation as he replies, "It is enough!"

Jesus will later make it clear to the apostles that he was speaking ironically when he suggested that the apostles buy swords: Jesus forbids the apostles to defend him with a sword as he is arrested. They ask, " 'Lord, shall we strike with a sword?' And one of them struck the high priest's servant and cut off his right ear. But Jesus said in reply, 'Stop, no more of this!' Then he touched the servant's ear and healed him."

Two other details unique to Luke, one before the arrest and one after, show Luke's gentle hand in describing the apostles' failures. In Mark (one of Luke's sources), during Jesus' passion in the garden, three times Jesus finds the apostles sleeping instead of praying. In Luke this happens only once, and Luke tells us that they were sleeping, "from grief."

Also in Luke, when Peter denies Jesus for the third time, Jesus is present. After being accused of having been with Jesus, Peter says, " 'My friend, I do not know what you are talking about.' Just as he was saying this, the cock crowed, and the Lord turned and looked at Peter.... " Peter weeps bitterly, undoubtedly because he saw only love in the eyes of Jesus after he denied him.

Although Luke certainly lets us see Jesus suffer during the events leading up to his crucifixion, Luke nevertheless presents Jesus not as a victim but as a healer. We have already noted that Jesus heals the servant's ear. In another ironic touch, Luke tells us that Jesus' very presence heals the relationship between Herod and Pilate: "Herod and Pilate became friends that very day, even though they had been enemies formerly." When Jesus responds to the women who are weeping over him he is not thinking about his own suffering but about theirs: "...do not weep for me; weep instead for yourselves and for your children.... " When the soldiers crucify Jesus he asks his Father to forgive them: "Father, forgive them, they know not what they do." He even comforts one of the criminals crucified with him: "...today you will be with me in Paradise."

As Luke tells his Gentile audience the story of Jesus' passion, death, and resurrection, he wants them to see that everyone, including them, is offered forgiveness and invited into the kingdom. Just as Jesus extended his healing power and his love to the apostles who denied and deserted him, and to the soldiers who arrested, ridiculed, and crucified him, so does Jesus extend God's healing love to the Gentiles who, for many years, did not know God. Gentiles, too, are invited into God's kingdom.

Isaiah 50:4–7 in its biblical context

Our reading today is part of one of the four suffering servant songs that appear in Second Isaiah. Chapters 40 to 55 of the Book of Isaiah date to the time when the Israelites were exiles in Babylon. The author of these chapters, whom we call Second Isaiah, was a prophet of hope who helped the Israelites find meaning in their suffering. The suffering servant poems, in the context in which they appear in Second Isaiah, are about the nation Israel. Israel is the Lord's suffering servant, and through Israel's suffering other nations will come to know God.

However, the suffering servant songs seem to be inserted into the text and may have been independent writings before they were included in Second Isaiah. In its original meaning, the poem we read today may well have been about the prophet himself. The Lord has given the prophet a well-trained tongue that he might

> know how to speak to the weary
> a word that will rouse them.

Second Isaiah did speak to the weary exiles a word that would rouse them. Prophets are often persecuted because they call others to fidelity and conversion. Even though the prophet has been abused he is not disgraced.

> The Lord GOD is my help,
> therefore I am not disgraced.

Because the prophet knows he is doing God's will, he has

> set [his] face like flint,
> knowing that [he] shall not be put to shame.

The suffering servant songs were not originally seen as messianic songs because no one expected the messiah to suffer. The messiah was expected to prevail over the Israelites' political enemies. However, after Jesus' passion, death, and resurrection, the early church found in the words of the suffering servant songs a way to probe the mystery of a suffering messiah. When we read the words in the context of the Lectionary we hear the words as referring to Jesus.

Philippians 2:6–11 in its biblical context

In the passage from Philippians Paul is encouraging the people to live selfless lives. Their model should be Jesus, who,

> . . . though he was in the form of God,
> did not regard equality with God
> something to be grasped.

Rather, Jesus took on "the form of a slave," "humbled himself," and became

> obedient to the point of death,
> even death on a cross.

By saying "even death on a cross," Paul is emphasizing the ignominious nature of Jesus' death, a death that was shameful. However, Jesus' death did not end in death.

> Because of this, God greatly exalted him. . . .
> Jesus Christ is Lord,
> to the glory of God the Father.

Today, as we read the passion of the Lord, we cannot but realize that the cross is a central mystery in our faith. Suffering is part of every person's life, just as it was part of Jesus' life. However, Jesus' suffering led to resurrection. Through his suffering Jesus redeemed the human race from sin. If we join Jesus in his suffering we will also join him in his victory over death.

Questions for Breaking Open the Word groups are on page 13.

Questions for other faith sharing groups

1. Do you remember times when you have disappointed someone you love? How did you feel? Did you need to know you were forgiven?

2. Do you remember times when someone you love has disappointed you? Were you able to forgive that person?

3. Have you experienced God's healing power? Do you think God wants you to experience it? Explain.

Bible study questions

1. What about Jesus does Luke emphasize?

2. How do we know that Jesus didn't want the apostles to defend him with swords?

3. In what ways does Luke picture Jesus as healing others during his own suffering?

4. Why were the suffering servant songs not at first thought of as messianic?

5. How were the suffering servant songs used by the early church?

THIRD SUNDAY OF LENT
CYCLE A

John 4:5–42 in its biblical context

As we read John's story of Jesus meeting a Samaritan woman we see a pattern that we will find throughout John's Gospel. Jesus will have a conversation in which he uses metaphors to talk about spiritual things. Those to whom Jesus is speaking will misunderstand Jesus' intent because they understand his words literally. The misunderstanding gives Jesus the opportunity to clarify his meaning. John uses this method because he is trying to teach his audience to think allegorically, to see levels of meaning. Through his Gospel John hopes to help his end-of-the-century contemporaries *see* that the risen Christ is in their midst.

Jesus comes to a Samaritan town. Jews considered Samaritans to be unclean because they were the descendants of the northern tribes who intermarried with their Assyrian conquerors after the fall of the northern kingdom. Jesus does something completely unexpected when he initiates a conversation with the Samaritan woman, not only because she is a Samaritan, but because she is a woman. John makes this clear as he tells us that the disciples "were amazed that he was talking with a woman."

Jesus says, "Give me a drink." The woman is taken aback by the impropriety of the request. She says, "How can you, a Jew, ask me, a Samaritan woman, for a drink?"

Jesus then makes the statement that the woman misunderstands. He says, "If you knew the gift of God and who is saying to you, 'Give me a drink,' you would have asked him and he would have given you living water."

Jesus is, of course, speaking of spiritual things. The living water that Jesus has to give is baptism. The sacrament of baptism is one of the ways in which John's audience can be with Christ, if only they can *see* that this is true. The woman, however, understands *water* to mean water. She points out to Jesus that he doesn't have a bucket so he couldn't possibly give her water, unless it were a miracle. Not even Jacob, the ancestor after whom the well is named, could do such a thing. Does Jesus think he is greater than Jacob?

The woman's misunderstanding gives Jesus an opportunity to elaborate: "Everyone who drinks this water will be thirsty again; but whoever drinks the water I shall give will never thirst; the water I shall give will become in him a spring of water welling up to eternal life."

If John's audience shared the woman's original misunderstanding, there is no way they could continue to misunderstand. The water that leads to eternal life is baptism. However, the woman does not yet understand. She says, "Sir, give me this water, so that I may not be thirsty or have to keep coming here to draw water." To her, *water* still means water.

Jesus now changes the subject. He asks the woman to get her husband. When she responds that she does not have a husband, Jesus commends her for telling the truth. "You are right in saying, 'I do not have a husband.' For you have had five husbands, and the one you have now is not your husband." With this statement we can surmise why the woman was at the well by herself in the heat of the day. Given her history, she must have been isolated from the company of the other women who also made daily trips to the well.

The woman does not try to defend herself. Rather, she has her first and partial insight as to the identity of the person with whom she is speaking. She says, "Sir, I can see that you are a prophet." She then brings up a matter of dispute between the Samaritans and the Jews: should people worship "on this mountain," that is, at a temple that had been built in Samaria for worship, or only at the temple in Jerusalem? Remember, by the time John is writing, the temple in Jerusalem no longer exists. It had been destroyed by the Romans. Jesus tells her that the time will come "when you will worship the Father neither on this mountain nor in Jerusalem.... But the hour is coming, and is now here, when true worshipers will worship the Father in Spirit and truth." For John's fellow Christians, worship is not tied to a geographic place. Rather, wherever people worship, the risen Christ is present.

The conversation then moves on to the identity of the messiah. Here the woman takes another step in recognizing Jesus' identity. Jesus tells the woman that he is the expected messiah. "I am he, the one speaking with you."

It is at this point that the disciples return and are amazed to see Jesus talking with a woman. They have a conversation with Jesus that illustrates the same pattern of misunderstanding that we saw with Jesus and the woman. The disciples urge Jesus to eat something. Jesus says, "I have food to eat of which you do not know." The disciples think *food to eat* means "food to eat." So they say, "Could someone have brought him something to eat?" Their misunderstanding gives Jesus the opportunity to explain. He says, "My food is to do the will of the one who sent me and to finish his work."

In the meantime, the woman had been so excited by her conversation with Jesus that she had left her bucket at the well and told everyone she met about her experience. The woman is a true evangelizer. However, she doesn't want people to rely on her word. She wants them to come and see for themselves. She says to her townspeople, "Come see a man who told me everything I have done. Could he possibly be the Christ?"

The Samaritans respond to her invitation to meet Jesus. After spending two days with Jesus, many of the Samaritans begin to believe. They then give witness to her: "We no longer believe because of your word; for we have heard for ourselves, and we know that this is truly the savior of the world."

By walking together in faith the woman and her townspeople have moved from understanding that Jesus is a prophet to understanding that he may be the messiah to understanding that Jesus is truly "the savior of the world." Their witness to one another has helped them accept the gift that Jesus wanted to give them all along.

Exodus 17:3–7 *in its biblical context*

Notice the question that the Israelites are asking in the desert, "Is the LORD in our midst or not?" This question ties today's Old Testament reading to the reading from John's Gospel because this is the very question to which John is responding by writing his Gospel. He wants his contemporaries to be able to see that Christ is in their midst in the church and in what we now call the sacraments: baptism and Eucharist.

Notice too that today's story is presented not as a test of the Israelites' fidelity to God, but as a test of God's fidelity to the Israelites. The people are thirsty and are grumbling about the hardships of life in the desert. When Moses asks God, "What shall I do with this people?" God could have responded, "Remind them that I freed them from slavery and tell them to stop grumbling." But God does not do that. Instead, God provides them with water. The story is told not to teach that the Israelites should not have grumbled, given God's mighty acts on their behalf, but to teach that God loves and saves. God did not lead the Israelites into the desert to let them die of thirst but to let them know that their God is in their midst.

Romans 5:1–2, 5–8 in its biblical context

Our Lectionary reading from Romans also emphasizes that God has taken the initiative to save us. We have not earned salvation. Rather, "the love of God has been poured out into our hearts through the Holy Spirit who has been given to us." Paul emphasizes this point by saying, "For Christ, while we were still helpless, died at the appointed time for the ungodly." In other words, we were sinners and God took the initiative to save us: "But God proves his love for us in that while we were still sinners Christ died for us."

Christ has offered salvation to the whole human race. However, Paul tells the Romans that "we have been justified by faith, we have peace with God through our Lord Jesus Christ, through whom we have gained access by faith to this grace in which we stand." Paul is saying that it is possible to refuse the gift of love and salvation that God longs to give us. Like the Samaritan woman, we must be open to new insights so that we can receive the gifts that we are offered and through faith come to know that Jesus Christ "truly is the savior of the world."

Questions for Breaking Open the Word groups are on page 13.

Questions for preparing for this week's Scrutiny

1. In what ways have you, like the Samaritan woman, sinned?

2. In what ways have you failed to receive the gifts that Christ longs to give you?

3. What can you do this week to prepare for your baptism?

Questions for other faith sharing groups

1. Who in our society is saying, "Give me a drink"? What is our response to this person?

2. Who in our society are marginalized because they have acted in ways that we believe to be wrong? How do we treat these people? How do you think Jesus would treat them?

3. Do you have positive or negative reactions to the word *evangelization*? What does this word mean to you? Based on today's readings, what do you think it means?

Bible study questions

1. What literary device does John use regularly to help his audience learn to think allegorically?

2. What does Jesus want to give the Samaritan woman?

3. In what way does the woman evangelize?

4. What does the passage from Romans emphasize?

5. To whom has Christ offered salvation?

FOURTH SUNDAY OF LENT
CYCLE A

John 9:1–41 in its biblical context

Today we read the story of a man who is given two kinds of sight, physical sight and spiritual sight. As John writes his Gospel at the end of the first century, he wants to help some of his contemporaries gain spiritual insight too. They have been expecting the return of the risen Christ on the clouds of heaven. John wants them to see that the risen Christ is in their midst.

When an author wants his audience to see more than one level of meaning in his writing, the author has to say something in the text that invites the audience to look beyond the surface meaning. We noted this in the commentary on last week's reading when we said that Jesus is in conversation with people who misunderstand what he is saying because they are thinking too literally. Their misunderstanding gives Jesus an opportunity to explain his real meaning. At the same time it gives the author the opportunity to help his audience learn to think allegorically. The mistake that Jesus is correcting in the mind of his listener the author is correcting in the mind of his reader.

John uses a different technique in today's Gospel to invite people to see two levels of meaning in his stories. Notice that when the parents of the blind man are asked how their son can now see they say, "We do not know how he sees now, nor do we know who opened his eyes. Ask him, he is of age; he can speak for himself."

Then John explains why the parents answered as they did: "His parents said this because they were afraid of the Jews, for the Jews had already agreed that if anyone acknowledged him as the Christ, he would be expelled from the synagogue." At the time that Jesus was working mighty signs as part of his public ministry, the Jews were not expelling other Jews from the synagogue because they were followers of Jesus. However, by the time John was writing, this is exactly what was happening. Those Jews who were expelled were put in terrible jeopardy because they were no longer exempt from emperor worship. It would have been a big temptation to refrain from acknowledging Jesus' divinity simply to avoid persecution and possible martyrdom.

By including a plot element that was contemporary with John and his audience rather than with Jesus and his contemporaries, John is inviting his readers to see an additional setting for his Gospel. They are invited to think of John's Gospel as being just as much about the risen Christ in their lives as it is about Jesus during his public ministry.

Notice how John pictures the blind man gradually coming to a full understanding of Jesus' identity. At first, when pressed by the Pharisees to say something about the man who gave him sight, he says only, "He is a prophet." Later, the Pharisees come to the healed man again and say that they know Jesus is a sinner. They have come to this conclusion because Jesus healed the man on the Sabbath. The once blind man insists that Jesus must be from God: "If this man were not from God, he would not be able to do anything." Of course, those who are reading John's Gospel see a double meaning in the words *from God,* a meaning that the blind man himself does not yet see. John has told us since the very beginning of his Gospel that Jesus is the preexistent Word who came from God.

The Pharisees are disgusted with this answer. They say, "You were born totally in sin, and are you trying to teach us?" The Pharisees believe the man was born totally in sin because he was born blind. They think that suffering is punishment for sin. If a man is born blind it must be because he or his parents sinned. As today's story begins, the disciples express this same belief when they say, "Rabbi, who sinned, this man or his parents, that he was born blind?" Jesus rejects this belief and says that the blindness is not a punishment for sin at all.

Jesus hears that the Pharisees have thrown the man born blind out. Jesus finds the man and asks him, "Do you believe in the Son of Man?" Remember that the phrase *Son of Man* is an allusion to the figure in the Book of Daniel who will come on the clouds of heaven to judge the nations (Dan 7:13). The man responds, "Who is he, sir, that I may believe in him?" When Jesus says, "You have seen him, and the one speaking with you is he," the man says, "I do believe, Lord," and he worships him. The man born blind sees Jesus' divinity.

The man has moved from understanding that Jesus is "a prophet," to understanding that he must be from God, to understanding that he is the Son of Man who was expected to come on the clouds of heaven. John wants his audience to be like the once blind man. He wants them to move to a belief that Jesus is divine and already present to them: "You have seen him." He wants them to be able to *see* that the risen Christ is in their midst.

Notice that when Jesus is healing the blind man of his physical blindness, after smearing clay on his eyes, he sends him to wash in the Pool of Siloam, "which means Sent." If you are thinking allegorically, as John wants you to, you will see a reference to baptism in these words. To be washed is to be baptized. When one is baptized one is sent on mission.

Notice too that just as John gives us a picture of a man learning to see, that is, coming to full faith in Christ, he also gives us a picture of the Pharisees choosing to remain blind. First, because of their legalistic understanding of Sabbath observance, they conclude that Jesus can't be from God. Next, because of their misunderstanding about the role of suffering, they reject not only the testimony of the man born blind, but the man himself. Finally, when they hear Jesus say, "I came into this world for judgment, so that those who do not see might see, and those who do see might become blind," they also reject an invitation to personal insight and conversion. They say, "Surely we are not also blind, are we?" Jesus tells them that the attitude that has been behind all of their misjudgments, the attitude that they already know everything and so have nothing to learn, has resulted in their remaining in sin: " . . . but now you are saying, 'We see,' so your sin remains."

The Gospel invites us to be like the man born blind, who grows in his spiritual insight, rather than to be like the Pharisees, who refuse to grow. Will we accept the invitation?

1 Samuel 16:1b, 6–7, 10–13a in its biblical context

Our reading from the First Book of Samuel is also about *seeing*. The setting for today's story is during the time when the future King David is still a youth tending his father's sheep. Samuel is a prophet of the Lord, and so he speaks for God. God tells Samuel to go to Bethlehem, to the house of Jesse, because, God says, "I have chosen my king from among his sons" (v. 1c).

As Samuel looks at Jesse's sons, he sees one who is particularly impressive, Eliab. However, the Lord says to Samuel, "Do not judge from his appearance or from his lofty stature, because I have rejected him. Not as man sees does God see, because man sees the appearance but the LORD looks into the heart."

Samuel listens to the Lord and asks Jesse, "Are these all the sons you have?" Only then is David brought in from the fields. Samuel "anointed David in the presence of his brothers" (v. 13b). This means that David is a *messiah*, an anointed one. God has a special job for David.

During Lent, as we all examine our consciences and as catechumens prepare for baptism, this reading reminds us that we must try to see, not as human beings see, but as God sees. We are also invited to consider the fact that at baptism we are all anointed with oil as a sign that God has a special mission for each of us too.

Ephesians 5:8–14 in its biblical context

The author of Ephesians invites his readers to "live as children of light." To live as children of light is to "learn what is pleasing to the Lord." The author reminds the Ephesians of a Christian hymn, probably used to celebrate baptism, when he says, "Therefore, it says:

> 'Awake, O sleeper,
> and arise from the dead,
> and Christ will give you light.' "

Notice that the Ephesians are not only urged to live as children of light, but are told that they are "light in the Lord." The light that they are will produce every kind of goodness, righteousness, and truth.

This week's Lectionary readings invite us to come into the light that is Christ, to walk in that light by doing God's will, and to realize that as baptized people we have been chosen and sent on mission to be that light for others.

Questions for Breaking Open the Word groups are on page 13.

Questions for preparing this week's Scrutiny

1. In what ways have you, like the man born blind, failed to see?

2. In what ways have you, like the Pharisees, been resistant to letting go of past misunderstandings so that you can grow in your knowledge of the truth?

3. What can you do this week to prepare for your baptism?

Questions for other faith sharing groups

1. Have you ever felt hesitant to profess your beliefs because of the reaction you think you would receive from others? Explain.

2. Have you had to discard some of what you were taught as a child in order to grow spiritually? Explain.

3. Are you baptized? If so, do you think of yourself as chosen by God and as sent on mission? Explain.

Bible study questions

1. In what two ways does John invite his readers to think allegorically as they read his Gospel?

2. What steps does the man born blind go through as he recognizes Jesus' identity?

3. Why do the Pharisees think Jesus cannot be from God?

4. Why does Jesus accuse the Pharisees of remaining in their sin?

5. How does the author of the Letter to the Ephesians encourage them to live?

FIFTH SUNDAY OF LENT
CYCLE A

John 11:1–45 in its biblical context

In our commentaries on the Gospel readings for the last two Sundays we pointed out the literary devices that John uses to alert his audience to the fact that his story has more than one level of meaning. That knowledge will be very helpful in understanding the full message of the story of the raising of Lazarus. As we will see, this story is about more than the raising of Mary and Martha's brother to an extended life on earth. It is about the raising of John's audience, including us, to eternal life.

John makes it clear that to understand his story we must learn to think allegorically by once again having Jesus engage in a conversation in which words that are intended to be metaphorical are understood to be literal. Jesus tells his disciples, " 'Our friend Lazarus is asleep, but I am going to awaken him.' So the disciples said to him, 'Master, if he is asleep, he will be saved.' But Jesus was talking about his death, while they thought that he meant ordinary sleep. So then Jesus said to them clearly, 'Lazarus has died.' "

Notice that John explains the mistake to his audience ("But Jesus was talking about his death, while they thought that he meant ordinary sleep") and Jesus explains the mistake to the disciples ("Lazarus has died"). This interchange prepares us to think allegorically as we read the story.

John gives us another clue to look for hidden meaning by saying something that doesn't appear, on first reading, to make sense. After Jesus is told that Lazarus is ill John tells us, "Now Jesus loved Martha and her sister and Lazarus. So when he heard that he was ill, he remained for two days in the place where he was." We would expect Jesus to have exactly the opposite reaction. If Jesus loved Martha and Mary we would expect him to leave immediately to help them in their time of need. When an author says something incongruous at the literal level it is an invitation to look for a reason. In looking for the reason we are drawn to probe the very point that the author wants us to probe.

Both Martha and Mary express their disappointment to Jesus about his absence. When Martha first sees Jesus she says to him, "Lord, if you had been here, my brother would not have died." When Mary first sees Jesus she also says, "Lord, if you had been here, my brother would not have died." Remember that this is exactly what John's audience is saying. They had expected Jesus to return on the clouds of heaven before their time, the end of the first century AD. In addition, many of those who believe in Jesus' divinity are being expelled from the synagogue, therefore being exposed to Roman persecution, even martyrdom. John's audience, too, is saying, "Lord, if you had been here, our relatives would not have died." Through this story John is teaching his audience that Jesus is with them, and, in fact, their relatives have not died. They have been raised to eternal life.

We hear this truth being taught just after Martha confronts Jesus with his absence. Jesus tells Martha, " 'Your brother will rise.' Martha said to him, 'I know he will rise, in the resurrection on the last day.' Jesus told her, 'I am the resurrection and the life; whoever believes in me, even if he dies, will live, and everyone who lives and believes in me will never die. Do you believe this?' " These words are being addressed both to Martha in the story and to John's end-of-the-century audience. The risen Christ is asking John's contemporaries and us, "Do you believe this?"

Martha's response is the one that John wants his audience to give: "Yes, Lord. I have come to believe that you are the Christ, the Son of God, the one who is coming into the world." Martha is affirming the core theological truths that John has been teaching throughout his Gospel. Jesus is the Christ. Jesus is the Son of God. Jesus is the one who came from the Father into the world, not to come and leave, but to stay. In fact, as John concludes his Gospel, he says that it is to teach these truths that he has written his Gospel in the first place: "But these are written that you may [come to] believe that Jesus is the Messiah, the Son of God, and that through this belief you may have life in his name" (John 20:31).

As the story continues, John emphasizes Jesus' deep love for Martha, Mary, and Lazarus. When the story began, John told us that "Jesus loved Martha and her sister and Lazarus." Now, as Jesus witnesses Mary's grief, John tells us that Jesus "became perturbed and deeply troubled.... And Jesus wept." The Jews, on seeing this, remark, "See how he loved him."

John also wants to emphasize that Jesus really does have power over life and death. In Mark's Gospel we read a story in which Jesus heals the daughter of Jairus (Mark 5:21–43). Jesus is told that the daughter has died, but it is not clear to the reader whether or not this information is correct. Here there is no doubt. Lazarus has been in the tomb for four days. Martha fears there will be a stench.

After the people remove the stone, an act of faith in itself, Jesus prays and then cries out, "Lazarus, come out!" Lazarus does come out, "tied hand and foot with burial bands, and his face was wrapped in a cloth." Jesus instructs the people to "Untie him and let him go."

Jesus had said immediately before performing this mighty sign, "Did I not tell you that if you believe you will see the glory of God?" To see the glory of God is to see God's divinity. As the story ends, John tells us that "many of the Jews who had come to Mary and seen what he had done began to believe in him." To believe in Jesus is to see Jesus' glory, to believe, with Martha, that Jesus is "the Christ, the Son of God, the one who is coming into the world." John wants his audience, including us, to believe this so that we too may have eternal life.

Ezekiel 37:12–14 in its biblical context

Since we have just read the story of the raising of Lazarus it would be easy to conclude that the prophet Ezekiel was promising his audience, the exiles in Babylon, that God would bring them back from the dead. However, Ezekiel prophesied from 593 BC to 571 BC, well before the Israelites came to any kind of belief in life after death.

Rather, Ezekiel is assuring the people that God will be faithful to his covenant promise of land. Being in exile in Babylon was like being dead and buried. The people longed to return to the land of the living, to Israel. Ezekiel assures them that their hopes would be fulfilled: "Thus says the LORD God: O my people, I will open your graves and have you rise from them, and bring you back to the land of Israel."

Ezekiel's oracle is wonderful news for the people. Because they are in exile and have lost all they thought God had promised them—their land, their king, and their temple—they are having to rethink their understanding of their covenant relationship with God. Does God still love them? Are they still God's people? In this oracle God assures them that they are still God's people, as God says, "O my people." God has not forgotten God's covenant promises. The people will be returned to their land. "I will put my spirit in you that you may live, and I will settle you upon your land; thus you shall know that I am the LORD. I have promised, and I will do it, says the LORD."

Ezekiel's prophecy was wonderful news for the exiles, but not as good as John's good news (the word *Gospel* means "good news") to his audience. Ezekiel was promising a return to Israel. John is promising eternal life.

Romans 8:8–11 in its biblical context

Paul, in his Letter to the Romans, is teaching that through Jesus we have eternal life: "If the Spirit of the one who raised Jesus from the dead dwells in you, the one who raised Christ from the dead will give life to your mortal bodies also, through his Spirit dwelling in you." This is the same truth that the story of the raising of Lazarus was teaching. Jesus has power over life and death. Those who believe in Jesus, who believe that Jesus is Christ, the Son of God, will have life in him, eternal life.

Questions for Breaking Open the Word groups are on page 13.

Questions for preparing for this week's Scrutiny

1. As a person who believes that Jesus is the Christ, the Son of God, how have you failed to live in fidelity to that belief?

2. As a person whom Christ loves, how have you failed to respond to that love?

3. What can you do this week to prepare for your baptism?

Questions for other faith sharing groups

1. Have you ever walked with someone to his or her death? Did you feel Christ's presence at that time? Explain.

2. Have you come to believe that Jesus is "the Christ, the Son of God, the one who is coming into the world"? Why do you believe this?

3. Do you believe that you belong to God? What ramifications does this belief have in your life?

Bible study questions

1. What words do both Martha and Mary say to Jesus?

2. Why are these words also on the lips of John's audience?

3. What is John teaching through the story of the raising of Lazarus?

4. Why were Ezekiel's words such good news for his audience?

5. What is Paul teaching the Romans in today's passage?

THE EASTER SEASON

EASTER VIGIL

Since one of the primary motives for writing this book is to serve RCIA groups who are *breaking open the word,* we have chosen the Easter Vigil readings to put in context since those preparing for baptism will be attending the Easter Vigil Mass.

Luke 24:1–12 *in its biblical context*

All of the Gospels claim that Jesus rose from the dead, but no Gospel describes the resurrection. The stories that claim Jesus' resurrection are empty tomb stories and postresurrection appearance stories. Today we read an empty tomb story.

As was true in the stories of Jesus' passion and death, the core of the empty tomb stories is consistent from one Gospel to another, but the details differ. In Luke three women, Mary Magdalene, Joanna, and Mary the mother of James, go to the tomb at daybreak on Sunday. You may remember that Palm Sunday's Gospel ended by telling us about these women: "The women who had come from Galilee with him followed behind, and when they had seen the tomb and the way in which his body was laid in it, they returned and prepared spices and perfumed oils. Then they rested on the sabbath according to the commandment" (Luke 23:55–56). Luke's Gospel, as well as his Acts of the Apostles, gives a unique role to women.

When the women arrive at the tomb the stone has already been rolled away. The narrator's voice tells us that "when they entered, they did not find the body of the Lord Jesus." The title "Lord Jesus" is a postresurrection title rooted in faith in the risen Christ. By using this title prior to the time when the women, or anyone else for that matter, fully understand what has happened, Luke is establishing dramatic irony between those reading the Gospel and the characters in the story: Luke and his audience already know what the characters do not yet understand. The presence of dramatic irony is important to note because it affects our understanding of the text. Because we, gathered at the Easter Vigil to celebrate Jesus' resurrection, believe in the risen Christ, we may forget just how difficult it was for the women and the apostles to comprehend the Easter good news.

In all three Synoptic Gospels (Mark, Matthew, and Luke) the women are met at the empty tomb and are told the significance of what they are seeing. In Luke they are met by two men in dazzling garments: "They said to [the women], 'Why do you seek the living one among the dead? He is not here, but he has been raised.' " This is the core Easter Gospel. Jesus has conquered death and is still alive.

Then the two men go on to say, " 'Remember what he said to you while he was still in Galilee, that the Son of Man must be handed over to sinners and be crucified, and rise on the third day.' And they remembered his words." Notice that the two men remind the women that they themselves heard what Jesus had said. Earlier in the Gospel Luke pictured three occasions on which Jesus warned his disciples of his impending death (see Luke 9:22; 9:44; 19:31). On none of these occasions does Luke specifically mention that women were among those disciples present. Here, however, Luke describes the women as remembering Jesus' words. Indeed they had been told. Remembering Jesus' words would now help them interpret the significance of the empty tomb.

The women then "returned from the tomb and announced all these things to the eleven and to all the others . . . but their story seemed like nonsense and they did not believe them." Notice that Jesus' predictions of the passion did not cause the apostles to expect that Jesus would rise from the dead. If they had expected the resurrection, the women's news would have confirmed their expectation and they would have believed them.

Today's Gospel ends with Luke telling us that Peter ran to the tomb, saw the burial cloths, and "went home amazed at what had happened." Again, remember that Peter does not yet understand what the reader understands. Peter is amazed at the empty tomb and at the women's story. That is Peter's understanding of "what had happened." Only when Peter experiences the presence of the risen Christ will he believe the good news that we celebrate on Easter Sunday: Jesus' body is not in the tomb. Jesus has risen from the dead and is still alive.

The Lectionary presents us with seven Old Testament passages to read at the Easter Vigil. We will say a few words about the context of each of these readings.

Genesis 1:1–2:2 *in its biblical context*

The story of our relationship with God begins with creation. God, out of love, creates the whole world and everything in it by the power of God's word. The crown of God's creative activity comes on the sixth day when God says, " 'Let us make man in our image, after our likeness.' . . . God created man in his image; / in the image of God he created him; / male and female he created them." Both men and women are created in the image of a loving God. Therefore, every human being has an innate dignity and the potential to become a loving human being. At the end of creating everything, including us, God "looked at everything he had made, and he found it very good." God finds us "very good."

Genesis 22:1–18 *in its biblical context*

The story of the sacrifice of Isaac is the story of Abraham (1850 BC) coming to a realization that God is too loving to want child sacrifice. Beginning in chapter 12 of Genesis we read that God called Abraham to leave his own country and to go to a land that God would show him. God entered into a covenant relationship with Abraham in which God promised Abraham land, protection, and descendants. Isaac is the child of the promise, Abraham's descendant whom Abraham's wife, Sarah, bore late in life.

Abraham lived in a polytheistic culture (a culture in which people believed in many gods) in which child sacrifice was routine. The expectation would be that Isaac, as the child who opened the womb, would be sacrificed. However, while Abraham was willing to do God's will, Abraham came to the understanding that God was too loving to want child sacrifice. Later this profound insight would be codified for the chosen people. They would sacrifice the firstfruits of their animals, but not of human beings (Exod 13:11).

Exodus 14:15–15:1 *in its biblical context*

Our reading from Exodus describes the parting of the sea that enabled the chosen people to escape from slavery in Egypt and return to the promised land (1250 BC). Four generations of patriarchs (Abraham, Isaac, Jacob, and Joseph) lived in Canaan after God first led Abraham there. When there was a famine in Canaan the people went to Egypt to get food. They remained in Egypt over five hundred years, becoming slaves to the Egyptians. However, God called Moses to lead the people back to the land that God had promised Abraham.

The Exodus was a profound experience of God's power and God's fidelity for the Israelites as a whole. All of the stories that we have in the Old Testament, even those that precede the Exodus, are told from a post-Exodus point of view. Who could ever doubt a God that would act so powerfully on behalf of God's chosen people?

Isaiah 54:5–14 *in its biblical context*

Our reading from Isaiah is from the part of the book known as Second Isaiah (Isa 40–55). Second Isaiah was a prophet who offered hope to the Israelites while they were in exile in Babylon (587 BC–537 BC). The period of the exile was the second most traumatic time in the history of Israel, second only to the time of slavery in Egypt. The people believed that God had promised to protect them. So when they lost their land, their king, and their temple they began to doubt their whole understanding of their covenant relationship with God. Were they still God's people or not? Isaiah assures the people that they still belong to God, who both made them and married them:

> The One who has become your husband is your Maker;
> his name is the Lord of hosts.

Isaiah also assures the people that the covenant is still intact:

> Though the mountains leave their place
>   and the hills be shaken,
> my love shall never leave you
>   nor my covenant of peace be shaken....

Isaiah 55:1–11 in its biblical context

In this reading Second Isaiah continues to comfort the people and to assure them that their covenant relationship with God still exists:

> I will renew with you the everlasting covenant,
>   the benefits assured to David.
> As I made him a witness to the peoples,
>   a leader and commander of nations,
> so shall you summon a nation you knew not,
>   and nations that knew you not shall run to you....

Isaiah is telling the Israelites that the covenant still exists. God is bestowing on all the people the role once personified by David, to become a witness to other nations of God's saving power.

This Lectionary selection ends with God assuring the people of the power of God's word:

> ...so shall my word be
>   that goes forth from my mouth;
> my word shall not return to me void,
>   but shall do my will,
>   achieving the end for which I sent it.

We have already read of the creative power of God's word in our first story from Genesis. Those of us who *break open the word* in the RCIA process are opening ourselves up to the power of God's word so that the living word will be fruitful in each of our lives.

Baruch 3:9–15, 32–4:4 in its biblical context

Baruch is one of the books that are in the Roman Catholic canon but not in the canon of other Christians. It was written about 150 BC by an Israelite who did not live in the promised land but who was completely faithful to the traditions of his ancestors. The setting of the book is the time of the Babylonian exile. The author attributes the book to Baruch, Jeremiah's scribe. By meditating on the time of the exile and its meaning, the author is teaching people like himself who are separated from their homeland to live in fidelity to their traditions.

Today the exiles are called to repent of their past sins and live a life of wisdom:

> Hear, O Israel, the commandments of life....
> You have forsaken the fountain of wisdom!
>   Had you walked in the way of God,
>   you would have dwelt in enduring peace.

The exiles are encouraged to remain faithful to wisdom despite the fact that they live in a foreign culture:

> Turn, O Jacob, and receive her:
>   walk by her light toward splendor.
> Give not your glory to another,
>   your privileges to an alien race.
> Blessed are we, O Israel;
>   for what pleases God is known to us!

There is no greater gift than the gift of revelation. Through God's gracious act we have been taught what the Lord would have us do. As we heard in the first reading, we are made in the image of a loving God. God wants us to learn to act lovingly in every situation. Learning wisdom will help us live as God would have us live.

Ezekiel 36:16–17a, 18–28 in its biblical context

Ezekiel was a prophet in Babylon during the exile. In today's reading Ezekiel is assuring the people that God will restore them to the promised land, not because they deserve it, but because the people have not been faithful witnesses to God in the foreign lands where they have gone. By bringing them back God will be glorifying God's name. "I will prove the holiness of my great name, profaned among the nations, in whose midst you have profaned it. . . . For I will take you away from among the nations, gather you from all the foreign lands, and bring you back to your own land."

Once the people are back God will forgive them for their sins and fill them with his spirit so that they will live according to God's statutes: "I will sprinkle clean water upon you to cleanse you from all your impurities, and from all your idols I will cleanse you. I will give you a new heart and place a new spirit within you. . . . You shall live in the land I gave your fathers; you shall be my people, and I will be your God."

Romans 6:3–11 in its biblical context

Paul is assuring the Romans that because they have been baptized they have died with Christ and will also be united with Christ in the resurrection: ". . . we who were baptized into Christ Jesus were baptized into his death. . . .

"For if we have grown into union with him through a death like his, we shall also be united with him in the resurrection." Because the baptized have died with Christ they are now "dead to sin." Their baptism means that they live a completely new life in Christ: "Consequently, you too must think of yourselves as being dead to sin and living for God in Christ Jesus."

On this most holy of all nights, as we welcome the newly baptized into the body of Christ and renew our own baptismal vows, we think once more of the women in Luke's empty tomb story who faithfully announced the good news "to the eleven and to all the others." We pray that we may accept the great gift we have received and become faithful witnesses of the risen Christ to all the nations in everything we say and in everything we do.

Questions for Breaking Open the Word groups are on page 13.

Questions for other faith sharing groups

1. What place do you think extravagant celebration plays in the life of a Christian?

2. Do you believe that Jesus rose from the dead? How do you give witness to this belief?

3. Do you think of yourself as having been made in God's image? What does this mean to you?

Bible study questions

1. What two kinds of stories claim that the resurrection occurred?

2. In Mark's empty tomb story, who comes to anoint Jesus?

3. What do they find?

4. What does the man clothed in white tell them to do?

5. According to Paul, what happens when a person is baptized?

SECOND SUNDAY OF EASTER

John 20:19–31 in its biblical context

We move now from Luke's empty tomb story to one of John's post-resurrection appearance stories. At the beginning of today's reading John tells us that it is evening of the first day of the week. Earlier in the day Mary Magdalene had discovered the empty tomb. She told Peter and the beloved disciple, who rushed to the site. The beloved disciple was the first to come to faith. John tells us that he "saw and believed" (John 20:8b). Peter and Mary Magdalene did not yet believe. "For they did not yet understand the scripture that he had to rise from the dead" (John 20:9). Just before today's reading picks up the story Jesus appeared to Mary Magdalene. She told the disciples, "I have seen the Lord" (John 20:18a).

Despite Mary Magdalene's witness, the disciples are locked in a room, "for fear of the Jews." This reference to "fear of the Jews" is one of many instances in John's Gospel in which he infuses his own historical setting, the end of the first century, into his story. At the time when John was writing, those Jews who did not believe in Jesus' divinity were persecuting those Jews who did. John was very angry at the Jews who were expelling their fellow Jews from the synagogue; by doing this they were endangering their lives. John's purpose in conflating the two historical times is to teach those in his audience that his story is just as much about the presence of the risen Christ in their lives as it is about the presence of the risen Christ in the lives of the original disciples. It is John's contemporaries, not the original disciples, who had reason to be fearful of some of their fellow Jews.

Jesus' first words to the disciples are "Peace be with you." Jesus had earlier given the disciples this same gift of peace. At his last meal with them before his death Jesus said, "Peace I leave with you; my peace I give to you. Not as the world gives do I give it to you. Do not let your hearts be troubled or afraid. You heard me tell you, 'I am going away and I will come back to you'" (John 14:27–28). Now, Jesus has come back to them, just as he promised, and he offers them peace.

Next Jesus shows the disciples his hands and his side. This is to demonstrate that the person who was crucified and died is the person who is before them now. The hands, of course, would show nail marks. The side would show the wound inflicted by the soldier after Jesus died. "But when they came to Jesus and saw that he was already dead, they did not break his legs, but one soldier thrust his lance into his side, and immediately blood and water flowed out" (John 19:33–34).

In John's Gospel the Spirit is given to the church during this first postresurrection appearance. We will discuss the disciples' commissioning ("As the Father has sent me, so I send you") and their reception of the Spirit ("Receive the Holy Spirit. Whose sins you forgive are forgiven them, and whose sins you retain are retained") at greater length on the feast of Pentecost when we will again read this same passage from John. For now let us simply say that the disciples are being commissioned to join in Jesus' mission. As the disciples succeed in spreading the good news of Jesus Christ they will invite people to baptism, the sacrament through which we receive forgiveness of our sins. To the extent that the disciples succeed in carrying out their mission, people will experience this forgiveness. To the extent that they fail, people will not.

Thomas is absent when Jesus appears to his disciples. The disciples tell him exactly what Mary Magdalene had told them: We have "seen the Lord." Remember, John's audience, living at the end of the first century, longs to see the Lord too. They had expected the second coming long before their time. Why had Jesus not returned in glory on the clouds of heaven as was expected? As he tells the story of Thomas, John is speaking directly to that audience.

Thomas will not believe on the word of another. He says, "Unless I see the mark of the nails in his hands and put my finger into the nailmarks and put my hand into his side, I will not believe." Thomas lives in his obstinate disbelief for a week. The disciples are once more gathered in a locked room when Jesus appears and once more gives them the gift of peace. This time the mention of the locked doors seems to emphasize that a locked door does not prevent Jesus from being with his disciples. Also, as we can tell by what Jesus will say to Thomas, Jesus is fully aware of the way in which Thomas expressed his doubt. Jesus' words to Thomas suggest that Jesus was not absent on that earlier occasion. One need not see Jesus' physical presence for Jesus to be with his disciples.

Jesus says to Thomas, "Put your finger here and see my hands, and bring your hand and put it into my side, and do not be unbelieving, but believe." When given the invitation to do exactly what he claimed that he must do in order to believe, Thomas does not accept the opportunity. Instead of touching Jesus' wounds, Thomas says, "My Lord and my God!" Thomas recognizes Jesus' divinity and worships him. The words that Jesus says to Thomas are words that John is speaking to his end-of-the-century audience: "Have you come to believe because you have seen me? Blessed are those who have not seen and have believed."

John then speaks directly to his audience, explaining why he has written the Gospel in the first place: "But these are written that you may come to believe that Jesus is the Christ, the Son of God, and that through this belief you may have life in his name." John wants his audience to be like the beloved disciple, the only one who believed without a postresurrection appearance. Mary Magdalene, Peter, and Thomas all believed after Jesus appeared to them personally. John is teaching his end-of-the-century audience that Jesus did return as he promised, in his postresurrection appearances. This means that Jesus is still alive. They are now called to believe this good news even though they have not personally seen Jesus in the flesh.

Acts 5:12–16 *in its biblical context*

In our reading from Acts we see the effect of Jesus' commissioning the apostles to carry on the work of his Father. Just as Jesus healed many, so are the apostles able to heal. "Many signs and wonders were done among the people at the hands of the apostles." As was true with Jesus, however, the healings are not an end in themselves; they are one form of preaching the good news of the coming of God's kingdom. The effect of the healings was that "more than ever, believers in the Lord, great numbers of men and women, were added to them."

Revelation 1:9–11a, 12–13, 17–19 *in its biblical context*

The Book of Revelation is a work of apocalyptic literature. This means that it was written in code to people suffering persecution in order to offer them hope. The author of the book introduces himself with the words, "I, John, your brother, who share with you the distress...." The hope that John offers those who are being persecuted is that Jesus, who also suffered persecution and died, has conquered death. In John's vision Jesus says, "Once I was dead, but now I am alive forever and ever." Jesus holds "the keys to death and the netherworld." No persecutor can defeat Jesus, nor can a persecutor defeat a disciple of Jesus.

Just as Jesus rose from the dead, so will those who remain faithful during persecution rise from the dead. Jesus now reigns in heaven. Jesus is "the one who lives." Once Jesus "was dead, but now I am alive forever and ever." It is this good news that we celebrate not only during the Easter season, but at every Sunday liturgy.

Questions for Breaking Open the Word groups are on page 13.

Questions for other faith sharing groups

1. Do you think of peace of mind and heart as a gift or as an accomplishment? Is it a gift that you have received? Explain.

2. Are you willing to believe something based on another person's witness or do you have to see for yourself? To what extent does your Christian faith rest on the witness of others? To what extent does it rely on personal experience?

3. Do you think the risen Christ is with you right now? Why or why not? If so, do you find it comforting or discomforting to think that Jesus hears the entire conversation?

Bible study questions

1. In John's Gospel, who is the first to believe?

2. In John's Gospel, when is the Spirit given to the church?

3. Why are Jesus' words to Thomas also especially appropriate for John's audience?

4. What kind of writing is the Book of Revelation?

5. What is the message of this kind of writing?

THIRD SUNDAY OF EASTER

John 21:1–19 in its biblical context

The end of our Gospel reading from last Sunday sounded like the conclusion to John's Gospel: "Now Jesus did many other signs in the presence of his disciples that are not written in this book. But these are written that you may come to believe that Jesus is the Christ, the Son of God, and that through this belief you may have life in his name" (John 20:30–31). Today's reading follows immediately after this conclusion. Scripture scholars think that chapter 21 of John's Gospel was added to the original Gospel in order to address some problems that the Johannine community was facing, but that it became part of John's Gospel before the original Gospel was published. As we will see, it is closely tied to what precedes it.

Today's reading begins with Jesus' appearance to the disciples at the Sea of Tiberias. John's Gospel had earlier pictured Jesus and his disciples together at the Sea of Tiberias. On that occasion the people were hungry and Jesus fed all of them with five barley loaves and two fish. After this great sign Jesus told his followers that he is "the bread of life" (John 6). Today's story has not only the same setting, but the same food—bread and fish. We are obviously invited to make a connection between the two accounts.

The disciples are fishing all through the night, but they catch nothing. In John's Gospel activities that take place in the night are activities that take place before people have seen the light, have recognized Christ. It is after dawn when the apostles find Jesus standing on the shore, but they do not recognize him. Jesus asks them if they have caught anything to eat. On hearing that they have not, Jesus tells them to cast their net once more. "So they cast it, and were not able to pull it in because of the number of fish." Based on this mighty sign, the beloved disciple recognizes Jesus. "So the disciple whom Jesus loved said to Peter, 'It is the Lord.' " As we noted last week with John's empty tomb story, the beloved disciple is always the first to believe. Love is the best soil for faith.

On hearing this great good news Peter cannot wait for the boat to reach the shore. He leaps into the water. The others soon arrive and find Jesus with "a charcoal fire with fish on it and bread." Jesus invites the disciples to eat. John makes a point of telling us that the disciples recognize Jesus as they eat. "And none of the disciples dared to ask him, 'Who are you?' because they realized it was the Lord." The recognition of Jesus' presence as they are being fed, along with the setting at the Sea of Tiberias, is an invitation to recall Jesus' "bread of life" discourse right after the multiplication of the loaves. John's end-of-the-century audience, looking for the risen Christ, is being invited to recognize that the risen Christ feeds and is present to them too, in Eucharist.

Next Jesus turns to Simon Peter and asks, "Simon, son of John, do you love me more than these?" Remember, we have already been told that this conversation is taking place around a charcoal fire. Earlier in the Gospel when John told us the story of Peter's threefold denial of Christ there was also a charcoal fire. "Now the slaves and the guard were standing around a charcoal fire that they had made. . . . Peter was also standing there keeping warm" (John 18:18a, c). As we read the story of Peter's profession of love we are invited to remember this earlier scene.

Three times Jesus asks Peter, "Do you love me?" Each time Peter responds that he does love Jesus. After each profession of love Jesus instructs Peter to take care of Jesus' flock. Peter is to *feed* and *tend* the sheep. However, Jesus never says, "tend *your* sheep." The sheep continue to belong to Jesus, but Peter is to become the good shepherd who lays down his life for the sheep. This passage reminds us of Jesus' earlier talk about himself as the good shepherd who lays down his life for his sheep (John 10:1–18).

Our passage ends with a warning about the kind of death that Peter will die. Remember, when this Gospel was written Peter had already died a martyr's death during Nero's persecution. Peter is told that someone will "lead you where you do not want to go." Like Jesus, Peter does not want to die, but his fidelity to the mission that

Christ has entrusted to him will end in martyrdom. To die a martyr's death is to glorify God. "He said this signifying by what kind of death he would glorify God."

Finally Jesus says to Peter, "Follow me." Peter did follow the risen Christ by becoming the shepherd of Christ's disciples. Jesus made it clear to Peter that service to his disciples must be rooted in love of Jesus. Love is the basis for the beloved disciple's faith. Love is the basis for Peter's ministry of leadership. John is teaching his end-of-the-century audience, and us, that love must be the basis for all that we do in the name of Jesus Christ.

Acts 5:27–32, 40b–41 in its biblical context

In last week's reading from Acts the apostles were adding greatly to the number of believers as they healed the sick. Between that reading and the appearance before the Sanhedrin that we read about today, a good deal has happened. Luke tells us that because the Sadducees were jealous of the apostles they put them in the public jail. During the night an angel opened the doors of the jail and let them out. The apostles returned to the temple to teach. Finding them teaching again, the court officers brought them to appear before the Sanhedrin. Today's reading begins at this point.

The high priest reminds the apostles that they have been warned to stop teaching in Jesus' name. They evidently do not want to be blamed for the part they played in Jesus' crucifixion: "We gave you strict orders, did we not, to stop teaching in that name? Yet you have filled Jerusalem with your teaching and want to bring this man's blood upon us."

Notice Peter is given prominence as the apostles reply: "But Peter and the apostles said in reply, 'We must obey God rather than men.'" They then report the good news of Easter: "The God of our ancestors raised Jesus, though you had him killed by hanging him on a tree. God exalted him at his right hand as leader and savior to grant Israel repentance and forgiveness of sins." The apostles are witnesses not only of Jesus' crucifixion, but also of his exaltation. There is no way that they can keep silent.

The Lectionary reading skips the next verses. In them Luke tells us that the Sanhedrin is so furious with the apostles that they want to put them to death. However, a Pharisee in the Sanhedrin, Gamaliel, offers his fellow Sanhedrin members some sage advice. He says, "...have nothing to do with these men, and let them go. For if this endeavor or this activity is of human origin, it will destroy itself. But if it comes from God, you will not be able to destroy them; you may even find yourselves fighting against God" (Acts 5:38b–39a).

Persuaded by Gamaliel, the members of the Sanhedrin do not send the apostles back to prison. They just order them once more "to stop speaking in the name of Jesus." The apostles leave rejoicing. They consider it an honor to "suffer dishonor for the sake of the name."

Peter and the other apostles have learned to model themselves after Jesus and to lay down their lives for Jesus' sheep.

Revelation 5:11–14 in its biblical context

In our reading from Acts we heard the apostles claim that God has exalted Jesus at God's right hand. Now, in the Book of Revelation, we see a picture of that exaltation. The scene is God's throne room in heaven. "Every creature in heaven and on earth and under the earth and in the sea, everything in the universe" is giving praise to God and to the lamb that was slain. All creatures cry out:

> "To the one who sits on the throne and to the Lamb
>   be blessing and honor, glory and might,
>   forever and ever."

The lamb, of course, is Jesus. Jesus is compared to a lamb for two reasons. First, Jesus is the new Passover lamb whose blood gives life. Second, Jesus is the lamb in Isaiah's suffering servant song who was "silent and opened not his mouth" (Isa 53:7b).

This song from the Book of Revelation not only claims that Jesus rose from the dead and now reigns with God in heaven; it also claims that Jesus is God. Both God on God's throne and the lamb receive identical praise. After this song proclaiming Jesus' divinity is sung, "the elders fell down and worshiped."

Jesus, who rose from the dead, is a divine person. He now reigns in heaven and all creation pays him homage.

Questions for Breaking Open the Word groups are on page 13.

Questions for other faith sharing groups

1. What do you think Jesus was trying to teach when he said that he is "the bread of life"?

2. Why is it essential that a person with authority act from love rather than from power?

3. Do you think of any other person as belonging to you? Explain. Why do you think Jesus told Peter to "feed my sheep," not "feed your sheep"?

Bible study questions

1. Who is the first to recognize Jesus? Why is this significant?

2. What is Peter's reaction?

3. What is John teaching his audience through this story?

4. Why does Jesus ask Peter, "Do you love me?" three times?

5. What good advice does Gamaliel give?

FOURTH SUNDAY OF EASTER

John 10:27–30 *in its biblical context*

The passage we read today from John's Gospel is part of a very contentious conversation that Jesus is having with some Jews. Immediately preceding today's reading John tells us that Jesus was walking around the temple area when some Jews said to him, " 'How long are you going to keep us in suspense? If you are the Messiah, tell us plainly.' Jesus answered them, 'I told you and you do not believe. The works I do in my Father's name testify to me. But you do not believe, because you are not among my sheep' " (John 10:24b–26). Today's reading picks up the story at this point and contrasts Jesus' sheep with those to whom he is speaking.

In order to understand John's intent in describing this conversation we should remember the situation in which John is writing. The first followers of Jesus did not have to choose between being a Jew and being a follower of Jesus Christ. There were both Jewish Christians and Gentile Christians. As we mentioned earlier, however, by the time John is writing, at the end of the first century AD, those Jews who believed in the divinity of Jesus were being expelled from the synagogues by their fellow Jews. As long as individuals belonged to the synagogue they did not have to participate in emperor worship, an abomination to all Jews, whether believers in Christ or not. Once expelled, however, they no longer had that protection and so would be expected to offer worship to the emperor. Those who refused were subject to persecution and death.

As John writes his Gospel he insists on the divinity of Christ, the very belief that his contemporary Jews might be tempted to deny. We see this in today's reading when Jesus says, "The Father and I are one." John does not want any of his fellow Jews to deny the divinity of Christ for the purpose of avoiding persecution.

So when Jesus tells these Jews, "My sheep hear my voice; I know them, and they follow me," he is contrasting his sheep to the people to whom he is speaking. They do not know Jesus, hear Jesus' voice, or follow him. Rather, they fail to understand what Jesus is saying. As Jesus continues, John pictures him emphasizing the point that John is trying to teach his audience. Jesus says, "I give [my sheep] eternal life, and they shall never perish. No one can take them out of my hand. My Father, who has given them to me, is greater than all, and no one can take them out of the Father's hand." In other words, John's audience need not fear persecution. Those who remain faithful to Christ will be safe in Christ's hands, in God's hands.

This passage recalls to our mind Jesus' description of the good shepherd that appears earlier in chapter 10. In that discourse Jesus drew an analogy between his relationship with the sheep and the Father's relationship with him: "I am the good shepherd, and I know mine and mine know me, just as the Father knows me and I know the Father..." (John 10:14). This relationship is the reason no one can snatch the sheep out of Jesus' hand. The sheep whom Jesus has been given have been given him by the Father, and no one can snatch anything from the Father. It is at this point that Jesus once again identifies himself with the Father. "The Father and I are one."

When Jesus says, "The Father and I are one," he has answered the original question that the Jews had asked regarding whether or not Jesus is the messiah. Jesus is the messiah. Our Gospel selection does not tell us their reaction. Jesus' answer so angers his listeners that they "picked up rocks to stone him" (John 10:31). When asked why they are stoning him they say, "We are not stoning you for a good work but for blasphemy. You, a man, are making yourself God" (John 10:33). Here John states very clearly, as a charge against Jesus, the truth that he is emphasizing: Jesus is God.

We read this Gospel from John during the Easter season because it does insist on Jesus' divinity. Jesus rose from the dead, thus revealing his true identity to his followers. Jesus will take care of his sheep. One need have no fear, even of martyrdom. Jesus gives his sheep "eternal life, and they shall never perish."

Acts 13:14, 43–52 in its biblical context

Our reading from Acts, too, describes a division among the Jews over the identity of Jesus Christ. As we begin today's reading we are told that "Paul and Barnabas continued on from Perga and reached Antioch in Pisidia." Our reading then skips over verses 15–42.

What happens in these intervening verses is that Paul is invited to speak in the synagogue. Paul uses the occasion to remind his fellow Israelites of their history, from the exodus, to David, to John the Baptist, to Jesus. Paul tells his listeners, "We ourselves are proclaiming this good news to you that what God promised our ancestors he has brought to fulfillment for us, [their] children, by raising up Jesus, as it is written in the second psalm, 'You are my son; this day I have begotten you' " (Acts 13:32–33). It is in response to this speech that we are told, "Many Jews and worshipers who were converts to Judaism followed Paul and Barnabas, who spoke to them and urged them to remain faithful to the grace of God."

Not all the Jews, however, were convinced that Jesus was the fulfillment of God's promises to their ancestors. It is these dissenting Jews who contradict Paul and Barnabas. Paul and Barnabas interpret their rejection as the fulfillment of a prophecy in Isaiah. In Isaiah the words are:

> I will make you a light to the nations,
>   that my salvation may reach to the ends of the earth.
>
>   (Isa 49:6b)

In their original context Isaiah was speaking to the exiles in Babylon, giving them hope that God would use their suffering to bring other nations to a knowledge of God. Paul and Barnabas interpret the words to mean that they should become a light to the Gentiles, that they should preach the risen Christ to everyone, not just their fellow Jews.

In the face of persecution, Paul and Barnabas simply move on to another town.

Revelation 7:9, 14b–17 in its biblical context

Again, let us remember the setting and purpose of the Book of Revelation. The book was written to those suffering persecution under the Emperor Domitian (AD 81–AD 96). It offers hope to those who have already lost loved ones to martyrdom and those who are themselves facing martyrdom. Their hope rests in Christ.

In today's reading John has a vision of the heavenly courtroom. In it a great multitude "from every nation, race, people, and tongue" is standing before God's throne and before the Lamb. An elder explains to John that these are the martyrs: "These are the ones who have survived the time of great distress; they have washed their robes and made them white in the blood of the Lamb." This is code for saying that those who were martyred, who remained faithful to Jesus even through death, have been redeemed by Jesus and now reign victorious with him in heaven.

Then John gives us a beautiful picture of just how safe these martyrs are now:

> The one who sits on the throne will shelter them.
> They will not hunger or thirst anymore,
>   nor will the sun or any heat strike them.
> For the Lamb who is in the center of the throne
>   will shepherd them
>   and lead them to springs of life-giving water,
>   and God will wipe away every tear from their eyes.

In all of our readings today we are presented with wonderful news. Jesus is God. Jesus has conquered death. Jesus is the good shepherd who takes care of his sheep. We need have no fear, even in the face of death. Just as Jesus rose from the dead, so shall we, if we but recognize his voice and follow him.

Questions for Breaking Open the Word groups are on page 13.

Questions for other faith sharing groups

1. Why do you think it is important to believe that Jesus is divine, not just that Jesus was a great person and a great teacher?

2. Do you think people are naturally attracted to goodness and truth? Why do you think this is? What do you think it means to "recognize Jesus' voice"?

3. What about Christianity do you think is most hopeful? Why?

Bible study questions

1. In what situation did the Jews in John's audience find themselves?

2. On what teaching is John insisting in the passage we read today?

3. How does Jesus answer the question that some Jews asked him?

4. What does John see in the heavenly courtroom?

5. Why are the martyrs safe?

FIFTH SUNDAY OF EASTER

John 13:31–33a, 34–35 in its biblical context

In last Sunday's reading from John's Gospel John was insisting on Jesus' divinity; not only is Jesus the messiah, but Jesus and the Father are one. In our reading today John is addressing the question, "If Jesus is truly divine, the Word incarnate, then why did he suffer the defeat of the cross?" Today we hear John teach that the cross is not a defeat but the occasion for Jesus' glorification.

The setting for today's reading is that of Judas's betrayal and Jesus' imminent crucifixion. This setting is established by the very first words: "When Judas had left them...." This reminds us that immediately preceding today's passage is Jesus' announcement of Judas's coming betrayal: "...Jesus was deeply troubled and testified, 'Amen, amen, I say to you, one of you will betray me....It is the one to whom I hand the morsel after I have dipped it.' So he dipped the morsel and [took it and] handed it to Judas..." (John 13:21b, 26b). Judas has now left, and Jesus, who, in John's Gospel, knows everything, knows that his crucifixion is imminent.

When Jesus says, "*Now* is the Son of Man glorified, and God is glorified in him," Jesus is teaching his disciples that his imminent crucifixion is not a defeat, but a victory. Through the crucifixion Jesus will be glorified, and the Father will be glorified. The passion and death will be Jesus' glorification because Jesus is choosing to lay down his life as a free gift of love. Jesus is not simply dying. Jesus is returning to the Father, having done what he came to do: to be a revelation of the Father's own love for Jesus and for us.

That the setting for Jesus' words is his imminent death is again made clear when Jesus tells the disciples, "My children, I will be with you only a little while longer." Jesus knows that when he leaves this meal he will be crucified, the most ignominious death possible in the eyes of the disciples. But even death, death on a cross, cannot thwart Jesus' accomplishing his Father's will—the revelation of God's love for God's people. Both Jesus and his Father will be glorified at once.

Next Jesus tells his disciples that he is giving them a new commandment: "I give you a new commandment: love one another. As I have loved you, so you also should love one another." Why is this a new commandment? After all, Deuteronomy has taught the Jews to love God with all their heart, all their soul, and all their strength (Deut 6:5). Leviticus has taught them to love not only their neighbor, but an alien, as themselves (Lev 19:34). Yet Jesus describes his commandment to love as a new commandment.

What is new about the commandment is that the disciples are to model their way of loving on Jesus himself: "As I have loved you, so you also should love one another." How has Jesus loved them? Jesus has loved them by freely laying down his life for them. It is to this kind of self-sacrificing love that Jesus is calling his disciples. In fact, their ability to love others as Jesus has loved them will be the sign through which people will recognize them as disciples of Jesus Christ: "This is how all will know that you are my disciples, if you have love for one another."

As we read this passage during the Easter season we are celebrating Jesus' and the Father's glorification through Christ having been raised up—on the cross and through the resurrection. As the Father has loved Jesus, and the Father and Jesus have loved us, so we are to love one another.

Acts 14:21–27 *in its biblical context*

Our reading from Acts also teaches that suffering is not necessarily a defeat. As today's reading begins, Paul and Barnabas are leaving Derbe and returning to Lystra, Iconium, and Antioch. We know from last Sunday's reading that Paul and Barnabas were persecuted and expelled from Antioch (Acts 13:50). The Lectionary does not include an account of what happened in Lystra and Iconium, but Barnabas and Paul suffered in those cities too. In Iconium there was an attempt to attack and stone them (Acts 14:5), and in Lystra Paul was stoned, dragged out of the city, and left for dead (Acts 14:19).

Why go back? As Paul and Barnabas tell their fellow disciples, exhorting them to persevere in the faith, "It is necessary for us to undergo many hardships to enter the kingdom of God." Paul, Barnabas, and the other disciples are loving both the Jews and the Gentiles of Lystra, Iconium, and Antioch as Jesus loved them. They are laying down their lives for them.

Today's reading also teaches us the importance that Luke places on what we call church structures. (Remember, the Acts of the Apostles is the second volume of a two-volume work, the first being the Gospel according to Luke.) Notice that Paul and Barnabas appoint elders for each church.

Paul and Barnabas are themselves not free agents. Rather, they were sent on mission, a mission that began at Antioch. There, while praying, the Christians in Antioch were told by the Holy Spirit to "set apart for me Barnabas and Saul for the work to which I have called them" (Acts 13:2b). After completing their prayer, " . . . they laid hands on them and sent them off" (Acts 13:3b). Today's reading concludes by describing the end of that mission. When they returned to Antioch, "they called the church together and reported what God had done with them and how he had opened the door of faith to the Gentiles." As teachers, Paul and Barnabas are accountable to the church that sent them on mission.

Revelation 21:1–5a in its biblical context

Our reading from the Book of Revelation is also teaching that suffering is not a defeat but part of the path to victory. Remember, the Book of Revelation is addressed to those suffering persecution. Many of them have lost loved ones to martyrdom. In today's passage John is picturing the final victory of good over evil.

The images John uses to describe the victory of good over evil are a city—"a new Jerusalem"—and "a bride adorned for her husband." The image of a city emphasizes the communal nature of the new order that God will establish. The image of the bride emphasizes the intimate relationship of love that will exist between God and God's people. "Behold, God's dwelling is with the human race. He will dwell with them and they will be his people and God himself will always be with them as their God."

In the new order suffering will be no more. "He will wipe every tear from their eyes, and there shall be no more death or mourning, wailing or pain, for the old order has passed away."

The One who sits on the throne, who makes all things new, is the risen Christ. During this Easter season we celebrate Jesus' victory over sin and suffering. By freely laying down his life, and by rising from the dead, Jesus has given us eternal life.

Questions for Breaking Open the Word groups are on page 13.

Questions for other faith sharing groups

1. Have you tried to come to terms with the mystery of suffering? If so, what thoughts about the mystery of suffering give you the most comfort and satisfaction?

2. How would you describe the way Jesus has loved you? As Jesus' disciple, how would you describe the way you are to love others? How are you doing?

3. Would you spare yourself the suffering you have experienced if you could? Why or why not?

Bible study questions

1. What question is John addressing in today's reading?

2. What response does John give to this question?

3. In what way is Jesus' commandment to love a new commandment?

4. How does Luke show his interest in church structure and accountability in today's reading from Acts?

5. What two images does John use to describe the victory of good over evil? What is he teaching through these images?

SIXTH SUNDAY OF EASTER

John 14:23–29 in its biblical context

In this week's Gospel Jesus is continuing what is called his farewell discourse, his final words to the disciples during his last meal with them on the night before he dies. Today's passage is Jesus' response to a question that one of the disciples has asked: "Judas, not the Iscariot, said to him, 'Master, [then] what happened that you will reveal yourself to us and not to the world?'" (John 14:22). Judas asks this question because Jesus has just assured the disciples, "I will not leave you orphans; I will come to you. In a little while the world will no longer see me, but you will see me, because I live and you will live" (John 14:18–19).

As is so often the case with John's Gospel, two levels of conversation are taking place at the same time. On the one level, Jesus is talking to his disciples on the night before he dies. On another level, John is talking to his end-of-the-century audience, who are disappointed that Jesus has not yet returned on the clouds of heaven. John wants his contemporaries to realize that the risen Jesus dwells in their midst.

Jesus responds to Judas's question by saying, "Whoever loves me will keep my word, and my Father will love him, and we will come to him and make our dwelling with him." In other words, love is the bond that results in Jesus and the Father dwelling with Jesus' disciples. The world, those who do not love Jesus or keep his word, will not be able to discern or experience this indwelling. Nevertheless, Jesus and the Father will be present to those who love them.

In addition to his own and the Father's presence, Jesus promises the disciples that they will receive "the Advocate, the Holy Spirit, whom the Father will send in my name...." John's is the only Gospel that uses the word *Advocate,* also translated *Paraclete,* to refer to the Holy Spirit. The word means a helper or counselor. Here Jesus tells his disciples what the role of the Spirit will be: the Holy Spirit "will teach you everything and remind you of all that I told you."

The disciples were not able to understand the significance of all they experienced when they were with Jesus before his crucifixion. The Holy Spirit will remind the disciples of all that Jesus told them, not just in the sense of helping them recall what Jesus said, but in the sense of helping them understand what they were previously unable to understand.

Next Jesus gives the disciples the gift of peace: "Peace I leave with you; my peace I give to you. Not as the world gives do I give it to you." Although Jesus instructs the disciples not to be troubled or afraid when he leaves them, the disciples are afraid. After the crucifixion they are huddled in a locked room in fear (see John 20:19). As we noted on the second Sunday of Easter, when Jesus appears to them he once again offers them the gift of peace (see John 20:19, 21).

Jesus tries to comfort the disciples by telling them that although he is going away, he will return. If they love Jesus they will rejoice that he is going to the Father.

Once more we see that love is the key to receiving the gifts that Jesus is offering. Those who love Jesus will experience the presence of Jesus, the Father, and the Spirit. Those who love Jesus will also experience the gift of peace.

Acts 15:1–2, 22–29 *in its biblical context*

In our reading from Acts we see the Holy Spirit teaching the church, just as Jesus promised the Spirit would in our Gospel reading from John. A problem has arisen: "Some who had come down from Judea were instructing the brothers, 'Unless you are circumcised according to the Mosaic practice, you cannot be saved.' " In other words, some were teaching that Gentiles who wanted to follow Christ must embrace Judaism, must follow the Jewish law, just as Jews who followed Christ followed the law.

Paul and Barnabas, who have just returned from preaching to the Gentiles, disagree strongly with this idea. Since neither side of this disagreement can simply ask Jesus what he would have them do, how can they come to an authoritative decision? The scene has been set for the first church council, the Council of Jerusalem.

The Lectionary passage tells us what led up to the Jerusalem council and describes how the decision was promulgated. However, it omits telling us how Paul and Barnabas arrived in Jerusalem, how the apostles and elders met and discussed the problem for a long time, how Peter insisted that the Gentiles should not have to follow the law since they are saved by grace, and how James contributed to their reaching a decision (see Acts 15:3–21). This section is very important because it illustrates how decisions were made in the early church. The Holy Spirit was understood to be with the early church leaders as they met and discussed the issues in an attempt to discern God's will.

As we can tell from the wording of the letter used to promulgate the decision, the church leaders believed that the Holy Spirit had guided them in their deliberations. "It is the decision of the Holy Spirit and of us...." The decision was that Gentiles who wanted to become disciples of Jesus Christ need only "abstain from meat sacrificed to idols, from blood, from meats of strangled animals, and from unlawful marriage." Circumcision was not required.

The reading from Acts illustrates the role of the Spirit that Jesus was teaching in our Gospel reading from John. The Spirit dwells in the church and instructs the church as we seek to be faithful disciples of Jesus Christ in new cultural situations.

Revelation 21:10–14, 22–23 *in its biblical context*

In the passage from the Book of Revelation we continue to read John's description of the heavenly Jerusalem, the final victory of good over evil. The heavenly Jerusalem is built on God's relationship of covenant love with Israel and on the church. That is why it has twelve gates inscribed with the names of the twelve tribes of the Israelites, and why the foundations of the stone walls are inscribed with the names of the twelve apostles.

The new Jerusalem has no temple. The Jewish temple in Jerusalem was understood to be the place where God dwelt with God's people. By the time the Book of Revelation was written, toward the end of the first century, the second temple in Jerusalem had been destroyed (AD 70). By saying that the new Jerusalem will have no temple the author is saying that a temple is no longer necessary because God dwells in the whole city. "I saw no temple in the city for its temple is the Lord God almighty and the Lamb." Nor will the city have need of sun or moon. "The glory of God gave it light, and its lamp was the Lamb."

In all three of our readings we are taught that God—Father, Son, and Spirit—dwells with us. If we love God and follow God's word we will experience God's indwelling and the gift of peace that accompanies the presence of God in our lives.

Questions for Breaking Open the Word groups are on page 13.

Questions for other faith sharing groups

1. When have you been most aware of God's dwelling with you?

2. Do you try to follow the guidance of the Spirit in your life? How do you go about discerning the Spirit's will?

3. Do you practice consensus decision making? How do you go about it? Why might a decision reached by consensus be wiser than a decision reached by oneself?

Bible study questions

1. What does Jesus promise the disciples during his last meal with them?

2. Why is this promise particularly important for John's end-of-the-century audience?

3. What problem that we read about in Acts confronted the early church?

4. What solution was reached? How was it reached?

5. Why is there no temple in the heavenly Jerusalem?

THE ASCENSION OF THE LORD

Luke 24:46–53 in its biblical context

In today's readings we have two accounts of the ascension by the same author, one from Luke's Gospel and one from the Acts of the

Apostles, the second volume of Luke's two-part work. Luke's two accounts differ in detail. By noting both the similarities and the differences in the two accounts, we will be able to discern what Luke is teaching by the way in which he tells the story.

Today's Gospel begins in the middle of an appearance story. Jesus appears in the midst of the disciples, who initially fail to recognize him. Jesus shows them his wounds, invites them to touch him, and eats with them. Next, Jesus uses the law, the prophets, and the psalms to show the disciples that, even though he is the crucified one, he is the fulfillment of God's promise to Israel. It is at this point that our Lectionary reading joins the story.

Today's reading begins with the commissioning of the disciples. The risen Christ tells the disciples that they are witnesses to the fact that "it is written that the Christ would suffer and rise from the dead on the third day and that repentance, for the forgiveness of sin, would be preached in his name to all the nations, beginning from Jerusalem." Here we see Luke's emphasis on forgiveness and universality. All nations are to hear the good news. We know from reading the Acts of the Apostles that the disciples did not understand that all nations were now invited into covenant love until sometime later (see Acts 10).

Jesus then tells the apostles to remain in Jerusalem until they are clothed with power from on high. After Jesus parts from them, that is, after Jesus ascends into heaven (more about this when we discuss today's reading from Acts), the disciples return to Jerusalem to await the coming of the Spirit. While they waited, "they were continually in the temple praising God."

The temple is where Luke began his story with Zechariah awaiting the fulfillment of God's promises. Jerusalem is central to the organization of both Luke and Acts. That is why Luke pictures the commissioning, along with the ascension, in Jerusalem and its environs rather than in Galilee (see Matt 28:16). From Jerusalem the good news of Jesus Christ, the fulfillment of God's promises, will be proclaimed to the whole world.

Acts 1:1–11 in its biblical context

Our reading from Acts is the very beginning of the second volume of Luke's two-volume work. At the beginning of his Gospel Luke also addresses Theophilus. Luke tells Theophilus that he is writing "an orderly sequence for you, most excellent Theophilus, so that you may realize the certainty of the teachings you have received" (Luke 1:3–4).

Luke begins Acts by summarizing what he wrote in the Gospel. "In the first book, Theophilus, I dealt with all that Jesus did and taught until the day he was taken up, after giving instructions through the Holy Spirit to the apostles whom he had chosen...." As Luke ended his Gospel he said that Jesus ascended into heaven: "As he [Jesus] blessed them he parted from them and was taken up to heaven" (Luke

24:51). In Luke's Gospel the ascension takes place on the first day of the week, the day on which the tomb is discovered empty and Jesus appears first to the two disciples on the road to Emmaus and then to the disciples in Jerusalem.

In Acts, however, the ascension is forty days later. Luke says that Jesus "presented himself alive to them [the disciples] by many proofs after he had suffered, appearing to them during forty days and speaking about the kingdom of God." The number forty often appears in scripture. The Israelites wandered forty years in the desert. Jesus was tempted for forty days. The number is not meant to be precise, but to say, "at the appointed time," at the time when God's work was accomplished and God's will was being fulfilled. Luke uses the occasion of the ascension both to conclude his account of Jesus' life, death, and resurrection, and to begin his account of the acts of Jesus' apostles and disciples who were acting in Jesus' name through the power of Jesus' Spirit.

As Luke ends his Gospel he pictures Jesus telling his disciples to "stay in the city until you are clothed with power from on high" (Luke 24:49). In today's reading from Acts Jesus repeats that instruction: "While meeting with them, he enjoined them not to depart from Jerusalem, but to wait for 'the promise of the Father about which you have heard me speak; for John baptized with water, but in a few days you will be baptized with the Holy Spirit.'"

The apostles then ask Jesus if he is "going to restore the kingdom to Israel." The apostles are evidently still hoping that Jesus will be a political messiah. Jesus tells them that the timing of God's actions is not for them to know, but he promises them, "you will receive power when the Holy Spirit comes upon you, and you will be my witnesses in Jerusalem, throughout Judea and Samaria, and to the ends of the earth." With these words Luke is summarizing the story he will tell in the Acts of the Apostles in which the apostles are Jesus' witnesses first in Jerusalem, then throughout Judea and Samaria, and finally to the ends of the then known world, Rome.

Luke is the only New Testament author to dramatize the ascension rather than just to report it. "When he had said this, as they were looking on, he was lifted up, and a cloud took him from their sight. While they were looking intently at the sky as he was going, suddenly two men dressed in white garments stood beside them." These two men are reminiscent of the "two men in dazzling garments" (Luke 24:4) who appeared at the empty tomb. In today's story they fulfill the same function that they did earlier; they explain the significance of the event that the apostles are witnessing. "Men of Galilee, why are you standing there looking at the sky? This Jesus who has been taken up from you into heaven will return in the same way as you have seen him going into heaven."

Today's Lectionary reading ends here. The Acts of the Apostles tells us that the apostles "returned to Jerusalem" (Acts 1:12), where they would await the coming of the Spirit.

Ephesians 1:17–23 in its biblical context

As the Letter to the Ephesians begins, the author prays that God will give the Ephesians "a Spirit of wisdom and revelation resulting in knowledge of him [God]." He then goes on to describe the exercise of God's might that God has revealed through Jesus Christ: "raising him from the dead and seating him at his right hand in the heavens, far above every principality, authority, power, and dominion, and every name that is named not only in this age but also in the one to come."

Today the church glorifies the Father and his Son, Jesus Christ, enthroned at God's right hand, as we wait in joyful expectation for the coming of his Spirit on Pentecost.

Questions for Breaking Open the Word groups are on page 13.

Questions for other faith sharing groups

1. In your own words, what do you think we are celebrating on the feast of the ascension?

2. Do you believe your baptism has commissioned you to do anything? What are you commissioned to do?

3. How do you personally carry on the mission of Jesus Christ?

Bible study questions

1. What did Jesus commission the disciples to do?

2. What two themes does Luke emphasize in his commissioning story?

3. What are the disciples instructed to do after the ascension?

4. What is meant by the number forty in Acts?

5. How does Ephesians describe the honor given Jesus after his resurrection?

SEVENTH SUNDAY OF EASTER

John 17:20–26 in its biblical context

Today's reading is the end of Jesus' farewell discourse to the disciples, which we have been reading over the last two Sundays. Jesus prays for those who will come to believe in him through the disciples' witness: "Holy Father, I pray not only for them, but also for those who will believe in me through their word, so that they may all be one. . . . " In other words, Jesus prays for those who will believe in him through the centuries, including us. If we look carefully at Jesus' prayer we can see both why Jesus wants his followers to remain one, and how we might succeed in doing that.

The reason unity among Jesus' followers is all-important is that our ability to witness to Jesus diminishes if we cannot maintain unity with one another. Jesus names this fact twice in today's reading. He prays that "they may all be one ... *that the world may believe that you sent me.*" He then repeats this prayer, "...that they may be brought to perfection as one, *that the world may know that you sent me....*" When Christians fail to be united with one another we are ineffective witnesses of the good news to those who do not yet know Christ.

Jesus and the Father are one because they love each other. Jesus prays that those who come to believe in him will be one as the Father and Son are one: "...so that they may all be one, as you, Father, are in me and I in you, that they also may be in us...." This prayer, too, Jesus repeats, "...that the love with which you loved me may be in them and I in them."

We see, then, that the source of unity among Christians is not merely the unity of human affection, or the bond that is formed from mutual effort and cooperation. Rather it is a participation in the mutual love the Father and the Son have for each other. Jesus, as the one who reveals the Father's love, does not want his followers simply to know that the Father and Son love each other, but to participate in that love, to live in it themselves. As we Christians learn to dwell in that love, we will learn to love one another and come to that unity for which Jesus prayed.

Jesus also prays that his followers may be with him so that they may see his glory: "I wish that where I am they also may be with me, that they may see my glory that you gave me, because you loved me before the foundation of the world." To see the glory of God is to witness God's saving acts, to witness some visible manifestation of God's divinity. In John's Gospel Jesus' glorification is his passion, death, and resurrection, because this is the manifestation of God's greatest saving act. Through Jesus God has redeemed the world.

However, the world has not received its Savior. Nevertheless, as John claims in his prologue:

> ...the Word became flesh
> and made his dwelling among us,
> and we saw his glory,
> the glory as of the Father's only Son,
> full of grace and truth. (John 1:14)

Only if we, Jesus' disciples, live in unity will Jesus' glory, Jesus' divinity and his saving acts, become a visible manifestation to the world of the Father's saving love.

Acts 7:55–60 in its biblical context

Today's reading from Acts is the middle of a story. Stephen is one of seven men chosen by the apostles and disciples to serve the church (Acts 6:5). As Luke tells the story, Stephen's ministry, made powerful by the Holy Spirit, reflects Jesus' own ministry. The scene we read today occurs just as Stephen finishes addressing the Sanhedrin after his arrest (see Acts 7:1–53).

Luke tells us that Stephen "looked up intently to heaven and saw the glory of God and Jesus standing at the right hand of God...." As we just discussed, to see God's glory is to see some manifestation of God's divinity and God's saving acts. Stephen sees exactly what we celebrated on the feast of the ascension: while Jesus' followers carry on his mission on earth Jesus already reigns victorious in heaven. This vision affirms the content of Stephen's speech to the Sanhedrin—that when they persecuted Jesus they persecuted God's holy one. The members of the Sanhedrin are so angry that they "covered their ears, and rushed upon him together."

As Stephen dies his words recall Jesus' words on the cross as they appear in Luke's Gospel: "Lord Jesus, receive my spirit" (see Luke 23:46), and, "Lord, do not hold this sin against them" (see Luke 23:34). These parallel accounts are teaching that those like Stephen, who become Jesus' witnesses to the world, are carrying on Jesus' own ministry.

Notice that the witnesses to Stephen's martyrdom "laid down their cloaks at the feet of a young man named Saul." Luke inserts this detail to introduce Paul, who will be the central figure of the second half of Acts. Before his conversion, Paul was a persecutor of the church. After his conversion Paul became the foremost witness to the Gentiles. Stephen's martyrdom was the beginning of a persecution in Jerusalem that caused many new Christians to flee, thus spreading the Gospel to Judea and Samaria.

Revelation 22:12–14, 16–17, 20 in its biblical context

Today's passage from the Book of Revelation, taken from the last verses of the book, continues to offer John's persecuted audience the hope that the book as a whole offers them. Their persecution will not last much longer. Jesus, already victorious in heaven, says, "Behold, I am coming soon. I bring with me the recompense I will give to each according to his deeds." The persecution will end soon. Those who have been faithful to Jesus will, like Jesus, have eternal life. Those who have not, as well as the persecutors, will be held accountable for their actions.

Nor need those who have lost relatives to martyrdom grieve over them. Those relatives are now with Jesus in heaven. Jesus assures those suffering persecution of this truth when he says, "Blessed are they who wash their robes so as to have the right to the tree of life and enter the city through its gates." The martyrs have washed their robes in the blood of the lamb (see Rev 7:14). Because of Jesus' redemptive acts they now have access to eternal life—they "have the right to the tree of life."

You might wonder why the Book of Revelation teaches its good news in code. This is a characteristic of all apocalyptic literature.

Code is used so that if the person suffering persecution—the Christian—is caught reading the message of hope by the persecutors (in this case, the Roman soldiers), the persecutors will not understand what the Christian is reading. Otherwise the Christian would be killed.

The book ends with an invitation to everyone to come to Christ: "Let the one who thirsts come forward, and the one who wants it receive the gift of life-giving water," an obvious reference to baptism. Jesus promises that the persecution will end soon: "Yes, I am coming soon." The people who long for Jesus' definitive victory over evil to be visible in their lives on earth pray, "Come, Lord Jesus!"

Questions for Breaking Open the Word groups are on page 13.

Questions for other faith sharing groups

1. Have you personally experienced the pain of disunity in Christ's body, the church? How?

2. What can you do personally to promote unity in the church?

3. In what ways do you witness to the world the good news of Jesus Christ?

Bible study questions

1. For whom and for what does Jesus pray in today's Gospel?

2. Why is unity essential for Christians?

3. What is the source of unity among Christians?

4. What is Luke teaching by drawing parallels between Stephen's ministry and Jesus' ministry?

5. Why is the Book of Revelation written in code?

Pentecost through Corpus Christi

Pentecost Sunday

John 20:19–23 in its biblical context

In John's Gospel the Spirit is given to the church on Easter evening during Jesus' first postresurrection appearance to the disciples. On "the first day of the week," that is, Easter Sunday morning, Mary Magdalene went to the tomb and discovered it empty. She told Peter and the beloved disciple, who also ran to the tomb and discovered only burial cloths. Next, Jesus appeared to Mary Magdalene and instructed her to tell the disciples that Jesus is "going to my Father and your Father, to my God and your God" (John 20:17). Mary does as she is instructed. It is on that same evening that the scene we read in today's Gospel occurs.

Today's Gospel is part of the Gospel selection that we read on the second Sunday of Easter (John 20:19–31). In the commentary for that Sunday we discussed Jesus' gift of peace, given both here and at the Last Supper (John 14:27–28). We also discussed why Jesus would have shown the disciples his hands and his side.

We did not discuss John's comment, "the disciples rejoiced when they saw the Lord." The fact that the disciples rejoiced is a fulfillment of a promise that Jesus made to the disciples at their last meal together (John 14:28). Jesus said to his disciples, "Are you discussing with one another what I said, 'A little while and you will not see me, and again a little while and you will see me'? Amen, amen, I say to you, you will weep and mourn, while the world rejoices; you will grieve, but your grief will become joy" (John 16:19–20). Then Jesus once more gives them the gift of peace: "Peace be with you."

Jesus then commissions the disciples to carry on his mission to the world. Jesus says, "As the Father has sent me, so I send you." At Jesus' last meal with the disciples he had earlier said what that mission is. Addressing his words to the Father, Jesus said that the Father has given his son "authority over all people, so that he may give eternal life to all you gave him. Now this is eternal life, that they should know you, the only true God, and the one whom you sent, Jesus Christ" (John 17:2–3).

How are the disciples to have the power to carry on Jesus' mission to the world? This ministry can be carried out only through the power of the Holy Spirit. "And when he had said this, he breathed on them and said to them, 'Receive the Holy Spirit.' " This description of Jesus *breathing* on the disciples is one of John's many allusions to the Book of Genesis. When God created the man in the garden God "formed man out of the clay of the ground and blew into his nostrils the breath of life, and so man became a living being" (Gen 2:7). Genesis is a story of creating the material world. John's Gospel is the story of God's re-creation, of God's establishing a new spiritual order through Jesus Christ.

In the new spiritual order people are offered not only eternal life but the forgiveness of their sins: "Whose sins you forgive are forgiven them, and whose sins you retain are retained." Scripture scholars suggest that with these words John is describing the effect of baptism, which is the forgiveness of sin. Those whose sins are retained are those who reject the gift of salvation that is offered them and are not initiated into the community. The disciples will have the power to carry on Jesus' mission only in and through the Spirit.

Acts 2:1–11 in its biblical context

In the Acts of the Apostles the Spirit is given to the church on the feast of Pentecost. Luke says, "When the time for Pentecost was fulfilled...." When we hear the word *Pentecost* we think of our celebration of the coming of the Spirit. However, Pentecost was a Jewish feast before it was a Christian feast. On the fiftieth day after Passover the Jews celebrated their covenant relationship with God by recalling Moses receiving the law on Mount Sinai. Just as the Gospel accounts reinterpret the significance of the meal celebrated on Passover by telling the story of Jesus instituting the Eucharist, so the Acts of the Apostles reinterprets the significance of the feast of Pentecost, making it a celebration of the gift of the Spirit to the church.

Notice that Luke says, "The time of Pentecost was *fulfilled.*" This is an expression used to describe the end of a time of waiting. Luke has used this traditional expression before. When Luke begins the story of Jesus' journey to Jerusalem to face his death, Luke says, "When the days for his being taken up were fulfilled, he resolutely determined to journey to Jerusalem" (Luke 9:51). The stage has been set for a momentous event.

Luke tells us that "suddenly there came from the sky a noise like a strong driving wind, and it filled the entire house in which they were. Then there appeared to them tongues as of fire, which parted and came to rest on each one of them." Wind and fire are traditional symbols for the presence of God. When Third Isaiah describes the coming of the Lord at the gathering of all the nations, he says, "Lo, the LORD shall come in fire, / his chariots like the whirlwind" (Isa 66:15). Notice that the fire rests on each person. This is to say that the Spirit has come to dwell in each person.

Luke then describes the coming of the Spirit by dramatizing its effect: because of the coming of the Spirit the apostles were able to preach the gospel to all nations. Earlier in Acts, when describing the ascension, Luke pictures Jesus telling the apostles, "But you will receive power when the holy Spirit comes upon you, and you will be my witnesses in Jerusalem, throughout Judea and Samaria, and to the ends of the earth" (Acts 1:8). At Pentecost the apostles did receive power from the Spirit. Luke says that "there were devout Jews from every nation under heaven staying in Jerusalem. At this sound, they gathered in a large crowd, but they were confused because each one heard them speaking in his own language." Because of the Spirit's power the gospel will be heard in every nation.

Although the two accounts that we read today about the Spirit being given to the church are very different, each does describe a very important result of the gift of the Spirit. John teaches us that it is the Spirit who gives disciples, including us, the power to carry on Jesus' mission to the world. Luke teaches us that through the power of the Spirit the gospel will be preached to every nation.

1 Corinthians 12:3b–7, 12–13 in its biblical context

In our reading from 1 Corinthians Paul teaches us that not only the power to carry on Jesus' ministry but the very ability to acknowledge that "Jesus is Lord" is a gift of the Holy Spirit. "No one can say, 'Jesus is Lord,' except by the Holy Spirit."

Many gifts are given to the church to carry out Jesus' mission. "To each individual the manifestation of the Spirit is given for some benefit." In Acts, as the tongue of fire appeared over each person's head, we understood that the Spirit dwells in each person. Now we learn that that indwelling is a gift not just to the individual but to the community. Individuals are to use their spiritual gifts for the good of Christ's body, the church.

Finally, Paul emphasizes the fact that Christ's body, the church, is one body: "As a body is one though it has many parts, and all the parts of the body, though many, are one body, so also Christ. For in one Spirit we were all baptized into one body, whether Jews or Greeks, slaves or free persons, and we were all given to drink of one Spirit." Last Sunday we heard Jesus pray fervently for the unity of his body, the church. Now we understand that all those who are baptized into Christ are baptized into one body, and that the Spirit is our source of unity.

Questions for Breaking Open the Word groups are on page 13.

Questions for other faith sharing groups

1. When you pray, to whom do you most often address your prayer: to the Father, to Jesus, to the Holy Spirit? Do you ever pray specifically to the Holy Spirit? When? Why?

2. Do you have a personal experience of the power of the Spirit? What is it?

3. Why do you think wind and fire are so often used as symbols to describe the presence of the Spirit?

Bible study questions

1. In John's Gospel when is the Spirit given to the church?

2. As the disciples carry on Jesus' mission, what two gifts will they offer the world?

3. In Acts when is the Spirit given to the church?

4. What is the effect of the coming of the Spirit in Acts? How is this effect described?

5. According to 1 Corinthians, why do people receive spiritual gifts?

The Solemnity of the Most Holy Trinity, Sunday after Pentecost

John 16:12–15 in its biblical context

The scene for today's reading is once more Jesus' farewell discourse to his disciples on the night before he dies. Jesus knows that the disciples are simply unable to understand what he is telling them and that they will be equally unable to understand the events that they will soon encounter: Jesus' arrest and his scandalous death on a cross. Jesus acknowledges their inability to understand when he says, "I have much more to tell you, but you cannot bear it now."

Once Jesus has departed, how are the disciples to learn the truth? Jesus assures the disciples that "the Spirit of truth . . . will guide you to all truth." We just read, on Pentecost Sunday, John's account of the disciples receiving that Spirit of truth on the evening of the resurrection when Jesus appears to them: " . . . he breathed on them and said to them, 'Receive the holy Spirit' " (John 20:22). In John's Gospel, Jesus fulfills both his promise to return and his promise of the gift of the Spirit on Easter Sunday evening.

Jesus tells the disciples that when the Spirit of truth comes, "he will guide you to all truth" and "will declare to you the things that are coming." Jesus is not saying that the gift that the Holy Spirit will give to the disciples is knowledge about inevitable future events. The "things that are coming," in this context, are Jesus' passion, death, and resurrection. The disciples will be frightened and disillusioned by these events. Once they receive the Spirit they will understand the events in an entirely new light.

The Spirit of truth will not "speak on his own," but "will speak what he hears." Jesus himself is the revelation of the Father's love. However, the world has not yet understood this revelation or the mighty saving act that the Father has accomplished through Jesus. So the Spirit will teach the same truth that Jesus has taught to a world that has not yet understood it.

The Spirit will glorify Jesus: "He will glorify me." As we discussed before, to see Jesus' glory is to witness Jesus' saving acts and to witness some visible manifestation of Jesus' divinity. In John's Gospel, Jesus' glory is revealed when he is lifted up, both on the cross and in the resurrection (John 12:27–36). The Spirit will glorify Jesus by making the truth about his death and resurrection known to his disciples.

Just before Jesus' arrest in the garden he showed that he understood that his crucifixion would reveal the Father's glory. Jesus said, " 'I am troubled now. Yet what should I say? "Father, save me from this hour"? But it was for this purpose that I came to this hour. Father, glorify your name.' Then a voice came from heaven, 'I have glorified it and will glorify it again' " (John 12:27–28). Unlike Jesus, the disciples will not immediately see Jesus' glory or the Father's glory in the "things that are to come," but with the help of the Spirit of truth they will eventually understand.

Our reading ends with an emphasis on the fact that the Holy Spirit will reveal not a new truth but the same truth that Jesus himself has revealed. Twice Jesus says, "he will take from what is mine and declare it to you." However, the truth that is Jesus' is also the Father's. "Everything that the Father has is mine." On this Trinity Sunday we celebrate the Father, Son, and Spirit, who share the same truth: God is love. The Son has revealed the Father's love, and the Spirit has continued to teach this revelation through the centuries.

Proverbs 8:22–31 in its biblical context

In today's passage from Proverbs, personified wisdom is describing her role in creation:

> "The LORD possessed me, the beginning of his ways,
> 　the forerunner of his prodigies of long ago;
> from of old I was poured forth,
> 　at the first, before the earth.... "

When we read of wisdom being poured forth before creation we think of the Holy Spirit. When we read of someone being present with the Father before the creation of the world we think of the preexistent Word who became flesh (John 1:1–14). However, the author of Proverbs did not share our belief in the Trinity. Rather, in describing wisdom, the author is personifying one of God's attributes.

Wisdom is responsible for the order of creation:

> " ...when he made firm the skies above,
> 　when he fixed fast the foundations of the earth;

when he set for the sea its limit,
    so that the waters should not transgress his command;
then was I beside him as his craftsman...."

The author's purpose in describing this order is to teach that, just as there is right order in creation, so should there be right order in relationships. In the passage immediately following today's Lectionary passage the author urges his readers to obey wisdom as they live their lives:

So now, O children, listen to me;
    instruction and wisdom do not reject!
Happy the man who obeys me,
    and happy those who keep my ways....
(Prov 8:32–33)

Romans 5:1–5 in its biblical context

Today, in his Letter to the Romans, Paul teaches us the truth that has been revealed through Jesus Christ: "...since we have been justified by faith, we have peace with God through our Lord Jesus Christ, through whom we have gained access by faith to this grace in which we stand."

Because we now have peace with God through Jesus, Paul boasts not only of this good news, but even of his afflictions. Afflictions work toward good in that they produce character and hope. Paul knows that hope will not be disappointed. Why? Because the Father's love, revealed through Christ, has been poured out into our hearts through the Holy Spirit.

In this passage the Spirit plays the role that, in the reading from John, Jesus promised the Spirit would play: the Spirit leads every generation to understand the truth of the Father's love that has been revealed by Jesus Christ.

Questions for Breaking Open the Word groups are on page 13.

Questions for other faith sharing groups

1. When you pray, do you pray to one person in the Trinity more than to another? If so, do you know why? Explain.

2. Why do you think Catholics begin and end their prayers with the sign of the cross? (Think both in terms of the words and of the motions.)

3. What role does the Spirit play in your life?

Bible study questions

1. Once Jesus has departed, how are the disciples to learn the truth?

2. What does Jesus mean when he says that the Spirit "will declare to you the things that are coming"?

3. What about creation is the author of Proverbs describing in today's reading?

4. What is his purpose in giving his audience this description?

5. Why is Paul certain that our hope will not be disappointed?

THE SOLEMNITY OF THE MOST HOLY BODY AND BLOOD OF CHRIST, CORPUS CHRISTI, SUNDAY AFTER TRINITY SUNDAY

Luke 9:11b–17 in its biblical context

Today, as we celebrate the great gift that we have been given in the Eucharist, the body and blood of Christ, our Gospel is not Luke's account of the Last Supper but his account of the multiplication of the loaves. However, today's story alludes to Luke's account of the Last Supper, at which Jesus institutes the Eucharist. As we look at today's story closely, remembering this allusion, we will see a meaning in the story that we may have previously missed.

On first reading today's Gospel appears to be a miracle story: There is not enough food for everyone. Jesus takes action. Everyone is fed and there is lots left over. The lesson: Jesus can work miracles. However, a miracle story, a distinct literary form, has certain characteristics and a certain emphasis that this story lacks. In a miracle story the storyteller makes a point of claiming that Jesus' mighty action brought about the miraculous result and emphasizes this fact by having the crowd react with awe (see Luke 5:12–16 as an example). Neither of these elements is present in today's Gospel. As the story is told, if you had been a member of the crowd, you would not have known that anything of an unusual nature had occurred.

In addition, miracle stories have a precise function: they center the reader's attention on the identity of Jesus, on Jesus' divinity and authority. In today's Gospel, the reader's attention is directed away from what Jesus can do and onto what the apostles are asked to do. Why?

As the story begins, Jesus is attending to the needs of the crowd: "Jesus spoke to the crowds about the kingdom of God, and he healed those who needed to be cured." The apostles bring an additional need to Jesus' attention: the crowd is hungry. However, the apostles are not asking Jesus to respond to this need. They are asking him to send the crowd away, to take no responsibility to feed them.

Jesus does not send the crowd away. Neither does Jesus say, "I will feed the crowd." Rather, he says, "Give them some food yourselves." With this response the storyteller puts the emphasis not on what Jesus can do, but on what Jesus is asking his followers to do. The Twelve think that Jesus' words are completely unrealistic. They say, "Five loaves and two fish are all we have, unless we ourselves go and buy food for all these people."

It is in the next scene that Luke alludes to the Last Supper. He describes Jesus' action with words that are very close to the words Jesus uses when he institutes the Eucharist. In today's story Luke tells us that "taking the five loaves and the two fish, and looking up to heaven, he said the blessing over them, broke them, and gave them to the disciples to set before the crowd." In describing the Last Supper, Luke will tell us that "he took the bread, said the blessing, broke it, and gave it to them, saying, 'This is my body, which will be given for you; do this in memory of me'" (Luke 22:19). Today's Gospel account is obviously alluding to the account of the institution of the Eucharist. Why?

Jesus told the disciples to feed the crowd themselves. They felt that this was beyond their ability. With Jesus' help, however, the crowd was fed: "They all ate and were satisfied. And when the leftover fragments were picked up, they filled twelve wicker baskets."

By alluding to the Eucharist Luke is reminding his readers that they—we—are not alone. Christ is present in us through the Eucharist. With Christ's help we have the power to respond to the hungry and not send them away. The twelve baskets left over symbolize Luke's teaching that if we respond to the needs of the hungry we will discover that there will be enough for everyone.

Genesis 14:18–20 in its biblical context

In its context in Genesis today's passage is about a king of Salem, Melchizedek, who brought bread and wine as gifts to Abraham after Abraham had defeated his political enemies. The enemies had captured Abraham's nephew, Lot, and had taken his goods. Salem is the same part of Canaan that will later become Jerusalem.

In addition to being a king, Melchizedek is described as "a priest of God Most High." Melchizedek blesses both Abraham and God, to whom he attributes Abraham's victory. In response Abraham gives Melchizedek "a tenth of everything."

We read this passage as we celebrate the Solemnity of the Body and Blood of Christ because this mysterious figure, Melchizedek, became a *type* for Christ. To say that Melchizedek is a type for Christ is to say that he prefigures or foreshadows Christ in some way. Melchizedek foreshadows Christ in that he is both king and priest, and he offers bread and wine as a gift and a blessing. However, the bread and wine that Jesus offers are his own body and blood.

1 Corinthians 11:23–26 in its biblical context

Our passage from 1 Corinthians comes in the midst of Paul's correcting the Corinthians for their failures. Immediately before today's passage Paul says, "When you meet in one place, then, it is not to eat the Lord's supper, for in eating, each one goes ahead with his own supper, and one goes hungry while another gets drunk. Do you not have houses in which you can eat and drink? Or do you show contempt for the church of God and make those who have nothing feel ashamed? What can I say to you?" (1 Cor 11:20–22).

We read what Paul does say in today's Gospel. Paul is reminding the Corinthians that their celebration of Eucharist is to be in remembrance of Jesus. Jesus was an example of self-sacrificing love, not an example of selfishness. After today's description of Jesus' institution of the Eucharist Paul concludes, "Therefore, whoever eats the bread or drinks the cup of the Lord unworthily will have to answer for the body and blood of the Lord" (1 Cor 11:27).

Both the Gospel and the reading from 1 Corinthians are teaching us that we are not really eucharistic people if we receive Jesus' body and blood ourselves and then act as though we have no responsibility for the poor.

Questions for Breaking Open the Word groups are on page 13.

Questions for other faith sharing groups

1. The Eucharist is central to Catholic worship and Catholic identity. Is the Eucharist central to your worship and identity? Explain.

2. What do you think it means to celebrate the Eucharist in remembrance of Christ?

3. What responsibilities do you think a person assumes by receiving the Eucharist?

Bible study questions

1. How does the story in today's Gospel differ from a miracle story?

2. What is Luke teaching by the way he tells this story?

3. What is a *type?* Why is Melchizedek a type for Christ?

4. What is the context for Paul's words to the Corinthians that we read this Sunday?

5. What is Paul teaching the Corinthians?

Ordinary Time: Sundays 10–34

Tenth Sunday in Ordinary Time

Luke 7:11–17 in its biblical context

On the Solemnity of the Most Holy Body and Blood of Christ we commented on the fact that the story of the multiplication of the loaves does not fit the form of a miracle story. Today's story, Jesus bringing the widow of Nain's son back to life, does fit the form of a miracle story.

When an author wants to claim a miracle he uses an identifiable form. First, a problem is brought to Jesus' attention. In today's story a funeral procession passes right in front of Jesus and the disciples: "a man who had died was being carried out." Next Jesus is specifically described as performing some action to solve the problem. Here Jesus steps forward, touches the coffin, and says, "Young man, I tell you, arise!" Then the author demonstrates that Jesus' actions solved the problem: "The dead man sat up and began to speak." Finally the crowd reacts to the marvelous deed in such a way that the reader's attention is brought to the identity of Jesus: "Fear seized them all, and they glorified God, exclaiming, 'A great prophet has arisen in our midst,' and 'God has visited his people.'"

Luke is claiming that Jesus brought the widow's son back to life.

There is no question that those who knew Jesus, whether or not they were his followers, experienced Jesus as a person of great power. Jesus worked mighty signs as part of his preaching about the imminent in-breaking of the kingdom of God. In the light of the resurrection, however, the focus of miracle stories changed from the kingdom of God to the identity of Jesus. Notice, the people who witness Jesus' mighty sign comment on Jesus' identity. They do not know what Luke has already told his audience, that Jesus is God's begotten Son. They come to the conclusion that Jesus is "a great prophet," and that "God has visited his people." The reader understands that there is a depth of meaning in the words of the crowd that those in the crowd do not themselves comprehend. In Jesus, God has visited his people in a unique way.

The story of Jesus bringing back to life the widow of Nain's son appears only in Luke. It has many details in it that are typical of Luke's Gospel. Luke emphasizes Jesus' interest in and compassion for women. Here Luke tells us that a widow has lost her only son. This is a terrible fate for anyone who lives in a patriarchal society.

The woman will certainly be marginalized and vulnerable with no husband and no son. Luke tells us that Jesus "was moved with pity for her and said to her, 'Do not weep.' "

Jesus cares much more about comforting the widow and restoring her son than he cares about the laws of ritual purity. Were Jesus a legalist he would not have touched a coffin, as this was expressly forbidden by the law (Num 19:16–21).

On seeing the man brought back to life the people call Jesus "a great prophet." This title and Luke's telling us that after bringing the man back to life "Jesus gave him to his mother" are allusions to a story about the prophet Elijah. We read the story of Elijah in today's Old Testament selection.

In Luke's Gospel, immediately after this story, the disciples of John the Baptist come and ask Jesus, "Are you the one who is to come, or should we look for another?" (Luke 7:19). The raising of the widow of Nain's son is part of the evidence that Jesus advises John and his disciples to ponder as they reach an answer to their question. Jesus says, "Go and tell John what you have seen and heard: the blind regain their sight, the lame walk, lepers are cleansed, the deaf hear, the dead are raised, the poor have the good news proclaimed to them" (Luke 7:22). Jesus is the one to come. In him God has truly visited his people.

1 Kings 17:17–24 *in its biblical context*

Today's Old Testament reading is the story to which Luke alludes as he tells us abut Jesus raising a widow's son. Elijah was a prophet in the northern kingdom during the reign of King Ahab (869–850 BC). King Ahab was not faithful to covenant love. He married Jezebel and "went over to the veneration and worship of Baal" (1 Kgs 16:31). It was the prophet Elijah's job to correct the king.

Just before the story we read today Elijah has told King Ahab that there is going to be a drought. God tells Elijah to go and hide. In Elijah's first hiding place the brook runs dry. The Lord then instructs Elijah to "Move on to Zarephath of Sidon and stay there. I have designated a widow there to provide for you" (1 Kgs 17:9). It is this widow who has lost her son.

This poor widow has literally been God's instrument to protect and save Elijah. She has sheltered and fed Elijah for a year when her son falls sick. That is why she remonstrates with Elijah as she does, and why Elijah remonstrates with God: "O Lord, my God, will you afflict even the widow with whom I am staying by killing her son?" Elijah prays that God will restore breath to the boy, and God does.

It is to the end of this story that Luke alludes when he says that Jesus gave the young man to his mother: "Elijah brought him down into the house from the upper room and gave him to his mother." The mother tells Elijah, "Now indeed I know that you are a man of God. The word of the Lord comes truly from your mouth." The story teaches that Elijah is a true prophet, as evidenced by the fact that God's power is present in him.

Galatians 1:11–19 in its biblical context

In today's reading from Galatians Paul is defending his authority to teach. Paul is angry because some missionaries are telling the Galatians that they must be circumcised. Paul has taught the Galatians that they are saved by faith, not by obedience to the law. Paul wants the Galatians to listen to him, not to the missionaries.

In his own defense Paul tells the Galatians that "the gospel preached by me is not of human origin." Paul received it directly from Jesus Christ. Paul admits that he initially persecuted the church. As a free gift of grace, however, God revealed his Son to Paul and called him to proclaim the gospel to the Gentiles. The Galatians have been the beneficiary of God's gift. Since Paul's authority is directly from God, the Galatians should believe him and not the missionaries who are preaching the necessity of circumcision.

Questions for Breaking Open the Word groups are on page 13.

Questions for other faith sharing groups

1. Do you believe in miracles? Do you have any personal experience of a miracle? Explain.

2. Do you ever find that a law gets in the way of your doing what you believe to be for another person's benefit? If so, what do you do to solve this dilemma?

3. What have you been given as a free gift of grace? What conclusion do you draw from the fact that these are gifts, not anything you have earned?

Bible study questions

1. What four elements are characteristic of the form *miracle story?*

2. How does today's Gospel story fulfill these characteristics?

3. In what two ways does Luke allude to the story of Elijah in today's Gospel story?

4. How does Paul defend himself in our reading from Galatians?

5. Why is Paul feeling it necessary to defend himself?

ELEVENTH SUNDAY IN ORDINARY TIME

Luke 7:36–8:3 in its biblical context

In today's Gospel we see both Jesus' love of sinners and Luke's unique interest in revealing the role that women played in Jesus' ministry.

Jesus is a guest in the house of a Pharisee when a woman comes and anoints his feet with costly oil. The Pharisee "said to himself,

'If this man [Jesus] were a prophet, he would know who and what sort of woman this is who is touching him, that she is a sinner.' " The reader's reaction to the Pharisee's thought is, "How does the Pharisee know that the woman is a sinner? Is the Pharisee a sinner too?" The Pharisee certainly does not consider himself a sinner. He is a self-righteous and judgmental person.

Jesus treats both the Pharisee, whose name is Simon, and the woman with love. Jesus realizes that his host is uncomfortable with the woman's behavior. He tells Simon a parable about two people who were both forgiven a debt, one a huge debt and the other a smaller debt. He then asks Simon, "Which of them will love him more?" Simon correctly replies, "The one, I suppose, whose larger debt was forgiven." Simon has no idea that in passing judgment on the characters in the parable he has passed judgment on himself. He does not know that the parable is calling him to self-knowledge and conversion.

Jesus then explains to Simon that he is like the debtor who has been forgiven less. Simon, of course, does not think of himself as a debtor at all. He feels worthy to have Jesus as a guest in his home. It has never entered his mind that Jesus would be associating with a sinner if Jesus associates with him. The woman, as Simon sees it, is in a different category entirely. She is a sinner, unclean. If Jesus knew who she is, Jesus would not allow the woman to touch him as she has, making him ritually unclean too.

Like the debtor who was aware of having been forgiven a great debt, the woman knows she is a sinner, but she also knows that she has been forgiven. Her deep expression of love is flowing from her knowledge that she has been forgiven. When Jesus tells Simon, " . . . her many sins have been forgiven because she has shown great love," he is not saying that she earned her forgiveness through her love. He is saying that she has obviously experienced forgiveness as exhibited by her great love. Simon, who has no sense of having been forgiven, exhibits much less love. Jesus then names the truth that was obvious to him when he observed the woman's behavior: "Your sins are forgiven."

Jesus then sends the woman on her way. "Your faith has saved you; go in peace." We do not know Jesus' parting words to Simon, nor his to Jesus. We do not know if Simon begins to understand that he too is a sinner and is in need of forgiveness. Once Simon understands this he will become more able to love his fellow sinner.

Luke then tells us something that we read only in Luke. Among Jesus' disciples who traveled with him on the road were a number of women. Mary Magdalene, who had been healed of possession (there is no evidence that Mary Magdalene was a prostitute or a notorious sinner of any kind) was with him, as well as a married woman of means, Joanna, and Susanna. Luke wants us to know that whenever we hear about Jesus and his disciples we should be aware that women are important members of that group.

2 Samuel 12:7–10, 13 in its biblical context

In our reading from 2 Samuel the prophet Nathan is trying to help David understand that he is a sinner, just as Jesus tried to help Simon understand that he is a sinner. In fact, Nathan picks the same way to help David see himself in this light as Jesus did with Simon: Nathan tells David a parable (2 Sam 12:1–4). Immediately before today's reading Nathan has told David a story about a rich man who had many sheep, but, in order to offer hospitality to a guest, he took a poor man's only lamb and prepared it for the meal. After David passes harsh judgment on this man Nathan tells David, "You are the man!" (2 Sam 12:7a).

Today's reading explains to David why he is that man. After all God has done for David, David "cut down Uriah the Hittite with the sword; you took his wife as your own, and him you killed with the sword of the Ammonites." In other words, David committed adultery when he slept with Bathsheba, and murder when he had Bathsheba's husband killed in battle (see 2 Sam 11). This sin would have dire political consequences: ". . . the sword shall never depart from your house. . . ."

Although we did not hear how Simon responded to Jesus, we do hear how David responds to Nathan. David listens to Nathan's words and realizes that he is a sinner. "I have sinned against the LORD." Nathan then assures David that God has forgiven him his sins. "The LORD on his part has forgiven your sin: you shall not die."

The good news in both the Gospel and the reading from 2 Samuel is that God forgives sinners. In order to experience that forgiveness, however, we must acknowledge that we are sinners. Once we have experienced our own sinfulness and realize that we have been forgiven, we will grow in our ability to love. We will be less self-righteous and less judgmental of others.

Galatians 2:16, 19–21 in its biblical context

Paul is still explaining to the Galatians that they should not listen to the missionaries who are telling them that they have to be circumcised. True, circumcision was demanded by the law, but they are not justified by obedience to the law. They are justified by faith in Jesus Christ.

Paul himself used to obey the law. But now he understands that this is not what God wants. Paul did not earn anything by that obedience. Rather, he has received a great gift: "I live by faith in the Son of God who has loved me and given himself up for me." If the Galatians agree to be circumcised they will as much as be saying that Christ's death was not effective: ". . . for if justification comes through the law, then Christ died for nothing."

Forgiveness is not earned. Salvation is not earned. Both are free gifts from a God who loves us. Our role is to receive these gifts gratefully and to express our gratitude by loving God and others, even our fellow sinners.

Questions for Breaking Open the Word groups are on page 13.

Questions for other faith sharing groups

1. Do you ever find yourself feeling more deserving or more worthy than someone else? In what settings? What are the dangers of this kind of thinking?

2. Do you examine your conscience routinely? If so, how do you go about it?

3. Do you believe that people who know they are loved are freer to love others? If so, why do you think this is true?

Bible study questions

1. What fault prevents Simon from loving more generously?

2. How does Jesus call Simon to self-knowledge and conversion?

3. Why does the woman love much?

4. With what sins did Nathan confront David?

5. What will the Galatians be saying about the effect of Jesus' death if they accept the necessity of circumcision?

TWELFTH SUNDAY IN ORDINARY TIME

Luke 9:18–24 in its biblical context

Notice that, as our Gospel begins, Jesus is at prayer. Luke often pictures Jesus praying, particularly at important times when decisions have to be made. In Luke it was while Jesus was praying after his baptism that the Holy Spirit descended upon him and the voice from heaven said, "You are my beloved son; with you I am well pleased" (Luke 3:22b). Jesus also spent the night in prayer before he selected his apostles (Luke 6:12, 13).

Now, in light of the conversation that follows, Jesus appears once more to be praying about his future ministry.

Jesus first asks his disciples who those in the crowd say that he is. Their answer is identical to what Luke has told his readers earlier: Luke said that Herod the tetrarch had heard about all that was going on surrounding Jesus and was very puzzled "because some were saying, 'John has been raised from the dead'; others were saying, 'Elijah has appeared'; still others, 'One of the ancient prophets has arisen'" (9:7b–8). Having heard this answer from the disciples, Jesus immediately moves on to a second question, "But who do you say that I am?"

It is Peter who responds for the group. Throughout his Gospel and in Acts Luke highlights Peter's unique role. However, the present story, also present in Mark (8:27–33) and Matthew (16:13–23), presents Luke with a problem. In Luke's source, the Gospel of Mark, Peter remonstrates with Jesus after Peter responds for the group and Jesus warns the apostles of his future suffering. Jesus then says to Peter, "Get behind me, Satan. You are thinking not as God does, but as human beings do" (Mark 8:33b). These are very harsh words directed at the person who will have a unique role of leadership in the church after the resurrection. Luke, in a characteristic way, simply omits them. He does not picture Jesus correcting Peter so severely.

What does Peter's response, "The Christ of God," mean to Peter? Certainly it does not mean what it means to us, that Jesus is a divine person. When Peter professes his belief that Jesus is the Christ of God he is saying that he recognizes Jesus as a person in whom God's power is at work, just as God's power has been at work in other great leaders, such as Moses and David. Through Moses God saved the people from slavery in Egypt. Through David God saved the people from the Philistines. Through Jesus God must be going to save the people from Roman domination.

It is because Peter understands the Christ to be a political figure through whom God's saving power will be manifest that Jesus warns the disciples "not to tell this to anyone." Jesus does not want the disciples to teach others their own misunderstanding. It is also because the disciples are expecting a messiah with political power that Jesus' next words are completely incomprehensible to them. Jesus warns the disciples that "the Son of Man [a messianic title from the Book of Daniel; see Dan 7:13] must suffer greatly and be rejected by the elders, the chief priests, and the scribes, and be killed and on the third day be raised." How could Jesus be the messiah, and at the same time be killed? Jesus' words are a total mystery to his disciples.

Not only does Jesus warn the disciples about his own coming suffering; he warns them that they too will suffer. "If anyone wishes to come after me, he must deny himself and take up his cross daily and follow me." The mystery of the cross is central not only to Jesus' vocation but to his disciples' as well.

Zechariah 12:10–11; 13:1 in its biblical context

Scripture scholars are puzzled by the passage from Zechariah that we read today. When Christians read about the inhabitants of Jerusalem grieving over "him whom they have pierced," we think of the passage as referring to Jesus. In fact, John quotes this passage in his Gospel. After Jesus has been taken down from the cross, and after a soldier thrusts a lance into Jesus' side, John says, "For this happened so that the scripture passage might be fulfilled: 'They will look upon him whom they have pierced' " (John 19:36a, 37b).

To understand the passage in its Old Testament context we must ask, "What would those to whom the passage was first addressed have understood the passage to be saying?" Chapters 12–14 of Zechariah are later works than most of the book (chapters 1–8), which dates to the time after the Babylonian exile, probably around

520 BC. Since chapters 12–14 do not have specifically historical language they cannot be dated exactly, but scholars believe today's oracle dates to the early Hellenistic period, after Alexander the Great (336 BC–323 BC) conquered the holy land.

The theme of the oracle is reconciliation and repentance. God will "pour out on the house of David and on the inhabitants of Jerusalem a spirit of grace and petition." Jerusalem will repent having killed someone—"him whom they have pierced." Scripture scholars do not know whom they have killed. Their mourning is compared to the mourning "of Hadadrimmon in the plain of Megiddo." Some believe that the reference to Megiddo refers to the occasion when King Josiah, the reformer, was killed in battle since that battle took place in Megiddo. "On that day," a phrase that is repeated and that refers to the great day of God's intervention, the inhabitants of Jerusalem will have access to "a fountain to purify from sin and uncleanness."

The prophet is telling his contemporaries that God will take the initiative to make it possible for them to see their sins and repent of them. Both the house of David and the inhabitants of Jerusalem are in need of repentance. The passage has been chosen today because, like the Gospel, for Christians it is focusing our attention on Jesus' suffering.

Galatians 3:26–29 in its biblical context

When you read the first sentence in today's passage from Galatians, you will better understand the context if you emphasize the words, "through faith." Paul wants the Galatians to know that it is through faith that they are "children of God in Christ Jesus," not through obedience to the law, not through being circumcised. The Galatians have been baptized; they don't need circumcision. Because they have become part of Christ's body, the church, distinctions among them are no longer important—Jew or Greek, slave or free, male or female— they are "all one in Christ Jesus." They do not need circumcision to make them Abraham's descendants and "heirs according to the promise."

Questions for Breaking Open the Word groups are on page 13.

Questions for other faith sharing groups

1. If Jesus asked you, "Who do you say that I am?" how would you respond?

2. Why do you think it mattered to Jesus what others said of him?

3. Why do you think Christianity and class systems are at odds? What effect does this fact have on your life?

Bible study questions

1. What does Peter mean by "the Christ of God"?

2. About what does Jesus warn the disciples?

3. Why are the disciples unable to understand Jesus' warning?

4. In the passage from Zechariah, what would the original audience have understood the prophet to be teaching?

5. What additional meaning do Christians see in the prophet's words?

THIRTEENTH SUNDAY IN ORDINARY TIME

Luke 9:51–62 in its biblical context

Our reading from the Gospel picks up the theme of suffering that we heard in last Sunday's Gospel: Today's reading begins: "When the days for Jesus' being taken up were fulfilled, he resolutely determined to journey to Jerusalem. . . . " The words "Jesus' being taken up" refer to all that Jesus has ahead of him—the trip to Jerusalem, his passion, death, resurrection, and ascension. To say that these days "were fulfilled" is to say that God's plan is coming to fulfillment through these events. Jesus knows suffering awaits him, but he is "resolutely determined" to do his Father's will.

Between last Sunday's reading and this reading several important stories have been passed over. One is the story of the transfiguration (Luke 9:28–36), which we read not only on the feast of the Transfiguration (August 6) but also on the second Sunday of Lent. In addition, the Lectionary does not include Jesus' second warning to his disciples about his coming death or two accounts of exorcisms. That James and John have witnessed the transfiguration, and have heard Jesus' second warning about his suffering, makes their behavior in today's Gospel all the more disappointing.

As Jesus passes through a Samaritan village he is confronted with the mutual prejudice that the Samaritans and the Jews had for each other. The Samaritans were descendants of the intermarriages that took place between the ten northern tribes and the Assyrians who had conquered them in the eighth century. From the Jewish point of view, the Samaritans were unclean. Jesus himself never let laws about people being unclean prevent him from ministering to them. Since Jesus is headed for Jerusalem the Samaritans realize he is a Jew and therefore they do not welcome him.

James and John want not only to retaliate, but to destroy these unclean Samaritans. They say, "Lord, do you want us to call down fire from heaven to consume them?"—this, after Jesus has taught his disciples to love their enemies: "But to you who hear I say, love your enemies, do good to those who hate you, bless those who curse you, pray for those who mistreat you" (Luke 6:27). James and John are not yet among those who are able to hear. Jesus has to rebuke them.

Luke then gives us three short interchanges that teach the hardships involved in being a disciple. First, someone makes a quick offer without realizing the ramifications of his words: "I will follow you wherever you go." Jesus tries to help this person comprehend how hard it is to be a disciple: Jesus is constantly on the move and has no place to call home.

To another Jesus extends the invitation to follow him. His answer, "Lord, let me go first and bury my father," means, "Yes, but not now." The man is making excuses. Maybe he will come in five or ten years, after his father has died. Jesus recognizes the empty excuse and calls him on it: "Let the dead bury their dead. But you, go and proclaim the kingdom of God." These words would be cruel if the man's father had actually died. We know from the story of the raising of the widow of Nain's son (Luke 7:11–17) that Jesus wants children to take care of their parents when they are in need. This man was simply making up excuses for rejecting the invitation.

In the third interchange another would-be disciple as much as says, "Yes, but not now." His response is: "I will follow you, Lord, but first let me say farewell to my family at home." This passage, as well as the previous one, is sometimes misinterpreted to mean that following Jesus' call and fulfilling family responsibilities are incompatible. Jesus is not saying that God is pleased when we fail to fulfill our responsibilities to our families (see Mark 7:9–13; Matt 15:3–7). Rather, he is teaching that the kingdom of God must be the top priority of his disciples. A true disciple does not say, "Yes, but not now." A true disciple gives a wholehearted "yes." Such a disciple is faithful even in the face of suffering and prays for his or her persecutors.

1 Kings 19:16b, 19–21 in its biblical context

We return to the story of the prophet Elijah, some of which we read on the Tenth Sunday in Ordinary Time. Elijah was a prophet in the northern kingdom during the reign of King Ahab (869–850 BC). In today's story Elijah is obeying God's command to pick his successor, Elisha.

Elijah finds Elisha going about his daily tasks. Elisha recognizes Elijah's gesture of throwing his cloak over him as an invitation to follow him. Elisha says, "Please, let me kiss my father and mother goodbye, and I will follow you." Elijah does not refuse this request. Instead he says, "Go back! Have I done anything to you?" Perhaps Elijah is reminding Elisha that the invitation to become a prophet is an invitation from God, not an invitation from Elijah. Elisha then completely leaves his former life by destroying his previous means of earning a living. He destroys his possessions to feed the people and then leaves to follow God's call.

Galatians 5:1, 13–18 in its biblical context

Once again, Paul is assuring the Galatians that they need not obey the law, which is a yoke of slavery. Christ has set them free of the law: "For freedom Christ set us free; so stand firm and do not submit again to the yoke of slavery." However, freedom is not license: "The whole law is fulfilled in one statement, namely, *You shall love your neighbor as yourself.*" Those who live in the freedom of Christ will live by the Spirit. Those who live by the Spirit will not give in to the desires of the flesh: "...these are opposed to each other." So, while the Galatians are freed from the law, as disciples of Christ they are called to live by the Spirit and to love one another.

Questions for Breaking Open the Word groups are on page 13.

Questions for other faith sharing groups

1. When you suffer, are you tempted to think that God has deserted you, or are you "resolutely determined" to see it through? Explain.

2. Do you understand your family responsibilities to be a way of doing God's will or as a burden that makes it difficult for you to be free to do God's will? Explain.

3. In your understanding, from what has Christ freed you? For what has Christ freed you?

Bible study questions

1. What do James and John fail to understand in today's Gospel?

2. What is Luke teaching through the three short interchanges with would-be disciples?

3. Does Luke's Gospel teach that following Christ and having family responsibilities are incompatible? Explain.

4. How does Elisha respond to God's call to succeed Elijah as a prophet?

5. In what statement is the whole law fulfilled?

FOURTEENTH SUNDAY IN ORDINARY TIME

Luke 10:1–12, 17–20 *in its biblical context*

In today's Gospel Jesus sends his disciples out to teach in both word and deed that "the kingdom of God is at hand." Jesus sends them out "in pairs" so that they will have companionship. As we learn from Genesis, it is not good for a person to be alone (Gen 2:18).

It is easier to understand the purpose of Jesus' instructions to the disciples, which make them dependent on the hospitality of others, after we have noted their reaction to the success of their ministry. The disciples say, "Lord, even the demons are subject to us because of your name." The disciples remark on their power. While discipleship involves power, it is not about power. Jesus' instructions to his disciples put them in a position of needing help, of being vulnerable. If they follow Jesus' instructions their relationship with others will be one of mutual gift-giving, not a relationship in which the disciples have all the power.

Jesus tells his disciples that he is sending them "like lambs among wolves. Carry no money bag, no sack, no sandals." That the disciples will be like lambs among wolves means that they will, in one sense, have less power, not more power, than those they serve. They will be dependent on the hospitality of others. The hope is, of course, that the wolves will not attack the lambs, but will lie down with them. This recalls Isaiah's image of peace:

> The wolf and the lamb shall graze alike....
> None shall hurt or destroy
>   on all my holy mountain, says the LORD.
>   (Isa 65:25a, c)

When the disciples arrive at a town they are to offer those in the town peace: "Peace to this household." Here, as in the post-resurrection appearance stories, peace is to be offered not just as a greeting, but as a gift. The peace that is offered is the peace that results from being freed from the power of evil. It is the disciples' power over evil that they are rejoicing over when they say, "even the demons are subject to us...." Jesus describes this power when he says, "Behold, I have given you the power to 'tread upon serpents' and scorpions and upon the full force of the enemy and nothing will harm you." Serpents and scorpions are symbols of evil.

If a town welcomes the disciples, they are to stay there, accept hospitality, and carry on their ministry: "...cure the sick in it and say to them, 'The kingdom of God is at hand for you.'" If the town does not receive them they are to say, "The dust of your town that clings to our feet, even that we shake off against you." This expression is similar to our expression, "Wash your hands of the matter." The disciples, if not received, are not simply to bang their heads against a brick wall; they are to move on to another town.

As our reading ends, Jesus gives the disciples one more warning about not getting too taken up with their power: "Nevertheless, do not rejoice because the spirits are subject to you, but rejoice because your names are written in heaven." The disciples are to rejoice in the fact that they are in right relationship with God. Their relationship with God is what is most important.

Isaiah 66:10–14c in its biblical context

Just as the disciples were rejoicing in the power over evil that they had in Jesus' name, so is the prophet in today's reading from Isaiah rejoicing in the Lord's power. Today's reading is from that part of the Book of Isaiah that scripture scholars refer to as written by Third Isaiah (Isa 56–66). Third Isaiah offered hope to those who returned to the holy land after the Babylonian exile. The returned exiles were faced with many hardships as they tried to rebuild Jerusalem, which had been ravaged by the Babylonians.

Third Isaiah's words are offering the returned exiles hope that Jerusalem would be rebuilt to its former glory:

> Lo, I will spread prosperity over Jerusalem like a river,
>   and the wealth of the nations like an overflowing torrent.
> As nurslings, you shall be carried in her arms,
>   and fondled in her lap;
> as a mother comforts her child,
>   so will I comfort you;
>   in Jerusalem you shall find your comfort.

Third Isaiah wants the returned exiles to rejoice in God's power, already made known to them by the fact that they have been allowed to return to the holy land. They need not be too discouraged by the burden of rebuilding. "The Lord's power shall be known to his servants."

Galatians 6:14–18 in its biblical context

As Paul ends his Letter to the Galatians he once again reminds them that they do not have to obey the law and be circumcised: "For neither does circumcision mean anything, nor does uncircumcision, but only a new creation." They have been created anew by Jesus' passion, death, and resurrection. From now on they should not let anyone who teaches anything else trouble them.

Although Paul has authority to teach as he does, he does not boast in his authority: "May I never boast except in the cross of our Lord Jesus Christ...." He knows that his authority comes from God and that it is to be used for only one purpose: to bring others to faith in Jesus Christ.

Questions for Breaking Open the Word groups are on page 13.

Questions for other faith sharing groups

1. Over whom do you have authority? What is the source of your authority? How do you think God wants you to use your authority?

2. Are you comfortable being dependent on others? Why do you think Jesus wants his disciples to experience dependency?

3. If you were to try to encourage others to trust in God's power, what examples from your own observation and experience would you give them?

Bible study questions

1. What instructions does Jesus give his disciples?

2. In what ways do the disciples have power? In what ways do they lack power?

3. Why should the disciples rejoice?

4. For whom was Third Isaiah a prophet?

5. What hope is Third Isaiah offering in today's reading?

FIFTEENTH SUNDAY IN ORDINARY TIME

Luke 10:25–37 *in its biblical context*

Today we read the parable of the good Samaritan. The Lectionary reading gives us the social setting for the parable, so we will have no trouble interpreting it. Since a parable is always the middle of a conversation, to interpret it we need to know its context. We need to ask ourselves, "To whom is Jesus speaking?" "What are Jesus and his audience discussing?" "With whom in the story does the audience identify?" "What is Jesus teaching the person to whom he tells the parable?" The story will be calling that person to self-knowledge and conversion of heart. The parable has this effect because the person to whom Jesus tells the story will pass judgment on the characters in the story. In doing so that person will unwittingly pass judgment on himself.

Luke tells us that a scholar of the law asked Jesus a question, not to learn from him but to test him. The question is, "Teacher, what must I do to inherit eternal life?" Jesus must have realized that he was being tested and that the lawyer already knew the answer because Jesus asks the lawyer, "What is written in the law?" The lawyer gives a perfect answer, quoting both Deuteronomy and Leviticus. Deuteronomy says, "Therefore, you shall love the Lord, your God, with all your heart, and with all your soul, and with all your strength" (Deut 6:5). Leviticus says, "You shall love your neighbor as yourself" (Lev 19:18b). The lawyer knows the law.

Luke then tells us that the lawyer felt the need to justify himself. By answering his own question he has revealed that he was not expecting to learn anything from Jesus, but was testing him. The lawyer asks, "And who is my neighbor?" It is in response to this question that Jesus tells the lawyer the story of the good Samaritan.

As the lawyer listens to this story he could identify with any character but the Samaritan. He could be the man who fell victim to robbers and needed help. He could be the priest or Levite, both well-respected people in society, who pass the man by. But the lawyer could never identify with the Samaritan. Samaritans, as we discussed on the Thirteenth Sunday in Ordinary Time, were considered unclean by the Jews. The lawyer felt perfectly justified in not regarding the Samaritan as his neighbor.

Yet, in Jesus' story the Samaritan is the good person. The Samaritan was "moved with compassion at the sight" of the poor man on the road. He lavishly took care of him, as he "poured oil and wine over his wounds and bandaged them." He even made sure the man would receive further care by promising to pay for it. After telling this story Jesus asks the lawyer, "Which of these three, in your opinion, was neighbor to the robbers' victim?"

The lawyer is obviously a very intelligent person. He understands that Jesus is teaching him that the answer to his question, "Who is my neighbor?" is that even Samaritans are his neighbor. But he cannot bring himself to answer Jesus' question by saying, "the Samaritan." Rather, he says, "The one who treated him with mercy." Jesus affirms this answer by saying to the lawyer, "Go and do likewise." Jesus is teaching the lawyer that he cannot use the law to justify his exclusion of certain people from the commandment to love. Even the Samaritans are the lawyer's neighbors, and he is required to love them.

Deuteronomy 30:10–14 in its biblical context

In our reading from Deuteronomy Moses is pleading with the people to return to the Lord with all their hearts and souls. "If only you would heed the voice of the LORD, your God, and keep his commandments and statutes that are written in this book of the law...."

While the statutes are written in the book of the law, they are also written in people's hearts. That is why Moses tells the people that the commandments are not too mysterious and remote for people to understand. They are not up in the sky, nor are they across the sea. "No, it is something very near to you, already in your mouths and in your hearts...."

Moses is telling the Israelites that they already know the difference between right and wrong. What is needed is that they heed God's voice and keep God's command: "...you have only to carry it out."

Colossians 1:15–20 in its biblical context

Today we read a high-Christology hymn from the Letter to the Colossians. To say that the hymn is "high Christology" is to say that it emphasizes Jesus' divinity. The hymn celebrates Christ not as an infant born in Bethlehem, but as "the firstborn of all creation."

> For in him were created all things in heaven and on earth,
>> the visible and the invisible,
>> whether thrones or dominions or principalities or powers;
>> all things were created through him and for him.

Christ existed before creation took place and is higher even than the angels.

Christ is also "the head of the body, the church." Here the author is using the word *church* to refer to a universal body, not to a particular local group gathering in Christ's name. The author's highly developed idea of church is one of the aspects of the letter that makes scripture scholars suggest that the letter is later than Paul's writings.

Christ is "the firstborn from the dead," that is, the first to experience resurrection. Through Christ all of creation has been reconciled to God:

> For in him all the fullness was pleased to dwell,
>> and through him to reconcile all things for him,
>> making peace by the blood of his cross
>> through him, whether those on earth or those in heaven.

Jesus is not just a great philosopher who lived at an identifiable time in history. Rather, Jesus preexisted his life on earth. Jesus is the "image of the invisible God...."

Questions for Breaking Open the Word groups are on page 13.

Questions for other faith sharing groups

1. Are there people in our society whom we have given ourselves permission not to love? Who are they? What are our reasons? What do you think Jesus would think of our reasons?

2. Do you feel that the law is written in your heart? Why or why not?

3. When you think of Jesus, do you prefer to emphasize his humanity or his divinity? Why?

Bible study questions

1. Why is it necessary to know the context of a parable in order to interpret it?

2. What questions should we ask ourselves in order to interpret a parable?

3. What is Jesus teaching the lawyer in today's parable?

4. What is Moses teaching the Israelites in today's reading from Deuteronomy?

5. What ideas in the hymn from Colossians make it a high-Christology hymn?

SIXTEENTH SUNDAY IN ORDINARY TIME

Luke 10:38–42 in its biblical context

Today we read a story that has annoyed many a housewife. However, when we look at the story carefully, we will see that Jesus has not criticized those who work hard to offer others the gift of hospitality. Rather, Jesus has refused to criticize, at another's request, a person who considers listening to his word more important than anything else.

Jesus enters a village and accepts the hospitality of a woman named Martha. In doing this Jesus is not following convention. It would be unusual for an itinerant preacher to accept the hospitality of a woman in her home. More than any other Gospel Luke makes a point of picturing Jesus in people's homes and accepting their hospitality, just as he instructed his disciples to do (Luke 9:4). By the time Luke is writing his Gospel, around AD 85, Christian churches are meeting in homes, and many women are offering them hospitality. Perhaps there will be a message for such women in today's Gospel.

Martha's sister, Mary, also acts unconventionally. She would be expected to busy herself with serving, not simply sitting at the feet of the teacher and listening to him. Luke tells us that Martha is "burdened with much serving." Martha wants everything to be perfect for her guest, and so she doesn't have time to be with her guest. She complains about Mary to Jesus. "Lord, do you not care that my sister has left me by myself to do the serving? Tell her to help me."

There is no instance in Luke's Gospel where Jesus criticizes one person at the invitation of another. Whenever one person finds fault with another Jesus tries to get that person to look first at his or her own faults. Jesus has earlier taught the crowd, "Why do you notice the splinter in your brother's eye, but do not perceive the wooden beam in your own? How can you say to your brother, 'Brother, let me remove that splinter in your eye,' when you do not even notice the wooden beam in your own eye?" (Luke 6:41–42a). Martha has found fault with her sister, but has not found any fault with herself.

Jesus treats both sisters lovingly and accepts each person's gift as that person has offered it. Martha's gift is her hospitality. Jesus accepts that gift. Mary's gift is her presence and attention. Jesus accepts that gift. However, when Martha criticizes Mary, Jesus points out to Martha that it is her behavior, not Mary's, that is lessening the gift of hospitality that Martha wants to offer. We can hear affection in Jesus' tone as he says, "Martha, Martha, you are anxious and worried about many things. There is need of only one thing. Mary has chosen the better part and it will not be taken from her." Jesus is not being ungrateful for Martha's hard work. He is just pointing out that Martha's serving seems to have become more important than her guest.

Family responsibilities, work responsibilities, hospitality responsibilities: all of these are important and good. However, none of these is more important than spending time with Jesus and listening to his word.

Genesis 18:1–10a in its biblical context

Our reading from Genesis is part of the story of the announcement of Isaac's birth to Abraham and Sarah (see Gen 18:1–15). On reading this account you might well ask, "Who is doing the announcing?" The reading begins, "The Lord appeared to Abraham. . . ." But then it says, "Looking up, Abraham saw three men standing nearby."

Abraham's reaction to his visitors makes it obvious that he is in the presence of the divine. First Abraham runs to greet his visitors and bows before them. "When he saw them, he ran from the entrance of the tent to greet them; and bowing to the ground, he said. . . ." He also acts as though he is not worthy to be in the presence of his visitors: "Now that you have come this close to your servant, let me bring a little food, that you may refresh yourselves." Abraham then fixes his guests the very best he has to offer.

Today's story is an example of the fact that the stories in this part of Genesis describe the presence of God in a variety of ways. Here the Lord's presence is described as "three men." Sometimes it is described as two men and the Lord (see Gen 18:22), and sometimes as two angels (Gen 19:1). Scripture scholars suggest that one reason for this variety is that the storytellers are trying to describe the mysterious nature of God's presence. The God of Abraham is a transcendent God, but at the same time a God who dwells among the people.

There is no question that the three men represent heavenly visitors because they announce the fulfillment of God's promise to Abraham. God had earlier promised Abraham a son. When Abraham said that his heir would be his steward because he had no children the Lord said, "No, that one shall not be your heir; your own issue shall be your heir" (Gen 15:4b). Now, in today's story, God is announcing the fulfillment of that promise: "I will surely return to you about this time next year, and Sarah will then have a son."

Colossians 1:24–28 in its biblical context

We continue reading the Letter to the Colossians. Remember, last week the author taught that Christ has already reconciled the whole world to God: "For in him all the fullness was pleased to dwell, and through him to reconcile all things for him..." (Col 1:19–20a). So when the author says, "Now I rejoice in my sufferings for your sake, and in my flesh I am filling up what is lacking in the afflictions of Christ..." he is not suggesting that Jesus' redemptive acts were incomplete, unfinished, or ineffective. Rather, he is teaching that ministers of Christ, who carry on Jesus' ministry, also participate in his suffering.

Through his suffering the author is bringing "to completion for you the word of God...." God has now chosen to make his mysteries known to the Gentiles. The author is spreading the good news of Christ's redemptive acts to the Gentiles, "admonishing everyone and teaching everyone with all wisdom, that we may present everyone perfect in Christ."

Questions for Breaking Open the Word groups are on page 13.

Questions for other faith sharing groups

1. Do you sometimes put your service to guests above the guests? Why is this not a true expression of hospitality? What could you do to prevent this from happening?

2. When you have a problem with someone do you speak to that person yourself or do you complain about the person to some third party? Why is the second approach not a good thing to do?

3. In what ways do you sit at Jesus' feet and listen to his word? Do you think you do enough of this? Explain.

Bible study questions

1. In what ways does Jesus treat both women lovingly in today's Gospel?

2. What is Luke teaching by telling this story of Jesus, Martha, and Mary?

3. What did God promise Abraham?

4. How is God's presence described in today's story?

5. What is one explanation for why God's presence is described in a variety of ways in the stories in Genesis?

SEVENTEENTH SUNDAY IN ORDINARY TIME

Luke 11:1–13 in its biblical context

Once more Luke pictures Jesus at prayer. When he has finished praying, one of the disciples asks Jesus to teach him or her, and the other disciples, how to pray. In answer to this request Jesus teaches the disciples what we have come to call the "Our Father."

Jesus first teaches the disciples to address God as *Father*. Jesus wants the disciples to think of God as a loving parent, someone who is with them day in and day out and who has both the desire and the power to act for their good. The disciples are then to say, "hallowed be your name." This is a prayer of petition, asking that everything that keeps God's name from being glorified on earth be remedied. So while Jesus wants the disciples to cultivate an intimate relationship with God, at the same time, he wants them to be aware of God's glory and majesty.

Next the disciples are to pray, "your kingdom come." A kingdom is a place where the king's will prevails. Therefore, to pray, "your kingdom come" is also to pray, "Your will be done." Luke's Our Father does not include this second line, as does Matthew's:

> your kingdom come,
> your will be done,
> on earth as in heaven.
> (Matt 6:10)

However, the meaning of the two versions is the same.

Jesus then teaches the disciples to pray for their daily necessities, not as individuals but as members of a community. "Give us each day our daily bread." Just as essential as bread is forgiveness: "and forgive us our sins." Our need for forgiveness obviously obliges us to forgive others; "for we ourselves forgive everyone in debt to us." Finally Jesus teaches the disciples to pray that they not be subjected to the final test. The final test appears to be the temptation to abandon God: apostasy. Jesus will twice more advise the disciples to pray that they not undergo the test, both times during his agony in the garden:

"Why are you sleeping? Get up and pray that you may not undergo the test" (Luke 22:46; see also Luke 22:40b).

Jesus then tells the disciples a parable, inviting them to compare themselves to one of the characters in the story: "Suppose one of you has a friend to whom he goes at midnight...." The friend gives the disciple what the disciple wants—bread to share with a guest—not because he wants to but because the disciple is so persistent. Later Jesus will tell a similar parable about an unscrupulous judge and a persevering widow (see Luke 18:1–5) to teach exactly the same lesson: perseverance in prayer. We make a big mistake if we allegorize either of these parables and make the unresponsive friend or the unscrupulous judge stand for God. Remember, the lesson from a parable comes from a single comparison between the audience and the story.

Jesus then assures the disciples that their prayers will be answered: "And I tell you, ask and you will receive; seek and you will find; knock and the door will be opened to you." As we read this we may think, "I know from experience that this is not true. I prayed hard for something and did not get it. Even Jesus prayed that he not have to drink the cup of his passion, but he was crucified just the same" (Luke 22:42). Jesus asks the disciples to believe that their prayers will be answered and that God's response will always be for their good. "What father among you would hand his son a snake when he asks for a fish?" It is because Jesus believes that his Father will do what is for the good, even if it is not what a beloved child wants, that Jesus himself will pray, "not my will but yours be done" (Luke 22:42b). God knows how to give good gifts to God's children.

Jesus ends his lesson on prayer by assuring the disciples that there is one good gift that the Father longs to give his disciples: the Holy Spirit. As we pray for the Holy Spirit, a prayer that will certainly be answered with a "yes," we will grow in our ability to trust in God's love and God's provident care in our lives.

Genesis 18:20–32 in its biblical context

Remember last week we commented on the variety of ways God is portrayed in various stories in the Book of Genesis. In today's story we have what is called an anthropomorphic picture of God, that is, God is pictured as though God were a human being. As the story begins, God is not all-knowing. God has heard the outcry against Sodom and Gomorrah and decides to go down and see if things are really as bad as have been reported.

On reading this introduction we might think that the story will be about whether or not Sodom and Gomorrah are sinful towns, but it is not. The story is about whether or not God is a just God. Abraham confronts God with the question: "Will you sweep away the innocent with the guilty? Suppose there were fifty innocent people in the city; would you wipe out the place, rather than spare it for the sake of the fifty innocent people within it? Far be it from you to do such a thing, to make the innocent die with the guilty so that the innocent and the guilty would be treated alike!"

Each time Abraham confronts God with the specter of innocent people being treated the same as the guilty, God admits that God would not destroy the city if that number of innocent people were in it. Through the story the author is teaching that God is just. The fate of the guilty and the fate of the innocent are not the same.

Colossians 2:12–14 in its biblical context

In our reading from Colossians the author is assuring the Colossians that they have been forgiven all their sins. They have been baptized into Christ's body, the church. Therefore, they have not only died with Christ ("You were buried with him in baptism"), but they have risen to new life with Christ ("he brought you to life along with him, having forgiven us all our transgressions"). Jesus accomplished our redemption through his obedience to his Father's will. He obliterated any charges against us due to our sins by nailing them to the cross.

Questions for Breaking Open the Word groups are on page 13.

Questions for other faith sharing groups

1. Do you, like Jesus, set aside time to pray? How would you describe your prayer life?

2. Is the prayer "Your kingdom come; your will be done" easy or hard for you to say? Do you know why?

3. When has God said yes to your prayer? When has God said, "I have a better idea"?

Bible study questions

1. How does Jesus teach the disciples to address God? Why?

2. In terms of petition, what does Jesus teach the disciples to request?

3. What is obviously required of us because we need forgiveness?

4. What is today's story from Genesis teaching?

5. According to our reading from Colossians, what is the effect of baptism?

EIGHTEENTH SUNDAY IN ORDINARY TIME

Luke 12:13–21 in its biblical context

Jesus is teaching a crowd, including his disciples, to trust God even during times of persecution when a person who has obviously not been listening interrupts and says, "Teacher, tell my brother to share the inheritance with me." Jesus does not respond with anger or impatience. He addresses the questioner as "friend." As we saw with the story of

Martha and Mary, however, Jesus is not willing to accept anyone's invitation to criticize someone else. He expresses his unwillingness to do this when he asks, "Who appointed me as your judge and arbitrator?"

Next Jesus addresses the crowd. Presumably, both the questioner and the brother are in the crowd, so Jesus is not judging either one of them, but is speaking to both of them. "Take care to guard against all greed, for though one may be rich, one's life does not consist of possessions." He then tells a parable to reinforce this teaching.

In the parable a rich man has a greater harvest than he himself can use. He asks himself, "What shall I do, for I do not have space to store my harvest?" In trying to come to an answer the rich man thinks of no one but himself. He never asks, "What would God have me do with my excess wealth?" Because he is trying to keep everything for himself he decides to build more storage space. That way he will have so much he will not have to work in the future. He says to himself, "you have so many good things stored up for many years, rest, eat, drink, be merry!"

On observing all this, God calls the man a "fool." Why? Because all of his decisions are based on a false presumption, and one about which he has no knowledge or control. The man is assuming that he will live a long life and will, over time, be able to enjoy his accumulated wealth. However, the man dies on the very night that he makes his selfish decision.

Both the questioner and the brother are compared to the rich man. They are being taught that, in deciding what should be done with an inheritance, they should remember that "one's life does not consist of possessions." Instead of thinking just of themselves, they should think about what God would have them do. What matters to God is that we use our possessions to care for those in need.

Ecclesiastes 1:2, 2:21–23 in its biblical context

The Book of Ecclesiastes, also called Qoheleth, is part of the Wisdom tradition of Israel. In the Wisdom books the authors rely on reason, rather than on revelation—on God's mighty interventions in history—to probe life's mysteries. The Book of Ecclesiastes begins and ends with the first line of our reading: "Vanity of vanities, says Qoheleth, all things are vanity!" (see Eccl 12:8). (The epilogue that follows this conclusion is thought to have been added by a disciple of the original author.)

Qoheleth (the word refers to the person who presides at an assembly) would agree entirely with Jesus' teaching in today's Gospel regarding wealth: It is foolish to spend one's life trying to amass wealth. However, their reasons for arriving at this conclusion are not identical. Jesus advised his disciples to use wealth in this life so as to please God. Jesus is assuming the context of life after death. The author of Ecclesiastes is not assuming that context. Rather, he is saying that amassing wealth is just not worth the effort. Those who spend their time trying to amass wealth do not enjoy the process: "All his days sorrow and grief is his occupation; even at night his mind is not at rest." Then, when he dies, he can't take it with him. He has to let someone else inherit it; someone who has not worked will benefit from all his labors: "and yet to another who has not labored over it, he must leave property." Qoheleth's conclusion? To seek wealth is one example of wasting one's time: "Vanity of vanities, says Qoheleth, / vanity of vanities! All things are vanity!"

Colossians 3:1–5, 9–11 in its biblical context

The Letter to the Colossians, like Jesus' teaching in the Gospel, is assuming that there is life after death. This perspective changes everything.

The author reminds the Colossians that life does not end with life on earth: "If you were raised with Christ [a reference to baptism, as we saw last week], seek what is above, where Christ is seated at the right hand of God." The Colossians should make their decisions based not on an earthly perspective, but on a heavenly one. "Think of what is above, not of what is on earth." The Colossians will then be able to share in Christ's resurrected glory: "When Christ your life appears, then you too will appear with him in glory."

Given this perspective the Colossians will live their lives differently. They will put to death "the parts of you that are earthly: immorality, impurity, passion, evil desire, and the greed that is idolatry." The Colossians have put on a new self. Now the old distinctions between Greeks and Jews, the circumcised and the uncircumcised, slaves and free, mean nothing. All people have been made one in Christ.

Questions for Breaking Open the Word groups are on page 13.

Questions for other faith sharing groups

1. Are you tempted to pursue a wealthy lifestyle? Why or why not? If so, how do you react to today's readings?

2. Think over the way you spent your time this past week. In what ways were you pursuing "vanity of vanities"? In what ways were you making decisions that will please God? Explain.

3. Do you make decisions in the context of a belief in life after death? If so, how does this belief affect your decisions?

Bible study questions

1. What does the person in the crowd ask Jesus to do? How does Jesus respond to this request?

2. What does Jesus teach the questioner through the parable?

3. Why does Qoheleth regard the accumulation of wealth as "vanity of vanities"?

4. What did Jesus and the author of Colossians know that the author of Qoheleth did not know?

5. How will the Colossians live their lives differently if they keep their eyes on Christ?

NINETEENTH SUNDAY IN ORDINARY TIME

Luke 12:32–48 *in its biblical context*

Today's Gospel is part of the talk we read last week: Jesus is teaching a large crowd, including his disciples. The Lectionary has skipped verses 12:22–31, which are much beloved. In the missing passage, often referred to as the "lilies of the field" speech, Jesus is teaching the crowd to seek first the kingdom of God and to rely on God's providence to provide for everything else that is needed.

In today's reading Jesus is telling the crowd that if they seek the kingdom they will surely find it, "for your Father is pleased to give you the kingdom." Once more, we see that living in the kingdom is not about earning something; it is about receiving a gift. While Jesus does not want the disciples to be afraid, or to think that they are earning the kingdom, he does want them to know that their response to God's love and God's invitation is very important. The two parables that Jesus tells in today's Gospel reemphasize the importance of a disciple's response, including ours.

The parables have an eschatological (end-time) tone. Servants are waiting for their master's return. Immediately after Jesus' resurrection the disciples expected Jesus to return in glory on the clouds of heaven at any moment. Luke is writing his Gospel around AD 85. The expectation of an imminent return is being revised. Obviously, no one knows exactly when the master will return. As a result, those in Luke's audience, as well as we who read the parable today, see an additional level of meaning. The parable is speaking not only about the parousia (Jesus' return at the end time), but about each of our individual deaths. None of us knows when our time will come. Those in the audience are compared to the servants who do not know when their master will return. The message is to be ready all the time. The master will be so pleased with such faithful servants that he will "have them recline at table, and proceed to wait on them." Notice, power is used to serve.

Peter then asks a question: "Lord, is this parable meant for us or for everyone?" Jesus does not give a direct answer to this question. Instead he tells another parable, similar to the preceding one. Notice, however, that it is Peter who has asked the question, and Jesus' response is about those given positions of leadership: "Who, then, is the faithful and prudent steward whom the master will put in charge of his servants to distribute the food allowance at the proper time?"

Those put in leadership must be faithful to the responsibilities entrusted to them. If a servant is always faithful, that is, no matter whether the master is present or absent all is done as it should be, "the master will put the servant in charge of all his property." However, if a servant who has been given responsibility lords it over others and mistreats them, that servant will be punished severely. A faithful servant knows his master's will and does it. An unfaithful servant, who intentionally acts contrary to his master's will, should expect serious punishment. Even a person who acts contrary to his master's will because he is ignorant of it will be punished, but not as severely. The lesson is clear: "Much will be required of the person entrusted with much, and still more will be demanded of the person entrusted with more."

Peter and the other disciples, who have been sent on mission and have been given a share in Jesus' power (see Luke 10:1–20), are being reminded, in front of the crowd, that they are accountable for the way in which they use their God-given gifts. They have been given power, not so that they can lord it over others, but so that they can serve others and participate in the coming of God's kingdom, a kingdom that God wants to give God's beloved people, God's "little flock."

Wisdom 18:6–9 in its biblical context

The Book of Wisdom is one of those books that appear in the Catholic canon but not in the canon of other Christian churches. It was originally written in Greek, probably in the first century BC, to Jews in Alexandria, Egypt. The Jewish author is praising the wisdom of their Jewish ancestors, encouraging the Jews in Alexandria to be faithful to their traditions in a world that has become Hellenized (that is, has adopted the Greek culture).

In today's reading the author is taking an ancient story, the story of the exodus, and retelling the story so that it is applicable to his first-century audience. He holds up the Jewish ancestors as people of wisdom who trusted God to keep God's promises. Because their ancestors, their "fathers," had "sure knowledge of the oaths in which they put their faith" (that is, God's promises of covenant love to the Israelites), they had courage. They knew that God would be faithful, that God would vindicate them: "Your people awaited / the salvation of the just and the destruction of their foes."

God did save the Israelites from slavery in Egypt. When God performed this mighty intervention in history, God not only punished the Egyptians, but glorified "us whom you had summoned."

The Jewish ancestors had been faithful to God when they lived in Egypt: "For in secret the holy children of the good were offering sacrifice / and putting into effect with one accord the divine institution." The author of Wisdom wants his fellow Jews, who are now living in Egypt in a Hellenized culture, to remain faithful to the wisdom of their ancestors, to remain faithful to covenant love.

Hebrews 11:1–2, 8–19 in its biblical context

The author of the Letter to the Hebrews is also holding up a Jewish ancestor, Abraham, as a model of fidelity. Abraham consistently acted in faith. He acted in faith when he left for the promised land. Why would he do such a thing? Because "he thought that the one who had made the promise was trustworthy." He acted in faith when he offered his son, Isaac, as a sacrifice. Why? "He reasoned that God was able to raise even from the dead. . . . " The author wants the Hebrews to have faith too. Faith will enable them to live in hope.

All of our readings are inviting us to live our lives in fidelity to a God who loves us and who wants to give us the kingdom. If we have faith we will live in hope, without fear, doing all that we can to carry out the Master's will. We will use our gifts, not to lord power over others, but to serve others in love, expecting the return of the master at any time.

Questions for Breaking Open the Word groups are on page 13.

Questions for other faith sharing groups

1. How have you experienced God's provident care? Has this experience helped you trust God's providence in the future? Explain.

2. If you, like Peter, asked Jesus, "Is this parable meant for us?" how do you think Jesus would respond? How does the parable apply specifically to your life?

3. Which of your ancestors in the faith do you most admire? What about this ancestor do you hope to emulate? Why?

Bible study questions

1. What two levels of meaning can be seen in today's parables?

2. What are the parables teaching?

3. To whom is the author of Wisdom writing?

4. What is he teaching his audience?

5. According to the author of Hebrews, why was Abraham able to be so faithful?

TWENTIETH SUNDAY IN ORDINARY TIME

Luke 12:49–53 in its biblical context

Jesus' words in today's Gospel are very puzzling, perhaps even impossible to understand, unless we put them in the context of the whole Gospel. After all, we know Jesus as the prince of peace. On Christmas day, as we celebrated Jesus' birth, we applied the words of the prophet Isaiah to Jesus' mission:

> How beautiful upon the mountains
>   are the feet of him who brings glad tidings,
> Announcing peace, bearing good news. . . .
>
> (Isa 52:7a)

Yet in today's Gospel Jesus says, "Do you think that I have come to establish peace on the earth? No, I tell you, but rather division." What could Jesus mean?

Jesus is not saying that the desired effect of his mission is to divide people, even family members, from one another, but he is saying that division will result from his ministry: Some will believe Jesus and become his followers. Others will not believe and will be angry, will even persecute those who do believe. Jesus knows this from experience.

Luke has certainly set the stage for this pronouncement through the stories he has already told us about Jesus' ministry. We have heard Jesus teach the disciples about the hardship of his and their calling (Luke 9:23–24). We have heard him twice tell the disciples that he will suffer and die (Luke 9:22, 44). Jesus has been accused of casting out evil spirits by the power of Beelzebub (Luke 11:15). He has experienced the inhospitality of the Samaritans (Luke 9:52–53). Now Jesus feels extreme urgency both about his mission and about his own suffering.

The image Jesus uses to describe both the effect of his ministry and the sense of urgency he feels about his ministry is fire: "I have come to set the earth on fire, and how I wish it were already blazing!" Fire symbolizes many things; one need not choose one meaning over another. For instance, fire symbolizes the judgment that is part and parcel of accountability. At the beginning of Jesus' ministry John the Baptist used fire as an image of judgment when he said, "Therefore every tree that does not produce good fruit will be cut down and thrown into the fire" (Luke 3:9b).

In addition, fire symbolizes the presence of God: Remember, God made his presence known to the Israelites through the burning bush and the pillar of fire that led them out of bondage. Fire also symbolizes the Holy Spirit: Tongues of fire rested over the head of each person at Pentecost. John the Baptist said that Jesus would baptize the people with the "holy Spirit and fire" (Luke 3:16). Finally, fire symbolizes purification. Jesus will set the earth ablaze with all of these fires.

Jesus' sense of urgency is not just about the fire he has to light, but about the baptism he has to receive: "There is a baptism with which I must be baptized, and how great is my anguish until it is accomplished!" Jesus is not speaking of ritual baptism. His meaning is closer to our expression, "baptism by fire." Jesus can feel the opposition and the evil building around him. Since persecution and death are inevitable, Jesus is anxious to get it over.

Jeremiah 38:4–6, 8–10 in its biblical context

Obviously our reading from Jeremiah is the middle of a story. The princes are angry with Jeremiah, so angry that they want him put to death, because Jeremiah is "demoralizing the soldiers who are left in this city, and all the people, by speaking such things to them." What did Jeremiah say?

The setting for today's reading is the southern kingdom, Judah, when it was being threatened by the Babylonians. Jeremiah preached a most unwelcome truth: that the Babylonians would be victorious in the coming battle. Jeremiah said, "Thus says the LORD: He who remains in this city shall die by sword, or famine, or pestilence; but he who goes out to the Chaldeans shall live; his life shall be spared him as booty, and he shall live. Thus says the LORD: This city shall certainly be handed over to the army of the king of Babylon; he shall capture it" (Jer 38:2–3).

The princes' response to Jeremiah is similar to the response of Jesus' adversaries to him. Instead of listening to the truth that Jeremiah is teaching, they want to silence him. So they throw him in a well and leave him for dead. The king, who had given permission to the princes to handle the problem as they saw fit, changes his mind after being informed of Jeremiah's situation. The king gives the court official permission to rescue Jeremiah.

Hebrews 12:1–4 in its biblical context

Last week in our reading from Hebrews the author was holding up Abraham as a model of faith. In the section between that reading and this Sunday's reading the author has held up many more models of faith from the Old Testament. It is to these examples that the author is referring when he says, "Since we are surrounded by so great a cloud of witnesses...."

In today's reading the author is urging the Hebrews to remain faithful themselves, to "persevere in running the race that lies before us...." He holds up Jesus as the preeminent model: "For the sake of the joy that lay before him he endured the cross, despising its shame, and has taken his seat at the right of the throne of God." True, the Hebrews are facing some opposition, but they have not had to resist their critics "to the point of shedding blood." In order to persevere the Hebrews should keep their "eyes fixed on Jesus, the leader and perfecter of faith."

Questions for Breaking Open the Word groups are on page 13.

Questions for other faith sharing groups

1. Has being faithful to your beliefs brought division rather than unity to some of your relationships? Explain. What do you think is the best way to respond to this fact?

2. Think of all of your experiences of fire. Why do you think fire appears so often in scripture as a symbol of God's presence and of Jesus' ministry?

3. Have you ever had to deliver truthful but bad news to someone? What were the circumstances? What were the effects of your words? Did you both dread, and want to accomplish, your task? Explain.

Bible study questions

1. Why is what Jesus says in today's Gospel so puzzling?

2. How has Luke set the stage for the passage that we read today?

3. What might Jesus have meant by the image of fire?

4. What did Jeremiah say that caused his critics to want him silenced?

5. What are the Hebrews being taught in today's reading?

TWENTY-FIRST SUNDAY IN ORDINARY TIME

Luke 13:22–30 in its biblical context

When Luke tells us that Jesus is on his way to Jerusalem, Luke is reminding us of the truth that we read in last week's Gospel: Jesus knows that when he reaches Jerusalem he will be killed. So Luke pictures Jesus on a journey, much as Jesus' disciples and we are on a journey. That journey will end when our life on earth ends. The choices we make on the journey will determine our ultimate destination.

Someone in the crowd asks Jesus, "Lord, will only a few people be saved?" Notice that Jesus does not directly answer this question. How many will be saved depends on the choices that people make on the journey. Jesus responds to the question by telling a parable.

In the parable a master of a house has locked his door. Some who are outside the house call and say, "Lord, open the door for us." The master does not open the door. Instead he says, "I do not know where you are from." Those outside remind the master, "We ate and drank in your company and you taught in our streets." Still, the master does not recognize them.

Remember that a parable is the middle of a conversation. The lesson comes from a single comparison between the person to whom Jesus is talking and someone in the story. In this story Jesus is comparing his audience, those whom he is inviting to become disciples, to the persons locked outside the house. One is not saved simply because one is present when Jesus teaches in the streets, or because Jesus eats and drinks with that person. Rather, one is saved when one becomes a disciple. To become a disciple is to put discipleship first, to choose the narrow door.

A parable is not an allegory. The lesson in a parable comes from the comparison between the audience and the characters in the story, not by having everything in the plot of the story stand for something else. It would be a mistake to think that the master in this story stands for God.

So, whether many are saved, or few, depends on whether many or few chose discipleship. If we heard only Jesus' parable we might think that Jesus has as much as said, "Few will be saved." That is not the case, however. Jesus then goes on to describe those who are saved, evidently a great number: First Jesus says that Abraham, Isaac, Jacob, and all the prophets will be in the kingdom of God. Next Jesus describes what could be a vast crowd: "And people will come from the east and the west and from the north and the south and will recline at table in the kingdom of God."

Although Jesus does not directly answer the question, "will only a few people be saved?" he does seem to imply that many will be saved. However, to have a casual acquaintance is not to be a disciple. To be saved one must respond to Jesus' invitation to discipleship with a wholehearted "yes." Since this response is a matter of the heart, those of us tempted to judge who is saved and who is not may be wrong: "some are last who will be first, and some are first who will be last."

Isaiah 66:18–21 *in its biblical context*

Today's Old Testament reading is from Third Isaiah, the prophet who offered hope to those who returned to the holy land after their exile in Babylon. During the exile some of the Israelites moved to various places in the then-known world, taking their knowledge of God with them. Through the exiles those in other nations came to know God. Third Isaiah teaches that God will send some from this group, from "nations of every language," to proclaim his glory to the world: " . . . from them I will send fugitives to the nations . . . that have never heard of my fame, or seen my glory; and they shall proclaim my glory among the nations."

Not only will the exiles return to Jerusalem, but people from every nation will hear about God and come to the holy city: "They shall bring all your brothers and sisters from all the nations as an offering to the LORD, on horses and in chariots, in carts, upon mules and dromedaries, to Jerusalem, my holy mountain, says the LORD. . . . "

Today's passage ends with a statement that would have been astounding to its original audience: the returned exiles. In reference to those from other nations Third Isaiah pictures God as saying, "Some of these I will take as priests and Levites." That people from other nations might become priests was not a given at the time of Third Isaiah's prophecy. In fact, Ezekiel, a prophet throughout the exile, did not think that people from other nations could become priests. Ezekiel taught that priesthood should be limited to Zadokite priests: "It is they who shall enter my sanctuary, they who shall approach my table to minister to me, and they who shall carry out my service" (Ezek 44:16).

Both our Gospel reading and our reading from Isaiah challenge us to realize that God may be more inclusive than are we. Some may be saved who, in our eyes, are lost. It is God's desire to save all. Whether many or few are saved depends on our response to God's love and God's invitation.

Hebrews 12:5–7, 11–13 *in its biblical context*

Today's reading from Hebrews is a continuation of last week's reading, in which the author is exhorting the Hebrews to remain faithful even though they are experiencing opposition. Today the Hebrews are told to regard their difficulties not as a sign of God's absence or displeasure, but as a sign of God's presence with them and God's love for them. God is treating the Hebrews as beloved children. "Endure your trials as 'discipline'; God treats you as sons. For what 'son' is there whom his father does not discipline?"

In teaching this lesson the author quotes Proverbs 3:11–12:

> "My son, do not disdain the discipline of the Lord
>   or lose heart when reproved by him;
> for whom the Lord loves, he disciplines;
>   he scourges every son he acknowledges."

If the Hebrews accept their difficulties in this spirit they will grow stronger. They will experience "the peaceful fruit of righteousness."

Questions for Breaking Open the Word groups are on page 13.

Questions for other faith sharing groups

1. Do you think many or few will be saved? Why?

2. In what ways are you a witness to God's love when you are "sent out" to your family, to work, and to your neighborhood? In what ways do you fail to be a witness?

3. In what ways has God disciplined you? What have you learned from this loving discipline?

Bible study questions

1. How does Jesus answer the question that he is asked in today's Gospel? What is Jesus teaching through this answer?

2. What is the setting for our reading from Isaiah?

3. What effect will those Jews who live in other nations have on those nations?

4. What does Third Isaiah say that would have struck his contemporaries as astounding?

5. How should the Hebrews regard their difficulties?

TWENTY-SECOND SUNDAY IN ORDINARY TIME

Luke 14:1, 7–14 in its biblical context

The passages immediately before and immediately after today's Lectionary reading affect our understanding of today's passage. Notice that the reading starts with chapter 14, verse 1, and then skips to verse 7. In the omitted passage Jesus heals a man with dropsy on the sabbath (Luke 14:1–6). Today's passage begins, "On the sabbath Jesus went to dine at the home of one of the leading Pharisees, and the people there were observing him carefully." The people are observing

Jesus carefully to see if he will heal on the Sabbath. After healing the man with dropsy Jesus dismisses him. Evidently the man with dropsy was not one of the invited guests at the Pharisee's house.

Just as the people who were invited to the banquet were observing Jesus carefully, so was he observing them. Jesus noticed "how they were choosing the places of honor at the table." We already know what Jesus thinks about seeking prestige. Earlier the disciples were having an argument over which of them was greatest. Jesus placed a child beside him and said, "Whoever receives this child in my name receives me, and whoever receives me receives the one who sent me. For the one who is least among all of you is the one who is the greatest" (Luke 9:48).

In today's passage Jesus uses humorous irony to correct the guests' desire to be noticed and to be honored. Jesus does not suggest that the guests stop seeking honor, but that they be craftier in the way they go about seeking honor. Instead of just brazenly taking the places of honor they should fake humility and take a back seat in hopes of being invited to a higher place. Jesus is gently correcting the guests for their constant concern about their own honor and prestige. Couldn't they just sit down without this concern even entering their minds?

Jesus then remarks to his host on the guest list. Perhaps this comment of Jesus' has been prompted by the fact that the man with dropsy was not an invited guest. Pharisees and scholars of the law, distinguished people, are the invited guests (Luke 14:3). Jesus tells his host that when he has a dinner party, instead of inviting friends, relatives, and wealthy neighbors, all of whom can reciprocate, he should "invite the poor, the crippled, the lame, the blind." They will not be able to reciprocate. The host will "be repaid at the resurrection of the righteous."

In a passage immediately following this exchange, but not included in the Lectionary, a man at the table says, "Blessed is the one who will dine in the kingdom of God" (Luke 14:15). In response to this remark Jesus tells the parable of the great feast to which are invited not only the host's friends, who turn down the invitation, but "the poor, the crippled, the lame, the blind." Still, the banquet is not full. This parable casts light on Jesus' previous remarks about whom the Pharisee should invite to his home. Perhaps the Pharisee believed, as did many of his contemporaries, that people who had disabilities were not in God's favor. Jesus corrects such a misunderstanding. Those who are suffering from physical ailments are not being punished. God loves them. They are invited to the heavenly banquet. The Pharisee would do well to invite them to his banquet too.

Sirach 3:17–18, 20, 28–29 *in its biblical context*

Sirach, also called Ecclesiasticus, is part of the Catholic canon, but not part of the canon of Protestant traditions. It was composed in Hebrew between 200 BC and 175 BC and translated into Greek by the original author's grandson sometime after 132 BC. The grandson wanted his

Greek-speaking contemporaries to benefit from the wisdom of his grandfather, Ben Sira. (*Sirach* is the Greek form of *Sira*.)

Ben Sirach wrote in the wisdom tradition. That is, he used reason to teach people both how to be in right relationship with God and others, and how to be successful in the world. In today's selection Ben Sirach is advising his readers to "conduct your affairs with humility." This is good practical advice as well as good spiritual advice. It is good practical advice because those who conduct themselves with humility "will be loved more than a giver of gifts." It is good spiritual advice because such persons "will find favor with God."

Ben Sirach also encourages his readers to be good to the poor.

> Water quenches a flaming fire,
> and alms atone for sins.

Sirach is not saying that an unconverted person can purchase forgiveness by giving money. Rather, he is saying that a wise man, out of kindness, will be constantly attentive to the needs of the poor. Sirach makes his meaning clear in the very next line:

> He who does a kindness is remembered afterward;
> when he falls, he finds a support. (Sir 3:30)

Sirach's teaching to take care of the poor, like his teaching to act humbly, is good advice for both spiritual and practical reasons.

Hebrews 12:18–19, 22–24a in its biblical context

Our passage from Hebrews is contrasting the Old Testament covenant made with Moses and the people at Mount Sinai to the New Testament covenant made with Jesus in the heavenly Jerusalem. The setting for the Old Testament covenant is described as "a blazing fire and gloomy darkness and storm and a trumpet blast and a voice speaking words such that those who heard begged that no message be further addressed to them" (see Exod 19–20). When God delivered the commandments the people were so afraid that they said to Moses, "You speak to us, and we will listen; but let not God speak to us, or we shall die" (Exod 20:19).

The setting for the New Testament covenant is the heavenly Jerusalem. Present are angels, God, the spirits of the just, and Jesus, whose blood did not call out for punishment, as did Abel's (see Gen 4:10), but for reconciliation.

The author of the Letter to the Hebrews makes this comparison as part of his plea that the Hebrews be a reconciling people. "Strive for peace with everyone, and for that holiness without which no one will see the Lord" (Heb 12:14). The Hebrews should strive for this peace and holiness because they are children of the new covenant. Jesus, the mediator of the new covenant, has reconciled the world to God.

Questions for Breaking Open the Word groups are on page 13.

Questions for other faith sharing groups

1. Why do you think that a concern about one's honor and prestige is a detriment to one's spiritual growth?

2. Do you think there is a relationship between what is spiritually wise and what is practically wise? Explain.

3. Why do you think that Christians are required to be reconciling people? Are you a reconciling person? How could you grow in your ability to be a reconciling person?

Bible study questions

1. What is Jesus teaching the guests at the Pharisee's dinner party through the parable he tells them?

2. What is Jesus teaching the host when he remarks on the guest list?

3. What reasons does Sirach give for why one should act humbly?

4. According to Sirach, in addition to being humble, what will a wise person do?

5. What comparison is the author of Hebrews making in today's reading?

Twenty-Third Sunday in Ordinary Time

Luke 14:25–33 in its biblical context

Once again, when we read the Gospel we are probably puzzled and resistant. Why would Jesus say, "If anyone comes to me without hating his father and mother, wife and children, brothers and sisters, and even his own life, he cannot be my disciple"? Jesus' words are particularly jarring because we know that Jesus has already told us that we are to love everyone, not only our family members, but even our enemies (see Luke 6:27–36). What could Jesus mean?

The main message in today's passage is a teaching that we have read at least four times previously (see Luke 5:1–11; 9:23–27, 57–62; 12:51–53): To be a disciple of Jesus Christ we must put discipleship first; we must put our relationship with Jesus before any other relationship. However, today's passage seems particularly harsh because of a problem with the translation. The Lectionary translation says that unless we "hate" others, and even our own lives, we cannot be Jesus' disciples.

In this passage the word *hate* means "love less." The meaning is clearer in Matthew's wording of the same teaching: "Whoever loves father or mother more than me is not worthy of me, and whoever loves son or daughter more than me is not worthy of me..." (Matt

10:37). Jesus is once more reminding his disciples that their response to his invitation to be a disciple must be a wholehearted "yes." No other relationship can be more important to us than our relationship with Christ.

Jesus then reminds those in the crowd that they should consider the cost of discipleship before they make a commitment. Discipleship is not easy. It will involve carrying one's cross. Any reasonable person considers the difficulty of a given course of action before deciding to do it. For instance, a person building a building does not lay the foundation without being sure that he can complete the project. A king does not go to battle without considering whether or not he will be able to win the battle. Just so, those who want to be disciples should think carefully before making such a decision; they should understand the cost before making the commitment.

Today's reading ends with Jesus saying, "In the same way, anyone of you who does not renounce all his possessions cannot be my disciple." Again we feel resistant. Surely Jesus couldn't be demanding that we renounce all our possessions. And how is this statement related to what precedes it? Jesus is implying some logical connection when he says, "In the same way.... " The connection seems to be a willingness to do what is necessary. The man who is building the building and the king who is going to battle both must be willing to do whatever is necessary in order to accomplish their goals. A disciple also must be willing to do what is necessary, even if that means renouncing one's property. Only a person who puts Jesus first can be Jesus' disciple.

Wisdom 9:13–18b in its biblical context

Our Old Testament reading is once more from the deuterocanonical Book of Wisdom (i.e., in the Catholic canon but not in the canon of Protestant churches; see the commentary for the Nineteenth Sunday in Ordinary Time, page 171 above). The author is meditating on how wonderful and necessary is God's gift of wisdom. First the author describes how difficult it is to know God's ways.

> Who can know God's counsel,
>   or who can conceive what the LORD intends? ...
> And scarce do we guess the things on earth,
>   and what is within our grasp we find with difficulty....

If we cannot perceive the things of earth how are we to perceive the things of heaven?

The author believes that human beings would not be able to perceive God's will or God's way were it not for the gift of wisdom that God has given the people.

> Or who ever knew your counsel, except you had given wisdom
>   and sent your holy spirit from on high?

The author uses the words *holy spirit* as a synonym for wisdom, not as a reference to the third person of the Trinity, a concept that developed later. Because God gave God's people wisdom, "the paths of those on earth" have been made straight. Human beings can know and act in ways that the Lord intends.

Philemon 9–10, 12–17 *in its biblical context*

Paul's Letter to Philemon is a very short letter (just one chapter) in which Paul asks Philemon, a slave owner, to welcome back, without inflicting any punishment, a runaway slave who has become a Christian and who has been serving Paul.

While Paul does not actually ask Philemon to free his slave, Onesimus, he does point out that now that both Philemon and Onesimus are baptized they have a new relationship with its own demands. "Perhaps this is why he was away from you for a while, that you might have him back forever, no longer as a slave but more than a slave, a brother, beloved . . . to you, as a man and in the Lord." Philemon is now to think of Onesimus as his partner in the Lord, not as his property. "So if you regard me as a partner, welcome him as you would me."

In addition, Paul, who is in prison, hints that Philemon might consider freeing Onesimus so that he could return to Paul. "I should have liked to retain him for myself, so that he might serve me on your behalf." Paul is not suggesting that Onesimus be his slave rather than Philemon's. He is suggesting that Philemon renounce his property, his rights as Onesimus's owner, so that Onesimus could help Paul in his ministry: " . . . so that he might serve me on your behalf in my imprisonment for the gospel. . . . "

In other words, Paul is challenging Philemon in the same way that Jesus challenged his would-be disciples, including us: In order to be faithful to his baptism, Philemon may have to renounce his *possession* and let Onesimus live as a free man.

Questions for Breaking Open the Word groups are on page 13.

Questions for other faith sharing groups

1. Do you find it hard to put Jesus and your relationship with him first? Explain.

2. What planning could you do in regard to time and possessions that would enable you to be a more faithful disciple?

3. Do you believe that wisdom is a gift? Whom do you know who has received this gift? Why do you think this person is wise?

Bible study questions

1. What is Jesus teaching in today's Gospel?

2. What does the word *hate* mean in today's passage? How does the same teaching appear in Matthew's Gospel?

3. What does the author of Wisdom mean by the *holy spirit?*

4. According to the Book of Wisdom, what does God's gift of wisdom make possible?

5. Why does Paul think that the relationship between Philemon and Onesimus should be different in the future than it has been in the past?

Twenty-Fourth Sunday in Ordinary Time

Luke 15:1–32 *in its biblical context*

In today's Gospel Jesus tells three parables, the parable of the lost sheep, the parable of the lost coin, and the parable of the older brother (more commonly called the parable of the prodigal son). Fortunately, our Lectionary selection includes both the audience to whom Jesus directs these parables and the topic that is under discussion. We need this information in order to interpret the parables correctly.

Luke tells us, "Tax collectors and sinners were all drawing near to listen to Jesus, but the Pharisees and scribes began to complain, saying, 'This man welcomes sinners and eats with them.'" It is in response to this criticism that Jesus tells today's parables. Jesus wants the Pharisees and scribes to understand that when Jesus eats and drinks with *them* he is eating and drinking with sinners. Jesus' parables are intended to call the Pharisees and scribes to self-knowledge and conversion.

The first parable is about a man who has one hundred sheep, but has lost one. He leaves the ninety-nine in the desert to search for the one. When he finds the lost sheep he calls all his friends together and rejoices. Luke helps us interpret the parable by having Jesus make the comparison between the audience and a character in the story himself. Jesus says to the Pharisees and scribes, "What man among you having a hundred sheep...." In other words, the Pharisees and scribes are compared to the man who has lost the sheep. They too would try to find that which they have lost and would rejoice when they found it.

The second parable is about a woman who has ten coins but has lost one. She searches diligently until she finds it. Then she too calls in her friends to rejoice with her. Once again, the Pharisees and scribes are compared to the woman. Like her, they would rejoice if they found what they had lost.

Finally Jesus tells the Pharisees and scribes a third parable, one that is designed to help them understand their own spiritual blindness. Jesus tells the story of a man who has two sons. The younger son is an obvious sinner. He asks his father to give him his inheritance early and then squanders it "on a life of dissipation." After sinking to the lowest of the low, he realizes that his father's servants have a better life than he is having. So he decides to go home and say, "Father, I have sinned against heaven and against you. I no longer deserve to be called your son; treat me as you would treat one of your hired workers." The younger son has come to the realization that he is a sinner. He does not feel superior to anyone.

The father is overjoyed that his son has returned and so throws a big party to celebrate. The older son, returning from the field, hears the party going on and asks a servant what is happening. On hearing that his brother has returned and that the party is in his brother's honor, he becomes angry and refuses to enter the house.

As the Pharisees and scribes listen to this story they would identify with the older brother. They feel just as that older brother does. The older brother says to his father, "Look, all these years I served you and not once did I disobey your orders; yet you never gave me even a young goat to feast on with my friends. But when your son returns, who swallowed up your property with prostitutes, for him you slaughter the fattened calf."

Like this older brother, the Pharisees and scribes feel that since they have obeyed the law they are better than those who have not. They feel self-righteous in regard to themselves and judgmental in regard to others. They want sinners named as sinners and marginalized as sinners. They do not want sinners to be invited to the banquet, much less have sinners be the guests of honor at the banquet.

Through the parable Jesus is teaching the Pharisees and scribes that they too are sinners. Their inability to love their brothers is a sin. The effect of their attitude will not be to exclude other sinners from the banquet, but to exclude themselves. Notice that the father invites both sons, both sinners, to the banquet. To the older son he says, "But now we must celebrate and rejoice, because your brother was dead and has come to life again; he was lost and has been found."

We do not know if the other brother accepts this invitation, repents, and joins the party. As the Gospel proceeds we will see that Jesus' self-righteous critics do not repent. Instead they want Jesus silenced (see Luke 20:19).

Exodus 32:7–11, 13–14 in its biblical context

On first reading, today's story from Exodus might seem to contradict our Gospel. In the Gospel Jesus told the Pharisees that there is a great deal of rejoicing in heaven when a sinner repents. This is not a picture of a punishing God. In the reading from Exodus, after the people have sinned, we hear God say to Moses, "Let me alone, then, that my wrath may blaze up against them to consume them." Are these contradictory pictures or not?

In order to respond to this question we need to know the literary form of the story from Exodus. This story is a legend. A legend has a historical core, but the author builds up an imaginative story around the historical core in order to teach a lesson. The historical core is the setting: the time when the Israelites were in the desert on their way to the holy land. The author uses a technique that we have seen before; he describes God anthropomorphically, that is, he describes God as though God were a human being. After seeing the people worship as God a golden calf that they have made with their own hands, God is so angry that God decides to destroy the people.

Moses intervenes on behalf of the people. He reminds God of all that God has done to save the people: "Why, O Lord, should your wrath blaze up against your own people, whom you brought out of the land of Egypt with such great power and with so strong a hand?" Moses then reminds God of his covenant promises to their ancestors, Abraham, Isaac, and Israel. On being reminded of all this God changes God's mind.

The lesson of the story is clear. God refrains from destroying sinners, not because sinners deserve to live, but because God is faithful to God's promises to love and protect. The Gospel, too, taught us that God loves, and therefore forgives, sinners. However, in order to receive forgiveness we first have to recognize that we are sinners and repent. Then there will be great rejoicing in heaven.

1 Timothy 1:12–17 in its biblical context

The First Letter of Paul to Timothy was probably attributed to Paul by one of his disciples who lived a generation later. Paul is pictured as meditating on God's abundant mercy: "I was once a blasphemer and a persecutor and arrogant, but I have been mercifully treated...." Paul describes himself as acting much as the Pharisees and scribes acted in today's Gospel. However, Paul did repent. Through his experience Paul learned that "Christ Jesus came into the world to save sinners." God not only forgave Paul but considered him trustworthy and appointed him to ministry. For this Paul is profoundly grateful. Paul hopes that his example will lead other sinners to Christ.

Questions for Breaking Open the Word groups are on page 13.

Questions for other faith sharing groups

1. Do you find it hard to forgive sinners? Do you believe that as a Christian you are required to do so? Explain.

2. Do you find it hard to believe that God has truly forgiven you for your sins? What effect does this belief have on your life?

3. Do you have a tendency to see others' sins more clearly than you see your own? If so, what could you do to remedy this situation?

Bible study questions

1. To whom does Jesus tell the parables in today's Gospel? What precipitated Jesus' telling these parables?

2. What is Jesus teaching through the first two parables?

3. What is Jesus teaching through the third parable?

4. What is the literary form of the story from Exodus? How would you describe this literary form?

5. What is the author teaching through the story from Exodus?

Twenty-Fifth Sunday in Ordinary Time

Luke 16:1–13 in its biblical context

Today we read a parable that has puzzled many people. A rich man has a steward (i.e., a person who manages his property), who "was reported to him for squandering his property." The rich man decides to fire the steward, and tells him so. While he still has his job the steward decides to use his master's money to make friends in hopes that the people he helps will be good to him later when he is unemployed, that they "may welcome me into their homes." We expect the master to be outraged at his steward. Instead he compliments him: "And the master commended that dishonest steward for acting prudently." What could Jesus possibly be teaching through this parable?

The Lectionary informs us that Jesus tells this parable to his disciples. In order to interpret the parable we have to figure out how the audience is compared to someone in the story. The disciples are compared to the dishonest steward for two reasons. First, the disciples are stewards of property, not owners, because everything belongs to God. As stewards it is the disciples' responsibility to share God's goods with those in need. Jesus has already taught the disciples how to regard personal property when he taught against greed and told them the parable of the rich fool (Luke 12:13–21; Eighteenth Sunday in Ordinary Time).

In addition, the disciples are compared to the steward because they, too, are in a temporary situation. Earth is a temporary situation. The disciples should keep in mind that the way they act in their present situation will affect the circumstances in which they find themselves in their next situation.

Notice that the master commends the dishonest steward not for acting dishonestly, but for acting prudently. All of his actions were motivated by the fact that he realized his present situation was temporary: "What shall I do, now that my master is taking the position of steward away from me?" It is this prudence upon which Jesus comments after telling the parable: "For the children of this world are more prudent in dealing with their own generation than are the children of light." In other words, Jesus is saying that if a dishonest person can prudently plan for his future, surely his disciples can do the same.

Jesus' next statement is ironic. Luke's Jesus often speaks ironically. Remember, we noticed that Jesus spoke ironically to the guests who were taking seats of honor at a banquet, suggesting that they add deviousness to their pride (see Luke 14:10; Twenty-Second Sunday in Ordinary Time). Here Jesus says, "I tell you, make friends for yourselves with dishonest wealth, so that when it fails, you will be welcomed into eternal dwellings." At face value these words do not make sense: If a person tries to make friends with dishonest wealth this behavior will not ensure the person's welcome into eternal dwellings. The meaning becomes clear if you invest the words with irony: If you make friends with dishonest wealth you will not be acting prudently, because, while such behavior might pave the way for you to be welcomed into an equally dishonest friend's home (this is what the dishonest steward did), it will not pave the way for you to be welcomed into eternal dwellings. If you want to be welcomed into eternal dwellings do not make friends with dishonest wealth.

Jesus then teaches without irony what he has just taught ironically. A disciple must be trustworthy in small matters as well as great matters. In addition, a disciple can serve only one master. "You cannot serve both God and mammon."

When reading Luke's Gospel, there are many times that you will better understand Jesus' words if you think of Jesus as having a sense of humor, as sometimes speaking playfully, and as using irony to gently correct his followers. Today's reading is just one example.

Amos 8:4–7 in its biblical context

Amos was the great eighth-century BC prophet who preached justice in the northern kingdom. In today's reading he is assailing those who grind down the poor. "Hear this, you who trample upon the needy / and destroy the poor of the land!"

Those who are mistreating the poor pretend to be religious. They obey the laws that forbid them from working when there is a new moon or on the Sabbath. " 'When will the new moon be over,' you ask, 'that we may sell our grain, / and the sabbath, that we may display the wheat?' " But even on these days of prayer they are plotting how they will cheat others. They will not give a full measure: "We will diminish the ephah" and will have things appear to weigh more than they do, and "add to the shekel."

In addition, those who are wealthy through their unfair practices are reducing the poor to slavery. Amos has earlier castigated the rich for their treatment of the poor:

> Because they sell the just man for silver,
>   and the poor man for a pair of sandals.
>   (Amos 2:6b)

Here he repeats the charge:

> We will buy the lowly for silver,
>   and the poor for a pair of sandals....

The rich have so little regard for the poor that to them the poor are worth no more than a pair of sandals. Amos warns the rich that God will never forget a thing they have done.

1 Timothy 2:1–8 in its biblical context

Last week the speaker in the First Letter to Timothy, Paul, thanked God for entrusting him with his ministry. This week he advises Timothy to have the people pray for others who have been given roles of leadership on their behalf: "...I ask that supplications, prayers, petitions, and thanksgivings be offered for everyone, for kings and for all in authority, that we may lead a quiet and tranquil life...." In other words, civil officials are also stewards. They too must use their power for the good of the people, that the people may lead tranquil lives.

It is pleasing to God that each person act for the good of others, for God "wills everyone to be saved." Because God wills everyone to be saved God has appointed Paul both preacher and apostle, to bring others to a knowledge of God and the "one mediator between God and men, / the man Christ Jesus...."

As disciples of Jesus Christ we are called to act as stewards, entrusted by God to use our gifts for the good of others. Our actions will be pleasing to God because God desires that all be saved, both ourselves and those we serve.

Questions for Breaking Open the Word groups are on page 13.

Questions for other faith sharing groups

1. Why do you think prudence is such an important virtue?

2. Are you a prudent person? Explain. What could you do to become more prudent?

3. Do you regard yourself as a steward of God's mission and God's property? If so, how does this belief affect your actions?

Bible study questions

1. In what two ways are the disciples compared to the steward in today's parable?

2. What is Jesus teaching through the parable?

3. What statement in today's reading is ironic? What is the intent of the statement?

4. What and to whom is Amos preaching in today's reading?

5. What does the author of 1 Timothy advise Timothy to do in today's reading? Why does the author say to do this?

Twenty-Sixth Sunday in Ordinary Time

Luke 16:19–31 in its biblical context

Last week our Gospel reading ended with Jesus telling the disciples, "You cannot serve God and mammon" (Luke 16:13b). This week we hear the story of the rich man and Lazarus. Between these two passages Luke's Gospel gives us some information that is not included in the Lectionary but that affects our understanding of today's parable.

Luke tells us that, as Jesus was teaching the disciples to be prudent stewards of property and not to allow love of riches to interfere with discipleship, the Pharisees were also listening: "The Pharisees, who loved money, heard all these things and sneered at him" (Luke 16:14). Jesus corrects the Pharisees by saying, "You justify yourselves in the sight of others, but God knows your hearts; for what is of human esteem is an abomination in the sight of God" (Luke 16:15).

Today's parable is part of this conversation. When we put the parable of the rich man and Lazarus in this context we see that it is not simply about the proper use of riches; it is also about whether or not the Pharisees accept the teaching authority of those whom God has sent them: Moses, the prophets, and Jesus himself. From the point of view of Luke and his reading audience, today's parable is about whether or not people will believe even if someone rises from the dead.

True, the parable of the rich man and Lazarus initially addresses the question raised last week with the parable of the crafty steward: how to use wealth on earth. The rich man in the story is in a temporary situation—earth. While on earth he "dressed in purple garments and fine linen and dined sumptuously each day," all the while completely ignoring the poor man, Lazarus, lying at his door. Both men die. Lazarus is "carried away by angels to the bosom of Abraham." The rich man goes to the netherworld and lives in torment.

Notice that Abraham does not tell the rich man he is being punished for not taking care of the poor; we assume he is in torment for this reason because of Jesus' previous teaching and because of what will follow. Abraham simply explains that the positions of the two have now been reversed. Lazarus is now comforted while the rich man is tormented. There is a great chasm between the two, and Lazarus cannot come to comfort the rich man.

At this point, the topic of the parable turns out to be something different than we expected. The rich man asks Abraham to send Lazarus to his father's house to warn his brothers "lest they too come to this place of torment." Abraham replies, "They have Moses and the prophets. Let them listen to them." The rich man, having not listened to Moses and the prophets himself, does not think that this is enough. He says, " 'Oh no, father Abraham, but if someone from the dead goes to them, they will repent.' Then Abraham said, 'If they will not listen to Moses and the prophets, neither will they be persuaded if someone should rise from the dead.' "

The Pharisees obviously are compared to the rich man. By telling them the story of the rich man and Lazarus Jesus is warning the Pharisees about two things: both their abuse of wealth and their rejection of him. The Pharisees have sneered at Jesus as he taught the proper use of wealth. In acting this way they are obviously acting like the rich man in that they are ignoring the needs of the poor. In addition, like the rich man, they are refusing to listen to the teachers whom God has sent them, to "Moses and the prophets," and, although they do not realize this, to Jesus himself.

This latter part of the parable, the part that takes place after the rich man and Lazarus die, is designed especially for the Pharisees. Unlike the Sadducees, they believed in the resurrection of the body. Jesus' suggestion that those who have died are still alive in bodily form on the other side would not have been preposterous to them. The Pharisees, of course, could not have known that Jesus would confirm the truth and authority of his teaching by rising from the dead. But for Luke and his audience, including us, the parable ends on a very ironic note. As Luke will tell us in the Acts of the Apostles, even when someone did rise from the dead, many still did not believe.

Amos 6:1a, 4–7 in its biblical context

In today's reading from Amos, the great prophet of justice is warning the Israelites that their rich lifestyle and their neglect of the poor will result in their experiencing political defeat. Notice that the Lectionary passage starts at 6:1 and then skips to 6:4. Our selection shows Amos warning Judah, the southern kingdom, "the complacent in Zion" (*Zion* is a reference to Jerusalem, the political and cultic center of the southern kingdom). The very next verse shows that the warning was also to the northern kingdom, Israel.

> Woe to the complacent in Zion,
>   to the overconfident on the mount of Samaria....

Samaria was the capital of the northern kingdom. While Amos was from the southern kingdom, his preaching was primarily in the northern kingdom.

Amos describes the rich lifestyle adopted by the wealthy: lying on beds of ivory, eating the best of food, listening to music, drinking wine, anointing themselves with fine oil, all the time ignoring "the collapse of Joseph," that is, the collapse of the nation. (The nation is often referred to by the name of one of the original twelve tribes; Joseph was one of the twelve sons of Jacob). Given this total infidelity to covenant love, the people should expect political defeat: "...now they shall be the first to go into exile."

1 Timothy 6:11–16 in its biblical context

In today's reading the author of 1 Timothy continues to give Timothy instructions on how to live. The author addresses Timothy as "man of God." Timothy is a "man of God" in two senses. We know from the beginning of the letter that Timothy was put in charge of the church in Ephesus (see 1 Tim 1:3). So Timothy is a "man of God" in the sense that he has been called to a specific ministry of leadership in the church. In addition, Timothy is, of course, among the baptized. It is to his baptism that the author refers when he admonishes Timothy, "Lay hold of eternal life, to which you were called when you made the noble confession in the presence of many witnesses." Timothy is encouraged to be faithful to his baptism and to his ministry, to keep the commandments "until the appearance of our Lord Jesus Christ."

Questions for Breaking Open the Word groups are on page 13.

Questions for other faith sharing groups

1. Whose teaching authority do you accept? Why?

2. Who are the poor lying at your doorstep? What is your response to them?

3. What about your lifestyle do you consider legitimate "taking care of yourself"? Does anything about your lifestyle reflect "excess wealth"? If so, what do you think you should do about that?

Bible study questions

1. About what two things is Jesus warning the Pharisees when he tells them the parable of the rich man and Lazarus?

2. Why is the plot of the parable especially suitable, given the Pharisees' beliefs?

3. What additional and ironic meaning is present for Luke's audience in the way the parable ends?

4. About what is Amos warning his contemporaries in today's reading?

5. In what two ways is Timothy a "man of God"?

TWENTY-SEVENTH SUNDAY IN ORDINARY TIME

Luke 17:5–10 in its biblical context

Our Gospel begins with the apostles saying to Jesus, "Increase our faith." This is the apostles' response to a very difficult direction that Jesus has just given them. Jesus has told the apostles that if their brother "wrongs you seven times in one day and returns to you seven times saying, 'I am sorry,' you should forgive him" (Luke 17:4). The apostles must realize that such generous forgiveness seems almost beyond human ability. So they ask Jesus to increase their faith.

This request reveals that the apostles are beginning to understand the spiritual order. They are beginning to understand that the spiritual life is not so much about what they are doing for God as it is about what God is doing for them through Jesus. They realize that if they are to live up to Jesus' teaching about forgiveness they will need more faith, and so they ask for this gift. Jesus affirms the power of faith when he says that with faith they could do what otherwise seems impossible; they could say to a mulberry tree, " 'Be uprooted and planted in the sea,' and it would obey [them]."

Next Jesus tells the apostles to think of themselves as "unprofitable servants." It is very likely that we feel some resistance to this direction because the words *unprofitable* and *servant* have negative connotations for us. The word *servant* or *slave* would not necessarily have had such negative connotations for the original audience. To be the slave of a king was considered a great honor. Jesus himself is elsewhere referred to as a slave (see Phil 2:7), as is Mary (Luke 1:38, 48). Luke has already made it clear, through Mary's example as well as Jesus' teaching, that it is right and good to be the one who serves.

Jesus is not teaching his apostles to have a subservient attitude or to lack self-respect. Rather, he is encouraging them to have an attitude of service rather than an attitude of pride. The apostles have had plenty of opportunity to witness a prideful attitude in Jesus' adversaries. As we have seen, because Jesus' adversaries obey the law more strictly than does Jesus, they feel that they have earned God's favor and are superior to Jesus and to "sinners."

By contrast, Jesus instructs the apostles to think of themselves as God's servants. However, no amount of service can earn God's love because God's love is a freely given gift. So, in this sense, the apostles are *unprofitable* servants. Rather than trying to earn God's love, the apostles are learning to serve in love as a response to God's initiative in their lives. Then, instead of being full of pride and self-righteousness, they will be full of love and gratitude. They will be able to say, "We are unprofitable servants; we have done what we were obliged to do," and mean it from their hearts.

Habakkuk 1:2–3; 2:2–4 in its biblical context

The prophet Habakkuk, like the apostles, needs to grow in faith. He is living through a most difficult time, the time shortly before the Babylonian exile (587 BC–537 BC), when the Babylonians have started to conquer the surrounding areas but before the fall of Jerusalem.

The Book of Habakkuk, which includes our reading, begins with the prophet's cry of "Why?" The prophet cannot understand why God is allowing events to unfold as they are unfolding.

> How long, O LORD? I cry for help
>   but you do not listen....
> Why do you let me see ruin;
>   why must I look at misery?

The Lectionary passage does not give us God's response to this initial question. God responds:

> Look over the nations and see,
> > and be utterly amazed!
> For a work is being done in your days
> > that you would not have believed, were it told.
> For see, I am raising up Chaldea,
> > that bitter and unruly people,
> That marches the breadth of the land
> > to take dwellings not his own. (Hab 1:5–6)

God is telling Habakkuk that God is raising up the Babylonians (i.e., Chaldea), who will conquer the unfaithful inhabitants of Judah.

Habakkuk cannot believe that God would do such a thing, and so, in a passage not included in the Lectionary, he remonstrates with God:

> Too pure are your eyes to look upon evil,
> > and the sight of misery you cannot endure.
> Why, then, do you gaze on the faithless in silence
> > while the wicked man devours
> > one more just than himself? (Hab 1:13)

God responds to this question with the words in the second half of today's reading. God's vision is coming to fulfillment. It "will not disappoint." Habakkuk must not be rash. He must wait and have faith in God's justice and fidelity.

> The rash one has no integrity;
> > but the just one, because of his faith, shall live.

2 Timothy 1:6–8, 13–14 in its biblical context

We move now from 1 Timothy to 2 Timothy. This letter, too, is thought by most scripture scholars to be attributed to Paul rather than written by Paul. The letters are called *Pastoral Letters* because they are written to pastors of churches rather than to the whole community.

One characteristic of the letters is that they show an interest in church organization. We notice this interest in today's selection as the author recalls a formal passing on of authority to Timothy by the imposition of hands: "I remind you to stir into flame the gift of God that you have through the imposition of my hands." The author wants Timothy to take Paul as his example, to bear any hardships that are his as he gives witness to the Gospel, and to guard "this rich trust with the help of the Holy Spirit that dwells within us."

Questions for Breaking Open the Word groups are on page 13.

Questions for other faith sharing groups

1. How would you describe the gift of faith? Have you personally experienced the power of faith, either in yourself or in someone else? Explain.

2. Do you feel resistant to the idea of being God's servant? Why or why not?

3. Have you, like the prophet Habakkuk, ever questioned God and asked "Why?" What were the circumstances? Did you receive an answer? Explain.

Bible study questions

1. Why did the apostles ask Jesus to increase their faith?

2. What does Jesus mean when he tells his apostles to think of themselves as "unprofitable servants"?

3. What questions does the prophet Habakkuk ask God? What is the setting for these questions?

4. What is God's response to Habakkuk?

5. Why is 2 Timothy called a *Pastoral Letter?* What pastoral interest is evident in today's reading?

TWENTY-EIGHTH SUNDAY IN ORDINARY TIME

Luke 17:11–19 *in its biblical context*

Today's Gospel, the story of Jesus curing ten lepers, follows immediately after last week's reading. Luke begins once again by reminding us that Jesus is on a journey to Jerusalem: "As Jesus continued his journey to Jerusalem...." We mentioned on the Twenty-First Sunday in Ordinary Time that this reference to a journey to Jerusalem is intended to remind us that even though Jesus knows what awaits him in Jerusalem he is choosing to make this journey in fidelity to his Father's will.

To understand the full significance of the story of the curing of the ten lepers, we must recall some earlier scenes in Luke's Gospel. Remember that when Jesus began his public ministry he read a scroll from the prophet Isaiah:

> The Spirit of the Lord is upon me,
>   because he has anointed me
>   to bring glad tidings to the poor.
> He has sent me to proclaim liberty to captives....
>
> > (Luke 4:18a)

After reading the scroll Jesus says, "Today this scripture passage is fulfilled in your hearing" (Luke 4:21b). Jesus is telling the people that they are living in the time when God is fulfilling God's promises, and that those promises are being fulfilled through him.

Jesus then goes on to tell his townspeople that no prophet is accepted in his native place, and he reminds them of times when non-Israelites have been the ones to benefit from a prophet's gift of healing (Luke 4:23–30). In fact, we will read one of Jesus' examples in today's Old Testament reading, when Elisha cures the leper Naaman.

Later John the Baptist's disciples come to Jesus and ask, "Are you the one who is to come, or should we look for another?" (Luke 7:19b). Jesus responds by holding up the mighty signs he has performed as evidence of his identity: "Go and tell John what you have seen and heard: the blind regain their sight, the lame walk, lepers are cleansed..." (Luke 7:22b). Jesus' curing of lepers is held up to John's disciples as a sign that Jesus is "the one who is to come," the fulfillment of God's promises.

In today's story all that Jesus has said is coming to fulfillment: Jesus cures ten lepers, and among them is a non-Israelite. As is true of other miracle stories, the account is designed to draw our attention to the identity of Jesus.

The lepers stand at a distance and call because they are unclean. They are not supposed to approach others or touch them. Jesus simply tells the lepers, "Go show yourselves to the priests." The purpose of showing themselves to the priests was to be declared clean so that they could be readmitted into the community (see Lev 14:2). So to obey this instruction was an act of faith on the part of each of them. While they were on the way they were cleansed.

Luke then tells us that one of the lepers, upon realizing that he was healed, "returned, glorifying God in a loud voice; and he fell at the feet of Jesus and thanked him. He was a Samaritan." As Jesus responds to the Samaritan he uses the occasion to emphasize three points: that only one returned to give thanks, that this one was a foreigner, and that the foreigner's faith has brought him salvation. In commenting on gratitude Jesus says that the gratitude should be directed toward God. However, Jesus is God's agent, and the man's realization of Jesus' identity has brought him not only a cure, but salvation: "...your faith has saved you."

2 Kings 5:14–17 in its biblical context

Naaman was the army commander of the king of Aram, a rival nation. The Arameans had previously captured an Israelite child who, when she saw that Naaman had leprosy, commented that the prophet in Samaria could cure him. With his king's permission, Naaman went to Elisha and asked to be cured. Elisha sent Naaman a message to wash seven times in the Jordan. After initial resistance to an apparently ridiculous demand, Naaman obeyed and was cured. Our Old Testament reading picks the story up here.

Naaman's cure results in his professing faith in the God for whom Elisha is a witness, the God of Israel. He says, "Now I know that there is no God in all the earth, except in Israel." Naaman asks for some soil to take home with him because, when he worships the God of Israel in his own country, he wants some of the soil of Israel to be with him.

Just as the story of Elisha's healing Naaman centers our attention on the God of Israel, so does the story of Jesus' healing of the ten lepers focus our attention on the identity of Jesus. If Jesus can heal lepers, who is he? Is he the one who is to come or not? Luke is teaching that Jesus is the fulfillment of God's promises to God's people. The Samaritan who had faith in Jesus was not only cleansed, but also saved.

2 Timothy 2:8–13 in its biblical context

The author of 2 Timothy pictures Paul writing from prison. Although Paul is in chains, "the word of God is not chained." Paul implores Timothy, "Remember Jesus Christ, raised from the dead, a descendant of David. . . . " Paul's mention that Jesus is a descendant of David is another way of saying that Jesus is the fulfillment of God's promises to the people.

Paul reminds Timothy that he can completely trust the truth that he has received and is now teaching others: "If we have died with him / we shall also live with him." This is to say that those who have been baptized ("died with him") will inherit eternal life ("live with him"). It is possible that Paul, Titus, and we could be unfaithful to Jesus. However, it is not possible that Jesus could be unfaithful to us or to God. The statement that if we deny Jesus "he will deny us" presupposes that Jesus has authority over others before God at judgment time (see Matt 10:32–33). Jesus could never be unfaithful because "he cannot deny himself."

Questions for Breaking Open the Word groups are on page 13.

Questions for other faith sharing groups

1. Think of a time in your life when you were overwhelmed with gratitude. What happened? Whom did you thank?

2. When have you had to walk in faith, trusting that things would work out before they actually had worked out? Are there times when you have failed to do this? Explain.

3. Do you completely trust the truth that since you have died with Christ you will also live with him? When do you think your "living with him" begins? Explain.

Bible study questions

1. Why was it an act of faith on the lepers' part to go and show themselves to the priests?

2. On what three things does Jesus remark when the leper returns to thank him?

3. Who is Naaman? In what way did Jesus speak of him as an example?

4. On what does the story of Naaman center our attention?

5. What truth does Paul tell Timothy he can completely trust?

TWENTY-NINTH SUNDAY IN ORDINARY TIME

Luke 18:1–8 in its biblical context

Today's parable about the widow and the dishonest judge is very similar to a parable that Jesus told earlier and that we discussed on the Seventeenth Sunday in Ordinary Time (see Luke 11:5–8). That parable was told in the context of Jesus' teaching the disciples how to pray. This parable is told in the context of Jesus giving a long eschatological sermon (i.e., one about the end times).

Immediately after the curing of the ten lepers, in a passage not included in the Lectionary, a Pharisee asks Jesus "when the kingdom of God would come" (Luke 17:20a). Jesus tells the Pharisee that the coming of the kingdom cannot be observed. "For behold, the kingdom of God is among you" (Luke 17:21b). Jesus then turns to his disciples and says, "The days will come when you will long to see one of the days of the Son of Man, but you will not see it" (Luke 17:22). As Jesus continues to teach about the coming of the kingdom he tells the parable of the persistent widow.

Luke introduces the parable by telling us what is being taught through the story. "Jesus told his disciples a parable about the necessity for them to pray always without becoming weary." In the story a widow asks for justice against her adversary. For a long time the judge, who cared neither for God nor for humanity, ignores her. However, the judge finally decides to do the right thing, not because it is the right thing to do, but because he fears that the woman might come and strike him. The disciples are compared to the woman. The lesson is perseverance in prayer.

As we have interpreted the parables in Luke's Gospel we have made a point of drawing the lesson from a single comparison between the audience and someone in the story. We have avoided the pitfall of allegorizing the parables. Today's parable is a perfect example of the danger of allegorizing a story that is not meant to be an allegory. If we allegorize this story the judge would have to stand for God.

As Jesus continues to explain his teaching, he does compare the judge to God, but not because they are similar. In fact, they are completely different. Jesus tells his disciples, "Pay attention to what the dishonest judge says. Will not God then secure the rights of his chosen ones who call out to him day and night? Will he be slow to answer them? I tell you, he will see to it that justice is done for them speedily." God is a just judge who will respond to the prayers of "his chosen ones."

Our reading ends with a statement that would seem completely unrelated to what precedes it if we were unaware of the larger context in which this passage appears in Luke's Gospel. Jesus says, "But when the Son of Man comes, will he find faith on earth?" Remember that Luke is writing this Gospel around AD 85, after the expected return of the Son of Man. As Luke pictures Jesus teaching his disciples to persevere in prayer in the context of the second coming, he knows that the words Jesus is saying hit home for them: Those in Luke's audience are longing to see the day of the Son of Man and have not seen it. Through Jesus' words Luke is reminding his audience to continue to pray and to continue to have faith so that when the Son of Man does come he will find faith on earth.

Exodus 17:8–13 in its biblical context

Our reading from the Book of Exodus is a response to the question, "Is God with us or not?" The story is teaching that God is with the Israelites, through Moses and the staff of God that he holds in his hand.

While the Israelites wandered in the desert they needed food and drink. They questioned whether or not God would take care of them. The stories immediately before the story we read today tell us how God provided the Israelites with manna, and then with water from a rock. The verse immediately before today's story says, "The place was called Massah and Meribah, because the Israelites quarreled there and tested the Lord, saying, "Is the LORD in our midst or not?" (Exod 17:7).

The staff that Moses is holding in today's reading has earlier been established as the sign that God is with him. When Moses was first given his mission he objected and said, "…suppose they will not believe me, nor listen to my plea? For they may say, 'The LORD did not appear to you'" (Exod 4:1). God's response is to point out Moses' staff and to show him that when he throws it on the ground it changes into a serpent, and when he picks it up it turns back into a staff (see Exod 4:2–4). God then tells Moses, "This will take place so that they may believe…that the LORD, the God of their fathers, the God of Abraham, the God of Isaac, the God of Jacob, did appear to you" (Exod 4:5).

In today's story, Moses, faced with war, tells Joshua that he "will be standing on top of the hill with the staff of God in my hand." This means that God will be with the Israelites as they fight. "As long as Moses kept his hands raised up, Israel had the better of the fight." Moses grew tired, however, and so Aaron and Hur had to support his hands. This is to say that even though Moses is God's chosen instrument, Moses cannot do everything alone. Moses needs the help of other leaders to make God's presence and power visible in the community.

2 Timothy 3:14–4:2 in its biblical context

Paul continues to encourage Timothy to remain faithful in carrying out his ministry. Timothy is to remain faithful to "the sacred Scriptures, which are capable of giving you wisdom for salvation through faith in Christ Jesus." Second Timothy was written before there was what we call the *New Testament,* so the author is referring to what we call the *Old Testament.* The author is claiming that when Old

Testament texts are read in the light of the events surrounding Jesus Christ they lead one to faith in Jesus Christ.

In addition, "All Scripture is inspired by God and is useful for teaching, for refutation, for correction, and for training in righteousness, so that one who belongs to God may be competent, equipped for every good work." Timothy is encouraged to continue to "proclaim the word . . . convince, reprimand, encourage through all patience and teaching."

In our Gospel reading we are assured that as we await the second coming, God hears us and will respond to our prayers. In the Old Testament reading we are assured that God was with God's people during the time of the exodus. In our reading from 2 Timothy we learn one of the ways in which God is constantly with us through the centuries; God is present in the inspired, living word, in scripture.

Questions for Breaking Open the Word groups are on page 13.

Questions for other faith sharing groups

1. How do you pray? Are most of your prayers petitions? Have you experienced the power of prayer? Explain.

2. In what ways do you experience God's presence? Have you considered the possibility that others might experience God's presence through you? Explain.

3. What role does scripture play in your life? Is it a living word? Is it integrated into your prayer life? Explain.

Bible study questions

1. In what context is today's parable told?

2. What is Jesus teaching through the parable?

3. What is being taught through the story from Exodus?

4. To what is the author of 2 Timothy referring when he speaks of scripture?

5. What does 2 Timothy say about scripture?

THIRTIETH SUNDAY IN ORDINARY TIME

Luke 18:9–14 in its biblical context

In Luke's Gospel today's parable about the Pharisee and the tax collector follows immediately after last week's parable about the persistent widow. The overall context is still an eschatological sermon. Just as last week's parable was about prayer, so is the parable of the Pharisee and the tax collector.

Luke gives us very clear information about the audience to whom Jesus tells this parable: "Jesus addressed this parable to those who were convinced of their own righteousness and despised everyone else." As we read the parable it is most likely that we do not identify with the Pharisee. However, if after reading the parable, we say to ourselves, "Thank God I am not like that Pharisee," we may have to take a closer look.

A Pharisee and a tax collector go up to the temple to pray. The Pharisee's prayer begins as though it were a prayer of gratitude, praising God: "O God, I thank you. . . . " However, the prayer immediately turns into a litany of self-congratulation. This Pharisee brings to his prayer an attitude that makes it impossible for him really to pray.

The Pharisee believes to the depths of his being that he is better than other people because he obeys the law. Instead of praying, the Pharisee lists the reasons why he feels superior to the tax collector. All of the qualities and actions the Pharisee claims as his own are good. However, they do not add up to righteousness, that is, to being in right relationship with God. The Pharisee has the idea that he has earned God's favor. Because he does not realize that he needs forgiveness for his pride and his judgmental attitude toward others, he does not ask for forgiveness. Because he does not realize that righteousness is a gift rather than something earned, he does not receive righteousness.

Those in Jesus' audience who are "convinced of their own righteousness and [despise] everyone else" are just like the Pharisee. However, the fact that they are like the Pharisee may prevent them from identifying with the Pharisee as they hear the story. After all, the Pharisee in this story turns out to be the "bad guy." Since the people to whom Jesus is directing the parable think of themselves as the "good guys," they may well miss the point.

Jesus' audience would never have identified with the tax collector. The tax collector would be looked down upon by the self-righteous people to whom Jesus is telling this parable. Tax collectors were hated by the Jews because they were seen as partners in Roman oppression. Since tax collectors received a cut of the taxes, they participated in what the Jews considered both an injustice and an idolatrous act: the coins collected had Caesar's image on them and were thus considered graven images.

Nevertheless, the tax collector is the "good guy" in the story. Unlike the Pharisee, the tax collector realizes that he is a sinner, confesses that he is a sinner, and asks for God's mercy. He knows that he has not earned God's mercy. He asks for it as a free gift.

The self-righteous and judgmental people in Jesus' audience are being taught that they, like the Pharisee, do not really pray and are not in right relationship with God, even though they think they are. If, when we read this parable, we say, "Thank God I am not like that Pharisee," then the parable is directed just as much at us as it is at Jesus' original audience.

Sirach 35:12–14, 16–18 in its biblical context

As we mentioned on the Twenty-Second Sunday in Ordinary Time, when the Old Testament reading was also from Sirach, this book is canonical for Catholics but apocryphal for Protestants. Like our Gospel, today's reading from Sirach gives us a lesson on prayer.

Because God is a God of justice, God has no favorites. God is not "unduly partial toward the weak," but, at the same time, God hears the cry of the oppressed, the orphan, and the widow. Sirach describes the cry of the oppressed much as Jesus described the prayer of the widow in last Sunday's Gospel:

> The prayer of the lowly pierces the clouds;
>   it does not rest till it reaches its goal,
> nor will it withdraw till the Most High responds,
>   judges justly and affirms the right,
> and the Lord will not delay.

Our God is not like a human king who might be inclined to respond more readily and more favorably to those who are wealthy and influential. Rather, while always acting justly, God is attentive to the cries of the poor and the powerless.

2 Timothy 4:6–8, 16–18 in its biblical context

As we read our passage from 2 Timothy we might be tempted to say, "Paul seems to be acting like the Pharisee in our Gospel reading. He is congratulating himself and calling himself 'righteous.'" However, this would be a mistaken impression, whether the author of the letters to Timothy is Paul or not.

Most scripture scholars believe the highly developed ideas in the letter date them as later than Paul. However, since there is not complete agreement on the subject, let us look at today's passage as though it were written by Paul himself. Paul is not like the Pharisee in today's Gospel because he understands that everything he has accomplished has been more God's work than his own. When describing his difficulties Paul says, "But the Lord stood by me and gave me strength, so that through me the proclamation might be complete and all the Gentiles might hear it." Paul does not rely on his own wits. Rather, he believes that the "Lord will rescue me from every evil threat. . . . " The glory does not belong to Paul: "To him be glory forever and ever. Amen."

However, it is more likely that a follower of Paul's wrote the letters to Timothy after Paul suffered a martyr's death and attributed them to Paul as a way of honoring him. The author is holding up Paul as a model for Timothy. Paul is a model because of his fidelity through suffering. "I am already being poured out like a libation, and the time of my departure is at hand. I have competed well; I have finished the race; I have kept the faith." The fact that Paul suffered opposition, even persecution, does not mean that God was not with him. It was the Lord who stood by Paul and gave him strength.

Paul was God's chosen instrument. He was faithful to his ministry until the end. Timothy is being urged to take Paul as a model and conduct himself in the same manner.

Questions for Breaking Open the Word groups are on page 13.

Questions for other faith sharing groups

1. What is your reaction to today's parable? Does your reaction teach you anything about yourself? If so, what?

2. Do you have a truth speaker in your life to whom you give permission to tell you something true about yourself when it is for your own good? If so, who is this person? If not, would you like to have such a person?

3. When you hear that God, although just, is quick to respond to the prayers of the oppressed, do you hear this as good news or not? Do you know why?

Bible study questions

1. Why is the Pharisee's prayer not really a prayer?

2. Why is the tax collector's prayer effective?

3. What is Jesus teaching his audience? Why is it likely that they will miss the message?

4. What is Sirach teaching us about prayer in today's reading?

5. What two interpretations could you give to Paul's words that we read today in the Letter to Timothy?

THIRTY-FIRST SUNDAY IN ORDINARY TIME

Luke 19:1–10 in its biblical context

We move on now to the story of Zacchaeus, the tax collector. The Lectionary has skipped over several important stories that help set the stage for today's story. One is a conversation that Jesus has with a rich official (Luke 18:18–23). Jesus invites the man to "sell all that you have and distribute it to the poor, and you will have a treasure in heaven. Then come, follow me" (Luke 18:22b). The man is greatly saddened by Jesus' words. He is rich and does not want to give up his possessions.

After discussing how difficult it is for a rich person to enter the kingdom of God, Jesus once more takes the Twelve aside and, for the third time, warns them that he is going to be killed but that he will rise on the third day. Luke tells us, "they understood nothing of this; the word remained hidden from them and they failed to comprehend what he said" (Luke 18:34). Luke has once again reminded us of what awaits Jesus in Jerusalem and of the urgency of his mission.

As we will see, awareness of the story of the reluctant rich man and of Jesus' third warning of his coming suffering and death helps us better understand the story we read today. A large crowd has gathered as Jesus passes through Jericho. Among the crowd are Zacchaeus, "a chief tax collector and also a wealthy man," as well as others who thoroughly disapprove of Zacchaeus. As we discussed last week, tax collectors were disliked by their fellow Jews because they were collecting taxes on behalf of the Roman occupiers. Zacchaeus's income would have been a percentage of the taxes he collected. That he was rich added insult to injury.

Jesus, of course, knows what people think of tax collectors. Nevertheless, when Jesus sees Zacchaeus up in the tree he makes a point of reaching out to him—he even invites himself to Zacchaeus's house. Jesus says, "Zacchaeus, come down quickly, for today I must stay at your house." As has happened many times before, Jesus is criticized for eating with sinners. The crowd grumbles, "He has gone to stay at the house of a sinner."

Zacchaeus responds immediately to Jesus' request and greets Jesus not only with joy, but with repentance. He must already be aware of Jesus' teaching on the proper use of wealth (see Luke 18:24–27), for he says, "Behold, half of my possessions, Lord, I shall give to the poor, and if I have extorted anything from anyone I shall repay it four times over." Zacchaeus is a great contrast to the sad rich man that Luke has just presented. On the other hand, he is much like the "sinful woman" who washed Jesus' feet, and like the two debtors in the parable Jesus told to the Pharisee who objected to Jesus' accepting that woman's gift (see Luke 8:36–50). Zacchaeus has repented not to earn Jesus' love but in response to his realization that Jesus already loves him.

Notice that Jesus tells Zacchaeus that he *must* stay at his house. There is a sense of urgency about that word. As we mentioned, Luke has been building up a sense of urgency as Jesus' trip to Jerusalem proceeds, constantly reminding the reader, through Jesus' predictions of his passion, of what awaits him there. Time is growing short to complete his mission. You may remember that we have seen Jesus use this expression before. In fact, Jesus' very first words in Luke's Gospel were to his mother when he said, "Why were you looking for me? Did you not know that I must be in my Father's house?" (Luke 2:49; see the Sunday after Christmas). Jesus must invite himself to Zacchaeus's house because Jesus must do his Father's will by seeking out the lost. In response to Zacchaeus's repentance Jesus says, "Today salvation has come to this house...." Zacchaeus has accepted the good news that Jesus must give: God loves sinners and calls them to repentance.

Wisdom 11:22–12:2 in its biblical context

The author of Wisdom has arrived by reason at the conclusion that God loves sinners. The first line of today's reading might make you think that the author is going to talk about the insignificance of human beings given the vastness of creation:

> Before the LORD the whole universe is as a grain from a balance
>> or a drop of morning dew come down upon the earth.

But that is not his point at all. Rather, he reasons that since all that exists was created by God, God must love all that exists. Why would God create something that God did not love and value?

> For you love all things that are
>> and loathe nothing that you have made;
>> for what you hated, you would not have fashioned.

Because God loves all of creation and God's spirit is in all that exists, God loves even sinners.

> But you have mercy on all, because you can do all things;
>> and you overlook people's sins that they may repent.

This does not mean that God permits people to keep on sinning without correction:

> Therefore you rebuke offenders little by little,
>> warn them and remind them of the sins they are committing,
>> that they may abandon their wickedness and believe in you,
>>> O LORD!

God loves sinners before they repent. God corrects sinners in order to call them back to be in right relationship with their loving God. Jesus was teaching Zacchaeus that God loves sinners when he told Zacchaeus that he must go to his house.

2 Thessalonians 1:11–2:2 in its biblical context

Both of the letters to the Thessalonians deal with questions surrounding the second coming. Our passage today begins with the prayer that the author offers for the Thessalonians as he begins his letter. He then quickly moves on to the problem at hand, the occasion for writing the letter.

Evidently someone in the community has been telling the Thessalonians that the second coming is at hand. Perhaps someone claiming to be inspired has said this. Perhaps someone has stated it as a word of prophecy in a community meeting. Perhaps someone has made this claim in a letter that has been attributed to Paul. In any case, it is not true, and the author does not want the Thessalonians to be disturbed about it: "We ask you, brothers and sisters, with regard to the coming of our Lord Jesus Christ and our assembling with him, not to be shaken out of your minds suddenly, or to be alarmed either by a 'spirit,' or by an oral statement, or by a letter allegedly from us to the effect that the day of the Lord is at hand."

Our reading ends at this point. However, in the letter the author goes on to argue against such an idea by pointing out that those signs that will precede the second coming have not yet occurred (see 2 Thess 2:3–12). The author of 2 Thessalonians does not want the people to be misled. Rather, he prays for them that God will "powerfully bring to fulfillment every good purpose and every effort of faith, that the name of our Lord Jesus may be glorified in you, and you in him...."

Questions for Breaking Open the Word groups are on page 13.

Questions for other faith sharing groups

1. If Jesus said to you, "I must come to your house," what would be your response?

2. In what ways has Jesus already come to your house?

3. Do you think it is reasonable to believe that God loves and forgives sinners? Why?

Bible study questions

1. How does Zacchaeus respond to Jesus' insistence that Jesus come to his house?

2. Why must Jesus go to Zacchaeus's house?

3. On what other occasion did Jesus say something similar?

4. How does the author of Wisdom reason his way to a belief that God loves sinners?

5. What misinformation does the author of 2 Thessalonians want to correct?

THIRTY-SECOND SUNDAY IN ORDINARY TIME

Luke 20:27–38 in its biblical context

Between last Sunday's story of Jesus and Zacchaeus and today's account of Jesus' argument with the Sadducees over the possibility of resurrection a great deal has occurred. Jesus has entered Jerusalem and has been greeted as a king (Luke 19:40). Once there, Jesus laments Jerusalem's coming destruction because she "did not recognize the time of [her] visitation" (Luke 19:44b). After cleansing the temple (Luke 19:45–46), Jesus continues to teach in the temple area. Luke tells us, "The chief priests, the scribes, and the leaders of the people, meanwhile, were seeking to put him to death, but they could find no way to accomplish their purpose because all the people were hanging on his words" (Luke 19:47b–48). It is in this context that Jesus has today's acrimonious discussion with the Sadducees.

The Sadducees were a powerful group within Judaism, made up of both the lay and priestly aristocracy. The Sadducees had control of the Sanhedrin, the Jews' supreme ruling council. Soon Luke will tell us that after his arrest Jesus will appear before the Sanhedrin: "When day came the council of elders of the people met, both chief priests and scribes, and they brought him before their Sanhedrin" (Luke 22:66). The chief priests who want Jesus dead, and who serve on the council of elders and on the Sanhedrin, are Sadducees.

The Sadducees do not believe in the resurrection. The question of life after death was a point of disagreement within Judaism at this time. Later in Acts Paul will appear before the Sanhedrin and will precipitate an argument among the members over the possibility of resurrection. Luke will set the scene by telling us, "the Sadducees say that there is no resurrection or angels or spirits, while the Pharisees acknowledge all three" (Acts 23:8). In today's Gospel the Sadducees argue their point of view with Jesus.

The Sadducees base their argument against the possibility of resurrection on the law (the first five books of the Old Testament). The Sadducees remind Jesus that the law requires a man to raise up an heir in the name of his brother should the brother die without having children (see Deut 25:5). The thinking behind this law was that since there is no life beyond earth, the way to give meaning to one's life and to extend it into the future was to have offspring. If a man died childless, his family had the obligation to raise up an heir in his name.

The Sadducees then point out that under no circumstances would it be considered moral for a woman to have more than one husband at a time. If there is life after death, wouldn't obedience to the law result in multiple husbands? Obviously, this would be wrong. Therefore there can be no life after death.

In response to this argument Jesus first challenges the Sadducees' assumption that life after resurrection is simply a continuation of life as it has been experienced on earth where people who have been married are still married. On earth people do enter into marriage to have children. Without procreation human life would not continue at all. However, in the world to come procreation will not be necessary to continue human life because people will not die. "They can no longer die, for they are like angels." The Sadducees' assumption that people are married in the world to come is wrong.

Next Jesus turns to the one authority he knows the Sadducees will accept, the same authority they used in posing their question: the law. Jesus points out that in the story of the burning bush, God is called the "God of Abraham, the God of Isaac, and the God of Jacob" (Exod 3:6). Since God is the God of the living, not the God of the dead, these patriarchs must still be alive. Therefore, Moses himself showed that the dead rise again.

Notice that when Jesus speaks of those who are judged worthy of a place in the resurrection he says that they *do* not marry, not that they *will* not marry: "those who are deemed worthy to attain to the coming age and to the resurrection of the dead neither marry nor are given in marriage." In other words, Jesus implies that for some "the age to come" is already present. The passage may be a hint that a vocation to the single life derives some of its meaning from the fact that it is a sign in this world of "the age to come."

2 Maccabees 7:1–2, 9–14 *in its biblical context*

Second Maccabees is part of the Catholic canon but not part of the canon of Protestant churches. Like many of the deuterocanonical books, it was originally written in Greek and was never included in the Hebrew canon. Second Maccabees tells us much of the history of Judaism from 180 BC to 161 BC. It was during this time in Jewish history that a belief in life after death entered Judaism.

Today's story, in which a mother and seven brothers are accepting death rather than disobeying the law, clearly expresses a belief in resurrection. At the point of death one of the brothers says, "You accursed fiend, you are depriving us of this present life, but the King of the world will raise us up to live again forever." When another brother is near death he says, "It is my choice to die at the hands of men with the hope God gives of being raised up by him."

In the end all seven brothers and their mother accept death bravely, believing firmly that they will drink "of never-failing life, under God's covenant" (2 Macc 7:36). This belief in a resurrection developed not from the conviction that human beings deserve life after death, but from the conviction that God in God's love will grant it.

2 Thessalonians 2:16–3:5 *in its biblical context*

The author of 2 Thessalonians continues to encourage the Thessalonians to remain faithful to what they have been taught rather than be misled by those who misinform them. In doing this the author reminds the Thessalonians that God the Father and Christ love them and give them "everlasting encouragement and good hope through his grace."

It was belief in God's everlasting love that allowed the Jews of the second century BC to arrive at a belief in life after death in the first place.

The author goes on to assure the Thessalonians that "the Lord is faithful; he will strengthen you and guard you from the evil one." In addition to a belief in God's love, a belief in God's justice enabled the Jews to believe in life after death. Surely God would not let evil prevail.

By the time the author of 2 Thessalonians is writing, Christ has risen from the dead. The author and the Thessalonians share a belief in life after death. They wait in joyful expectation for the time when Jesus will return and raise them to eternal life as well.

Questions for Breaking Open the Word groups are on page 13.

Questions for other faith sharing groups

1. On what do we, as Christians, base our belief in life after death?

2. What difference does a belief in life after death make in the way you live your life?

3. Do you think it is reasonable to believe in life after death? Why?

Bible study questions

1. Who were the Sadducees? What roles did they play in Jewish society?

2. Over what question do the Sadducees argue with Jesus? What is their argument?

3. What response does Jesus give to the Sadducees' argument?

4. Based on what two beliefs did some Jews arrive at a belief in resurrection?

5. Why do the Thessalonians have "everlasting encouragement and good hope"?

THIRTY-THIRD SUNDAY IN ORDINARY TIME

Luke 21:5–19 in its biblical context

Jesus is still teaching in the temple area. Some people are speaking about the temple, noting how it is "adorned with costly stones and votive offerings." Jesus warns the people that the temple is going to be destroyed. "All that you see here—the days will come when there will not be left a stone upon another stone that will not be thrown down."

This passage recalls Jesus' earlier statement, not included in the Lectionary, when he lamented over Jerusalem: "For the days are coming upon you when your enemies will raise a palisade against you; they will encircle you and hem you in on all sides. They will smash you to the ground and your children within you, and they will not leave one stone upon another within you . . ." (Luke 19:43–44a).

The people then ask Jesus, "Teacher, when will this happen? And what sign will there be when all these things are about to happen?" As we can tell from the way Luke has pictured the people wording this question, the topic of the destruction of the temple ("when will this happen?") and the topic of the end times ("when all these things are about to happen") are one and the same in their minds. For Jesus' contemporaries the end times were the times when God would take decisive action and vindicate God's people by punishing evil and rewarding good. In today's passage we see that the destruction of the temple would be one of the signs that the end times were near.

Jesus, too, speaks of the destruction of the temple and the end times in relationship to each other. As he responds to the people's question he talks not only about the destruction of the temple, but also about the coming of the Son of Man. One of the signs of the end times that Jesus describes, in a verse immediately after today's Lectionary reading, is the desolation of Jerusalem: "When you see Jerusalem surrounded by armies, know that its desolation is at hand" (Luke 21:20).

After describing this sign, along with the signs that we read in today's Gospel, Jesus says, "And then they will see the Son of Man coming in a cloud with power and great glory. But when these signs begin to happen, stand erect and raise your heads because your redemption is at hand" (Luke 21:27–28). So Luke pictures both Jesus and his contemporaries treating the destruction of the temple and the end times, the coming of the Son of Man, as related events.

By the time Luke is writing his Gospel (AD 85) the temple has been destroyed, but the Son of Man has not yet come in glory. So for Luke and his contemporaries, as for us, the destruction of the temple and the coming of the Son of Man are two separate topics. In addition, Jesus' followers have suffered severe persecution. Many have died before the coming of the Son of Man. Luke's description of the coming of the end times is influenced by these facts.

First Luke has Jesus point out that many will think they are seeing the signs of the imminent coming of the Son of Man, but they will be mistaken. "See that you not be deceived, for many will come in my name, saying, 'I am he,' and 'The time has come.' Do not follow them!" As we recently read in our Lectionary selections from 2 Thessalonians, this was the experience of the Thessalonians. They were being told that "the time has come," when it had not come. Jesus warns his followers not to be deceived by such false prophets.

Jesus also warns his followers that they will suffer persecution. "Before all this happens, however, they will seize and persecute you, they will hand you over to the synagogues and to prisons.... You will even be handed over by parents, brothers, relatives, and friends, and they will put some of you to death."

As Jesus describes this terrible persecution, even death, he says, "but not a hair on your head will be destroyed. By your perseverance you will secure your lives." What could Jesus mean? Remember, just last week we read Jesus' argument with the Sadducees over the possibility of life after death. Jesus can now assure his followers that if they remain faithful to him through persecution "not a hair on your head will be destroyed," because there is life after death. The life that his followers will secure by faithfully suffering persecution is not life on earth, but life in the world to come.

Malachi 3:19–20a in its biblical context

Our reading from Malachi is also about the end times, that is, the time when God will intervene in history to vindicate God's people.

God will punish evil and reward good. The word *Malachi* means "my messenger." The author of Malachi lived during the time when the Israelites were rebuilding Jerusalem after the Babylonian exile (587 BC–537 BC). He was extremely critical of what he saw as violations of the people's covenant relationship with God. After telling of abuses Malachi asks, "Where is the just God?" (Mal 2:17b).

The passage we read today is part of Malachi's response. The just God will come soon: "Lo, the day is coming, blazing like an oven. . . ." When God comes, "all the proud and all evildoers will be stubble." For those who have been faithful, however, "there will arise / the sun of justice with its healing rays." When God comes those who are evil will be punished and those who are good will be vindicated.

2 Thessalonians 3:7–12 in its biblical context

As he brings his letter to a close, the author of 2 Thessalonians pictures Paul addressing a problem that has arisen in the community. Evidently some of the Thessalonians are unwilling to work, presumably because they believe those who are saying that the second coming is at hand. If the world as we know it is coming to an end, why bother working? Paul has no patience with this attitude. If a person will not work, that person should not eat.

The author pictures Paul presenting himself as a model for the Thessalonians. "You know how one must imitate us. For we did not act in a disorderly way among you, nor did we eat food received free from anyone." The Thessalonians should go about their business in a quiet and orderly way and not keep busy by "minding the business of others."

Questions for Breaking Open the Word groups are on page 13.

Questions for other faith sharing groups

1. When you hear the phrase *end times*, what do you understand it to mean?

2. When you think about Jesus' coming in glory to judge the living and the dead do you want it to happen soon or not? Why?

3. What do you need to do to be prepared for the end times?

Bible study questions

1. What two events are connected topics for Jesus and his contemporaries but not for Luke or for us?

2. What has occurred, and what has not occurred, that has separated the topics in Luke's mind and in ours?

3. What does Luke mean when he pictures Jesus telling his followers that not a hair on their heads will be harmed?

4. Why is Malachi longing for the end times?

5. What problem has arisen among the Thessalonians that is addressed in today's reading?

The Solemnity of Our Lord Jesus Christ the King, Thirty-Fourth Sunday in Ordinary Time

Luke 23:35–43 in its biblical context

On the feast of Christ the King the Gospel reading focuses our attention not on Christ in glory at the right hand of the Father, but on Christ crucified and taunted. The reading is full of dramatic irony: that is, the characters in the story and the readers of the Gospel have completely different understandings of what is taking place. While the soldiers intend to ridicule Jesus by calling him a king, the reader knows that their words are true. Christ is a king.

Luke has already told us that the Jewish leaders want to kill Jesus (see Luke 19:47). However, since theirs is an occupied country, the Sanhedrin, the Jewish high court, does not have the authority to put Jesus to death. In order to receive the death penalty Jesus would have to be found guilty in a Roman court. That is why Jesus was taken before Pilate and accused of claiming to be a king.

When Jesus is before the Sanhedrin the charge is blasphemy. The members of the Sanhedrin first ask Jesus if he is the messiah. Jesus responds, "If I tell you, you will not believe, and if I question, you will not respond. But from this time on the Son of Man will be seated at the right hand of the power of God" (Luke 22:67b–69). They then ask, "Are you then the Son of God?" He replies, "You say that I am" (Luke 22:70). This settles the matter for the members of the Sanhedrin. They consider Jesus' words to be blasphemy.

When Jesus is brought before Pilate, the Roman procurator, the charge is different. Jesus' accusers say, "We found this man misleading our people; he opposes the payment of taxes to Caesar and maintains that he is the Messiah, a king" (Luke 23:2). Before Roman authorities the charge is sedition, not blasphemy. By claiming to be a king Jesus would be challenging the authority of the Roman emperor. Although Pilate finds Jesus innocent, he succumbs to the demands of the crowd and turns Jesus over to be crucified.

In today's Gospel Jesus has already been crucified. The rulers who sneer at Christ as he hangs on the cross, and the soldiers who jeer at him, have no idea in the world that Jesus is a king and could save himself. Their intent is to ridicule Jesus when they say, "If you are King of the Jews, save yourself." However, the reader knows both that Jesus is a king and that he will not use his power to save himself. Luke showed us that Jesus overcame the temptation to use his power in self-serving ways before his public ministry ever began (see Luke 4:1–13).

In a story found only in Luke we read that one of the criminals crucified with Jesus defends him. After telling a fellow criminal that the two of them deserve the punishments they have received but Jesus does not, he turns to Jesus and says, "Jesus, remember me when you come into your kingdom." This is a most remarkable statement. It presumes that the criminal understands that Jesus, as a king, has the power to forgive, and that even though Jesus himself is facing death, Jesus will enter his kingdom and reign.

In response Jesus tells the criminal, "Amen, I say to you, today you will be with me in Paradise." Jesus' words reflect the understanding that Jesus' reign will not be at some far off "end time" but this day. However, Jesus does not use the word *kingdom* to describe the place where he and the criminal will be. Rather, he calls it *paradise. Paradise* is the word used in the Septuagint (the Greek translation of the Old Testament) to describe the garden of Eden, the garden in which God placed Adam and Eve. By placing this word on Jesus' lips, Luke implies that Jesus' death reverses the effects of sin.

The fact that Jesus forgives sinners has been a great emphasis throughout Luke's Gospel. The church chooses to join Luke in emphasizing this theme on the feast of Christ the King. In today's Gospel we see that Jesus did not come to save himself, but to save sinners, including us. Luke wants us to understand that the jeerers' words are true. Jesus is king, not only of the Jews, but of the whole world. Christ, the king, has reconciled the world to God.

2 Samuel 5:1–3 in its biblical context

In today's reading from 2 Samuel all the tribes of Israel (that is, the northern tribes) come to David and ask him to be their king. First they acknowledge that they are all one people, although they have not yet had a single king over all twelve tribes: "Here we are, your bone and your flesh." Then they affirm that David was a great leader in battle while Saul was king: "In days past, when Saul was our king, it was you who led the Israelites out and brought them back." Now Saul is dead, and so they need a new king.

The leaders of the tribes believe that in choosing David they are confirming God's choice: "And the LORD said to you, 'You shall shepherd my people Israel and shall become commander of Israel.'" Earlier in 2 Samuel we were told that David was God's choice for king when Abner, one of Saul's soldiers, said that the Lord swore to David to "take away the kingdom from the house of Saul and establish the throne of David over Israel and over Judah from Dan to Beer-sheba" (2 Sam 3:10). David is anointed the first king of all the tribes: " . . . they anointed him king of Israel."

David will go on to become the greatest king that Israel ever had. Later God will promise David that his kingdom will be secure forever (see 2 Sam 7:8–17). It was because of this promise that the Jews expected one from David's line, an anointed one, a Christ (*Christ* means *anointed*) to come and save them from the Romans. Jesus was the fulfillment of God's promise to the house of David, but Jesus was a very different kind of king from the one they expected.

1 Colossians 1:12–20 in its biblical context

Our reading from Colossians includes a hymn that honors Jesus as "the firstborn of all creation." By *firstborn* the author means that Jesus existed before anything else was created: "For in him were created all things in heaven and on earth, / the visible and the invisible / . . . all things were created though him and for him." Jesus is also the "firstborn from the dead." In Luke, and only in Luke, Jesus is called the *firstborn* in the infancy narrative: " . . . and she gave birth to her firstborn son. She wrapped him in swaddling clothes and laid him in a manger . . . " (see Luke 2:7). As we see from Colossians, *firstborn* is a high-Christology title; that is, it is claiming that Jesus is divine.

The Colossians are urged to give thanks to the Father for Christ: "He delivered us from the power of darkness and transferred us to the kingdom of his beloved Son, in whom we have redemption, the forgiveness of sins." Through Jesus, God has reconciled all things to himself, "making peace by the blood of his cross. . . . "

On the feast of Christ the King we recognize the firstborn on the cross. We give thanks that we, like the man crucified with Jesus, have been forgiven our sins. We join the whole church in praising Christ, our king.

Questions for Breaking Open the Word groups are on page 13.

Questions for other faith sharing groups

1. In what ways is Christ the king in your life?

2. When you pray, "thy kingdom come," for what do you understand yourself to be praying?

3. Why do you think the church has chosen to focus our attention on Christ crucified on the feast of Christ the King?

Bible study questions

1. Why was Jesus charged before the Roman court with claiming to be a king?

2. In what way is the scene in today's Gospel full of dramatic irony?

3. What is the criminal's request to Jesus? What does this request presume that the criminal understands?

4. What is Jesus' response? What is Luke teaching through this response?

5. What does the word *firstborn* mean when applied to Jesus?